Precarious Protections

The publisher and the University of California Press Foundation gratefully acknowledge the generous support of the Barbara S. Isgur Endowment Fund in Public Affairs.

Precarious Protections

UNACCOMPANIED MINORS SEEKING
ASYLUM IN THE UNITED STATES

Chiara Galli

UNIVERSITY OF CALIFORNIA PRESS

University of California Press
Oakland, California

© 2023 by Chiara Galli

Library of Congress Cataloging-in-Publication Data

Names: Galli, Chiara, 1987– author.
Title: Precarious protections : unaccompanied minors seeking asylum in
  the United States / Chiara Galli.
Description: Oakland, California : University of California Press, [2023]
  | Includes bibliographical references and index.
Identifiers: LCCN 2022037191 (print) | LCCN 2022037192 (ebook) |
  ISBN 9780520391895 (cloth) | ISBN 9780520391918 (paperback) |
  ISBN 9780520391925 (epub)
Subjects: LCSH: Unaccompanied immigrant children—Legal status,
  laws, etc.—United States. | Central Americans—Legal status, laws,
  etc.—United States. | Asylum, Right of—United States. | Legal
  assistance to children—United States. | Legal assistance to
  immigrants—United States.
Classification: LCC KF4837 .G35 2023 (print) | LCC KF4837 (ebook) |
  DDC 342.7308/2—dc23/eng/20221003
LC record available at https://lccn.loc.gov/2022037191
LC ebook record available at https://lccn.loc.gov/2022037192

32 31 30 29 28 27 26 25 24 23
10 9 8 7 6 5 4 3 2 1

Contents

Illustrations

Acknowledgments

This book was eight years in the making, and I have incurred countless debts to many, many amazing people who helped me along the journey. I want to take this space to thank them.

First and foremost, I am immensely indebted and eternally grateful to my research participants, whom I unfortunately cannot thank by name since I promised them anonymity. The immigration attorneys and other advocates working in Los Angeles legal clinics were incredibly generous and patient in helping me decipher the complex realm of the law and teaching me about the important phenomenon of immigrant children facing removal proceedings. I also want to thank each of the Central American immigrant youths and their family members who put their trust in me, allowing me into their lives and sharing their stories with me for this research. Telling their stories is a privilege and a great responsibility; I hope I have done them justice.

This book is based on my dissertation, and this project simply would not have been possible had I not been lucky enough to call the University of California Los Angeles (UCLA) my intellectual home and to find such exceptional and supportive mentors there. At UCLA, I was incredibly privileged to work with an amazing dissertation committee: Roger Waldinger,

Cecilia Menjivar, Ruben Hernandez-Leon, Stefan Timmermans, and Susan Terrio. I cannot thank each of them enough for their critical and insightful feedback, which crucially shaped this book and the underlying research, and for their never-ending patience in reading countless drafts of the dissertation chapters, related articles, and parts of the book. For their mentorship and support, I also want to thank Gail Kligman, Leisy Abrego, Hiroshi Motomura, and Marjorie Orellana. Thanks also to C. K. Lee; it was in her notoriously challenging and rigorous ethnographic methods class that the seeds of this project were planted during my first year in grad school.

The UCLA Migration Working Group was my intellectual family as I developed this project, and there I built a lasting community of cherished friends and colleagues whom I could always count on to brainstorm ideas, to cheer me on, to celebrate successes, and to read drafts. Among them, a special thanks to Molly Fee, Andrew Le, Tianjian Lai, Estefania Castaneda Perez, Fernando Villegas, Nihal Kayali, Leydy Diossa, Mirian Martinez-Aranda, Deisy Del Real, Irene Vega, Tahseen Shams, Phi Su, Ian Peacock, Nathan Hoffman, and Peter Catron. Also, among my UCLA colleagues, thanks to Juan Delgado, Eleni Skaperdas, Alina Arseniev, Wisam Alshaibi, Luis Manuel Olguin, and Matias Fernandez for your friendship during the trials and tribulations of grad school.

A huge thank you to David Scott Fitzgerald and Lauren Duquette Rury, who reviewed the book manuscript as incredibly generous readers and who gave me the most constructive feedback and critique; thanks as well to Gail Kligman and Filiz Garip, each of whom read a full draft of the book at key moments of its development, providing insightful and detailed feedback; all of them helped me sharpen and improve the book immensely. Thank you also to Susan Coutin, Amada Armenta, Leisy Abrego, Lucy Mayblin, and Adrian Favel, who were kind enough to read and comment on chapters of the dissertation and book. I also want to thank Rawan Arar for always being there to exchange ideas and help me solve pressing dilemmas during the various phases of the book-writing process.

I was able to dedicate myself full time to writing this book for two years thanks to the generous support of the Klarman family, who created the Klarman postdoctoral fellowship program at Cornell. I was so fortunate to be able to spend this time fully immersed in this project; writing the book during the difficult first two years of the COVID pandemic gave me joy, purpose, and a formidable challenge. I am grateful to my mentors and colleagues at Cornell, in particular at the Migrations Initiative, for their support, for the many stimulating conversations, and for reading and commenting on my book proposal and parts of the book: Filiz Garip, Shannon Gleeson, Beth Lyon, Maria Cristina Garcia, Matt Hall, Steve Yale-Loehr, Eleanor Paynter, Angel Escamilla Garcia, Grace Kao, Tatiana Padilla, Molly O'Toole, Celene Reynolds, Tristan Ivory, Peter Rich, Mabel Berezin, and Kim Weeden. I also want to thank my colleagues in the Department of Comparative Human Development and in the Migrations Workshop at the University of Chicago for their enthusiasm about my work, which they expressed through dozens of stimulating questions, and for their warm welcome to the University of Chicago.

The research and writing of this book were generously supported by the National Science Foundation Graduate Research Fellowship Program, the National Science Foundation Dissertation Improvement Grant, the Haynes Foundation, the Latino Center for Leadership Development, the California Immigration Research Initiative, the P.E.O. sisterhood, the Klarman Fellowship, and the University of Chicago.

At the University of California Press, I want to thank Naomi Schneider and the editorial board members for believing in and supporting the book project and Summer Farah, Jon Dertien, LeKeisha Hughes, and Gary Hamel for their editorial assistance. Thanks also to Bill Nelson for designing the map of Central America in chapter 2. A big thank you goes to Los Angeles–based Salvadoran artist Victor Interiano who enthusiastically agreed to allow us to reproduce his art on the cover of the book; the piece was inspired by his own experience as an advocate for Central American unaccompanied youth in Los Angeles.

Last, but certainly not least, I want to thank my family. When my parents, Piero and Francesca, decided that we would migrate to this country when I was just six years old, they altered the course of my life indelibly, vastly expanding the opportunities afforded to me and my perspective on the world; I am deeply grateful for their courage and their love. My mother also deserves a special thanks for instilling in me my love of books so successfully that I have now managed to write one of my own. And my husband, Pedro, who has followed me to the other side of the world and then some and with whom I have been truly lucky to share many adventures. *Gracias*, Pedro, for always being by my side; writing this book would have been impossible without your unwavering support and good humor, I dedicate it to you.

1 Exclusion and Protection in US Immigration Law and Policy

I answered my phone to hear a young voice: "Hi, this is Jocelyn.[1] I saw a flyer at my immigration attorney's office about a study on Central American unaccompanied minors. I'd like to participate." Driving through the Los Angeles traffic, I made my way to the predominantly Latino neighborhood where Jocelyn shared a tiny apartment with her aunt and two cousins. We sat at the kitchen table together, and, after overcoming some initial shyness, Jocelyn told me her story. Her father had never been a part of her life. Her mother migrated to the United States when she was just a baby. They had barely kept in touch. In El Salvador, Jocelyn was raised by her grandmother, whom she considered to be her "real mom." Jocelyn also felt close to her aunt, who had called her often and sent remittances from the United States. When Jocelyn was twelve, one of her classmates was murdered by MS-13 gang members at school. Her grandmother decided that it was no longer safe for her to attend. Jocelyn would spend the next three years barely leaving her house before she finally fled the country in 2015. The violence in her hometown had escalated, a microcosm of the national trends of rising homicide rates in El Salvador.

In the meantime, Jocelyn's aunt had been saving up for her quinceañera, a rite of passage that marks the life-course transition from girlhood to womanhood in Latin America. Yet violence had put Jocelyn's coming-of-age on hold: she had left school but was unable to work. Her family decided to use the quinceañera savings to extract her from her risky life as a teenager in El Salvador instead. They paid a *coyote* to smuggle Jocelyn out of the country, leading her along the dangerous, unauthorized migration route to the US-Mexico border, the only travel option available for children who migrate alone to join undocumented parents and relatives in the United States.[2] Then fifteen-year-old Jocelyn was apprehended at the US-Mexico border and admitted as an unaccompanied minor, a formally recognized vulnerable category in US immigration law.[3] She was detained in an Office of Refugee Resettlement (ORR) shelter, where she would spend six months before joining her aunt in Los Angeles. Upon release, Jocelyn was one of the lucky youths represented by a free immigration attorney paid for by the limited government funding available for the legal representation of unaccompanied minors in removal proceedings.

In the United States, Jocelyn found temporary refuge from the risks she faced in El Salvador. Yet, despite her formally protected status, even with high-quality legal representation, she would face an arduous journey to lasting protection and legal status. Despite the fact that Jocelyn had escaped from violence, her attorney told her that she had slim odds of winning her asylum case. People assume that asylum protects those who fear returning to their homes. Yet this commonsense understanding is a far cry from how asylum law works in practice. The United States interprets the refugee definition narrowly and fails to adequately recognize the age-specific forms of violence and persecution that cause children and youths to flee their homes today. Expertly working within the constraints of this legal system, Jocelyn's attorney strategically advised her to apply for Special Immigrant Juvenile Status (SIJS) instead, a form of immigration relief for children abandoned, abused, or neglected by their parents. The process would be longer, but Jocelyn was far more likely to win her case and eventually become a lawful permanent resident and then a US citizen. When I met her, Jocelyn was eighteen years old and still in legal limbo, waiting for the result of her case. She had crossed the threshold of the age of majority but was still unable to legally work, her rite of passage to adulthood on hold even as a young immigrant in the United States.

Jocelyn is one of the over three-quarters of a million unaccompanied minors who have arrived at the US-Mexico border since 2009 (Figure 1),

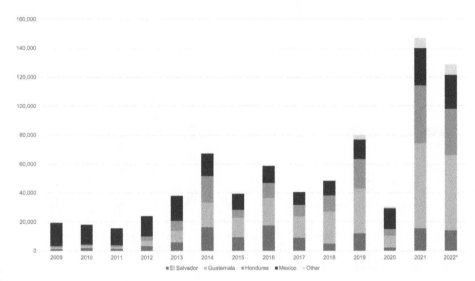

Fig. 1. Unaccompanied minors apprehended at the US-Mexico border, 2009–2022. *FY 2022, partial data through July. (US Border Patrol Southwest Border Apprehension Statistics, Unaccompanied Children, www. cbp.gov)

as violence, human rights violations, and deprivation have triggered out-flows from El Salvador, Guatemala, and Honduras, where teenagers are especially at risk of being targeted and victimized by gangs. This migration stream reflects broader global trends: children make up over half of the world's displaced population; and more children than ever before are crossing international borders alone to seek asylum in rich liberal democracies in the Global North.[4] In the United States, unaccompanied minors' asylum applications have increased exponentially from just over four hundred in 2009 to a high of more than twenty thousand per year during the years this research took place (Figure 2).[5]

Like all countries party to the United Nations Refugee Convention and Protocol, the United States must abide by its commitment to *non-refoulement*, which prohibits states from returning individuals to countries of origin where they fear for their lives, at least until their asylum claims have been examined.[6] Yet asylum seekers are perceived as ethno-racial, cultural, and economic threats. Countries like the United States try to keep them far away from the physical space where non-refoulement is activated—namely, the territorial border—and thereby from the advocates

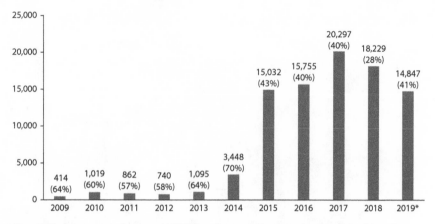

Fig. 2. Unaccompanied minors' USCIS asylum applications (and approval rates), 2009–2019. *FY 2019, partial data through March. (USCIS Quarterly Stakeholder Meetings, Minor Principal Applicant Reports, www.uscis.gov)

who can help them claim rights and protection. These same countries externalize migration control through a combination of walls, visa restrictions, and bilateral agreements with transit countries that restrict mobility and fund camps that both aid and contain refugees in the Global South, where 85 percent of the world's displaced people live.[7]

All immigrants who circumvent these obstacles and show up "uninvited" at the border to seek asylum pose a challenge for immigration control. Receiving states have sought to chip away at their rights to exclude them. Yet unaccompanied asylum-seeking children present an especially exacting dilemma because they are considered too innocent and vulnerable to be morally excluded outright. Children are the social group perhaps best able to tap into the emotional nature of compassion. Widely accepted ideals of children's "natural" role as dependents mark childhood as a time to be protected by adults. Indeed, over the course of the past two decades, advocacy on behalf of unaccompanied minors has become a major force in US immigration politics, securing gains such as funding to represent children like Jocelyn in removal proceedings. Lawmakers have responded to pressures from advocates by introducing humanitarian laws that exempt unaccompanied minors from aspects of immigration enforcement aimed at adults at the border and in detention facilities, as well as granting them special due process protections as asylum seekers.

Since their numbers first grew sharply during the Obama administration (Figure 1), unaccompanied minors have been portrayed by policy makers and the media with starkly contrasting narratives that highlight the liminal, or in-between, position that these youths occupy in the United States. At times, they are seen as scared and helpless victims of violent home countries, innocent children allowed to migrate alone by irresponsible parents. Other times, they are perceived as "bogus" refugees who file fraudulent asylum claims or—merely by virtue of being teenagers from Central America—even as dangerous MS-13 gang members, deviously making their way into the country by taking advantage of the misplaced generosity of protective laws. In recent years, these laws have transitioned from being relatively obscure, and agreed upon across the political spectrum, to being extremely visible. Proponents of immigration restriction—former President Donald Trump and his senior adviser Stephen Miller prominent among them—politicized and tried to delegitimize these protections by framing them as "loopholes" that allow unwanted immigrants to cheat the system. In contrast, immigration advocates argue that these laws are too limited in scope and should be expanded to provide more protection to a greater number of vulnerable immigrant children.

Social scientists have investigated unaccompanied minors' detention in federal facilities and the perspectives of the state actors who manage them.[8] We know far less about youths' perspectives and their experiences *after* they are released from federal custody, as they adapt to their new homes while navigating the US asylum process. Legal scholars have highlighted the inadequacy of an asylum institution created for adults as a means to protect children, as well as the "ambivalence" of immigration laws targeting unaccompanied minors.[9] On the one hand, like adults who are undesired immigrants from the Global South, the state seeks to *exclude* unaccompanied minors. On the other hand, as legal minors—and children who enter the United States alone, without their parents—they are seen as deserving of *protection*. Following a tradition of sociolegal ethnographic scholarship, this study takes a step further to examine the gaps between the law in books and the law in action.[10] This book asks how the contradictory legal context of reception—characterized by exclusion and protection—shapes the lives of immigrant youths and the legal strategies of those who advocate on their behalf.

This book centers the experiences and perspectives of my two groups of key informants—unaccompanied minors and their immigration attorneys—and describes how they work together to navigate the US asylum bureaucracy, seeking protection, refugee recognition, and membership rights. This is a story about the contradictions of asylum law and other categories of humanitarian admission that are fraught to begin with; about the young immigrants who, often uncomfortably, inhabit them; and about the legal advocates whose professional motivation is rooted in social justice, who try to expand these categories but face many constraints in doing so. The chapters that follow guide the reader along the arduous journeys that youths undertake from sending countries, where their lives are at risk, and through the multi-agency maze of the US immigration system. My goal is to demystify the highly politicized, yet little understood and complex asylum process, illustrating the challenges that youths and their advocates face. In this way, I aim to disrupt discourses that portray unaccompanied minors as either innocent children deserving of protection or menacing teenagers and quasi-adult "illegal" immigrants to be excluded and expelled.[11]

These youths are migrating to the United States to flee violence and deprivation, to survive and find hope, to join their families, to pursue their dreams and aspirations, to work and study, and to continue transitions to adulthood put on hold due to insecurity in their home countries. I highlight both the real vulnerabilities and agency of Central American unaccompanied minors and the repercussions of inhabiting a dual liminal position in the United States: as teenagers, suspended between the social positions of childhood and adulthood; as asylum seekers, in legal limbo between protected refugee status and deportable "illegality." I argue that these young asylum seekers are de facto refugees because they escaped life-threatening violence in Central America. Yet, despite the strides made, thanks to decades of advocacy work, to recognize their unique vulnerabilities in the US asylum process, youths' lived experiences still too often fail to match the narrow refugee category.

To qualify for asylum, youths must demonstrate that they experienced the "right" *amount* and *types* of suffering prior to fleeing their homes. The timing of their escape hence goes on to influence their chances of success in the asylum process. But when and how youths make it out of their home countries depends on a combination of resources and sheer luck. In addition to meeting legal definitions, youths must also elicit the compassion of the asylum officers and immigration judges who make discretionary decisions on their cases. This compassion is conditional on embodying a one-dimensional identity as a helpless refugee child.

Although under some conditions advocates can expand eligibility categories and challenge this rigid legal system, the narrow refugee category is often perpetuated through organizational practices and lawyering strategies. As a result, vulnerable youths who escaped from violence are frequently denied protection in paradoxical ways or face lengthy legal limbo. The asylum process, in turn, spills over to affect youths' everyday lives as their legal and social liminality interact. Unlike their peers for whom adolescence marks a moment of transition to adulthood, I demonstrate that youths like Jocelyn undergo a *rite of reverse passage* in the United States.[12] To be seen as deserving of free legal representation, refugee status, protections for abandoned children, and, more broadly, of aid and support, unaccompanied minors must distance themselves from markers of adulthood and instead present childlike narratives and behaviors.

The findings I present in this book are based on six years of research (2015–2021), spanning the Obama and Trump administrations. I conducted longitudinal and multi-sited ethnographic fieldwork in various nonprofit legal aid organizations that represent unaccompanied minors in Los Angeles. There, I shadowed immigration attorneys and other staff as they helped nearly eighty youths apply for asylum and/or SIJS and navigate challenges beyond the legal realm. Many of these staff members had a personal connection to this phenomenon as Latinx immigrants or as the children of immigrants. They entered and persevered in the stressful and poorly paid profession of public interest immigration lawyering because they wanted to give back to their communities. In these same legal aid organizations, I also spent countless hours working as a volunteer legal assistant and English-Spanish interpreter to help attorneys prepare asylum cases. Playing an active role in the process I was studying positioned me in the field as an advocate as well as a researcher-volunteer. This experience allowed me to acquire firsthand knowledge about the challenges of working with asylum-seeking youth. I complemented the ethnography by conducting 122 in-depth interviews, 55 of which were with immigration attorneys, other advocates, and asylum officers. The rest of my interviews were with 45 Central American unaccompanied minors and 10 of their caretakers; I stayed in touch with many of these youths over an extended period of time and re-interviewed 12 of them roughly two years after we first met. I point those interested in reading more about how I carried out the research and the characteristics of study participants to the methods appendix at the end of the book.

The rest of this introductory chapter is structured as follows. First, I situate the book's intervention in the academic literature and broader debates on immigration law, refugee flows, and childhood and the life course. Second, I discuss how protections for unaccompanied minors and asylum seekers came to exist in US immigration law and policy, developments that are, in part, tied to a longer history of Central American immigration to this country. Third, I briefly anticipate how these protections uniquely shape youths' trajectories in the US immigration bureaucracy. Last, I discuss why Los Angeles was a strategic site to conduct this research. I end by outlining the structure of the book.

WHAT CAN WE LEARN BY STUDYING THE CASE OF UNACCOMPANIED MINORS?

This book bridges and extends two strands of international migration scholarship, while also informing academic and real-world debates on refugee flows. Child-centered migration studies have focused on how an individual's stage in the life course shapes migratory aspirations and assimilation, but they have neglected to examine the role of the state and its immigration laws in these processes. Conversely, a burgeoning socio-legal scholarship has focused on how immigration laws affect the lives of *adults*. With few exceptions, studies about how lawyers broker immigrants' applications for legal status have likewise focused only on adults.[13] This is perhaps unsurprising since minors—those under age eighteen—are generally invisibilized in the realm of immigration law and considered derivatives on parents' applications.[14] Their fate depends on how the state treats their parents. The case of unaccompanied minors—who migrate without their parents or legal guardians and hence must make independent claims vis-à-vis the state—provides a strategic opportunity to study children and youths as legal subjects in their own right.

EXCLUSION AND PROTECTION IN THE IMMIGRATION LAW IN ACTION

Revising our adult-centric theories of the immigration law in action is urgent in today's world, one where both immigration control and child migration are on the rise. While past research focused on advancing a critique of the exclusionary dynamics at play in the immigration and asylum system, the case of unaccompanied minors brings protective forces into stronger relief.

Problematizing the taken-for-granted notion that states can and should exclude immigrants, sociologists Cecilia Menjívar and Leisy Abrego have conceptualized the enforcement laws targeting undocumented adults and those with temporary statuses as "legal violence."[15] These laws not only restrict cross-border mobility, but also separate families, make immigrants vulnerable to exploitation, and negatively affect their health and well-being, as well as the well-being of their offspring, many of whom are US citizens.[16] Since suffering is inflicted on immigrants through laws and regulations—in other words, it is *legal*—this exercise of state power is widely perceived as legitimate. For the over ten million undocumented immigrants in the United States, the constant threat of deportation—their "deportability"—serves as a powerful disciplining force.[17] The "illegality" of these individuals is actively *produced* by the state as it deprives those it deems undesirable of membership rights, relegating them to a subordinate position in society. Legal status works as a new axis of inequality that stratifies the immigrant experience like other dimensions of an individual's social position, like race, class, gender, and age.[18]

To be sure, receiving countries like the United States have enacted immigration enforcement laws that inflict suffering on immigrants and exclude them. Yet they have also implemented *humanitarian* laws that instead reflect the opposite intention: to alleviate the suffering of immigrants considered vulnerable by providing them pathways to inclusion and legal status. These laws reflect what some have called the "humanitarian ethos," an emotional sentiment based on the notion that suffering is a universal human experience that knows no distinction based on nationality or legal status.[19] At the same time, humanitarian admissions are self-serving because they validate the nation's identity as good and generous, a bastion of human rights and the rule of law.[20] Critical humanitarianism scholars have examined the implementation of various humanitarian immigration laws, including asylum and policies that allow the ill, trafficking victims, and battered women to obtain deportation relief.[21] These scholars rightly argue that humanitarian admissions favor the plight of select subgroups while ignoring the fact that *all* undocumented immigrants are vulnerable precisely because the state deprives them of legal status. Yet advocates would take issue with the somewhat cynical extension of this argument: that all humanitarian admissions are inherently conservative and compatible with immigration control.[22]

Immigrants' rights advocates have always selected subgroups of undocumented immigrants to prioritize making their cases for legalization on legal and normative grounds.[23] Children have proved to be a particularly successful advocacy category, and unaccompanied minors are a protected group in liberal democracies worldwide. The concept of childhood as a vulnerable category emerged gradually over centuries as the social value of children changed from being understood in terms of economic utility to the family to a sentimental conception of childhood as "priceless," a time of innocence to be sheltered by adults and devoted to school and play rather than work.[24] These conceptions of childhood innocence originated vis-à-vis middle-class white children and later percolated through society at large, although class and race biases in considerations of which children deserve compassion and protection still persist. Nonetheless, childhood is a formally protected status recognized by the international community at large today, as reflected in the near-universal acceptance of the 1989 UN Convention on the Rights of the Child (CRC) and its underlying principle of the *best interests of the child*. The CRC establishes that all children (individuals under age eighteen), irrespective of immigration status, are both independent rights-holders and entitled to special, supplemental protections because they are physiologically and developmentally distinct from adults.

As a case study of a country of reception for unaccompanied minors, the United States presents similarities and differences to other liberal democracies. Most European countries provide more protections to unaccompanied minors than the United States, including special permits that allow them to reside there legally until age eighteen.[25] Of course, in those contexts, reaching the legal threshold of adulthood comes with the loss of the protective status and significant new vulnerabilities, including the risk of deportation. Further, the US has set itself apart from the world as the only country that has not ratified the CRC. Recognizing that children have rights independent of their parents was grounds for alarm in a country with strong ideological resistance to state intervention in families and private life more broadly.[26] The US juvenile justice system ostensibly takes into the account the best interests of US citizen children. Yet, in practice, the system is plagued with racial and class inequalities, and it disproportionately adultifies and denies special treatment and discounted penalties to young people of color and those living in disadvantaged neighborhoods.[27] When it comes to deciding whether to grant legal status to undocumented immigrant children, with the exception of SIJS applicants, the United States does not take into account the best interests of the child. Nonetheless, as I will discuss throughout the book, the United States provides a host of other protections to unaccompanied minors that have important implications.

Humanitarian policies protecting unaccompanied minors do not negate legal violence, but they interact with exclusionary forces in important ways. These policies provide tools that advocates can use to keep in check state interests to exclude immigrants. These policies also position unaccompanied minors relatively more favorably than adults, which explains why they have recently provoked the ire of proponents of immigration restriction. Yet, at the same time, this book demonstrates that these protections are an imperfect fix in light of rigid US asylum law that fails to adequately recognize how an individual's age and the stage in the life course shapes experiences of escape. I demonstrate how immigration attorneys bridge the gaps between youths' lived experiences and the refugee category by adopting creative legal strategies, thus playing a key role in enabling youths to gain inclusion—deportation relief, legal status—in a country that would otherwise reject them. Indeed, legal representation has been found to drastically increase unaccompanied minors' chances of being allowed to stay in the United States from 15 to 73 percent.[28] At the same time, I also show the limitations of these legal strategies, thus exposing the protection gaps that exist despite well-intentioned humanitarian law, which leave too many vulnerable youths at risk of deportation back to home countries where their lives are in danger.

IMMIGRATION LAWYERING
WITH UNACCOMPANIED MINORS

I use the concept of "legal brokers" to examine the work of advocates— immigration attorneys, legal assistants, and other support staff—who help unaccompanied minors navigate asylum proceedings. These advocates work in nonprofit, migrant-serving legal aid organizations or legal clinics. Legal brokers carry out a "legal translation role" by reducing gaps in meaning between the institutions of the receiving country and newly arrived immigrants, who have little or no knowledge of complex immigration laws and bureaucracies.[29]

Ethnographers have conducted various case studies examining how legal brokers mediate access to legal status for immigrants. In her seminal ethnography of Salvadoran asylum seekers' struggles to obtain refugee status in the United States in the 1980s and 1990s, anthropologist Susan Coutin argues that legal brokers act as "agents and critics of the law" who simultaneously reinforce and challenge official legal categories as they help their clients apply for relief.[30] Some studies have emphasized the former role, arguing that lawyers reproduce narrow categories by acknowledging restrictive eligibility criteria as the "rules of the game," at the expense of advocating for policy change that would expand access to legal status to more immigrants.[31] Legal brokers can also create *additional* barriers for access to legal status when they choose to represent only clients who are "easy" to work with because they have recovered from past victimization and otherwise fit what are often biased client selection and management criteria.[32]

Conversely, other studies have emphasized legal brokers' roles in expanding access to legal status. The lawyers who represented Salvadoran asylum seekers largely excluded from protection in the 1980s believed that "law is one thing, justice is another."[33] This led them to advocate for policy changes that transformed the US asylum system and created new opportunities for Central Americans to obtain legal status. The legal brokers who helped undocumented immigrants apply for the last large-scale legalization in the United States under the Immigration Reform and control Act of 1984 (IRCA) also carried out an activist role.[34] They implemented "street-level revisions" to expand eligibility criteria and promote legalization beyond policy makers' initial intentions.[35]

In light of these two contrasting characterizations of immigration lawyering, in this book, I am interested in asking: what conditions allow legal brokers to play an activist role and what others instead limit their ability to challenge narrow humanitarian categories of admission? While the literature suggests a dichotomy, I use strategic comparisons to understand what factors enable and constrain legal brokers' ability to engage in the creative manipulation of legal categories and proceedings. I do so by comparing the different organizational strategies that nonprofits use to select clients (chapter 4). I also compare lawyering in two different political contexts (chapter 5): the Obama administration, which was characterized by the ambivalent approach to children identified in existing legal scholarship; and the Trump administration, characterized by a sole focus on exclusion to undermine the established rights of unaccompanied minors and asylum seekers.[36] I thus demonstrate how structural, organizational, and political factors crucially shape legal strategies, determining whether the goal of obtaining relief for each individual immigrant client is at odds or in synch with the goal of expanding eligibility categories to benefit more immigrants.

HUMANITARIAN CAPITAL: UNDERSTANDING HOW LAWYERS BROKER APPLICATIONS FOR LEGAL STATUS

At the individual level, the humanitarian legalization process is one where the immigrant's intangible emotions and lived experiences of suffering can be mobilized to obtain key tangible benefits: legal status and membership rights. Humanitarian policies exist based on the assumption that suffering is measurable and that deserving vulnerable immigrants will be adequately identified through a bureaucratic selection process. Yet uncertainty and discretion are key defining features of the asylum system and other humanitarian categories of admission.

It has been well documented by scholarship on adults' asylum cases that the bureaucratic selection process that sorts refugees apart from immigrants is fraught with inconsistencies, inequality, and a good measure of chance. Different countries diverge in their interpretation of the refugee definition and in their asylum grant rates. To give just one example, grant rates for Afghanis ranged from 5 to 95 percent in European Union countries.[37] In the United States, grant rates vary widely between different immigration courts and asylum offices across the country and even among decision-makers in the same agency, who exercise significant discretion in deciding whether to grant cases. Their personal characteristics, including gender, partisanship, and professional background, are among the key determinants of asylum outcomes.[38] Uncertainty is so rife in the process that the US bureaucracies that decide asylum claims have earned the moniker of "refugee roulette."[39]

Given these conditions, my goal with this book is not to elaborate a grand theory to predict case outcomes: why some Central American unaccompanied minors are awarded refugee status and others are not. Rather, I address the following question: how do legal brokers navigate the indeterminate humanitarian legalization process to try to obtain favorable outcomes for their clients? To explain their brokerage work between the state bureaucrats who decide whether to grant cases and the immigrant applicant, I introduce the concept of *humanitarian capital*.[40] I define humanitarian capital as a form of "symbolic capital" that legal brokers activate relationally as they interview their clients by recognizing specific instances of suffering in their lived experiences and attributing differential value to each.[41]

In this exercise of translation of human suffering, legal brokers determine the "worth" of each experience by using their expertise to mine formal legal definitions and eligibility criteria. Legal brokers also draw on their past experience working with other clients to compare, contrast, and rank each immigrant's experiences in a constructed hierarchy of suffering. Assessing humanitarian capital in each client's lived experiences allows legal brokers to anticipate how adjudicators—asylum officers, immigration judges— will evaluate each case, deciding whether to grant legal status and rights. Legal brokers thus estimate the likelihood of success for each application to decide what forms of relief to pursue and which cases to represent. In preparing their clients' applications for humanitarian relief, legal brokers consolidate humanitarian capital by meticulously documenting—usually in written declarations, supported by documentation—human suffering, emotions, and inherently imperfect memories of past experiences. They thus make immigrants' lived experiences of suffering legible to the asylum officers and immigration judges who have the power to either grant protection or send asylum seekers back to dangerous home countries. By finding ways to give value to the unmeasurable, legal brokers manage risk and uncertainty in an inherently indeterminate process.

In the chapters that follow, I illustrate how legal brokers elicit and attribute value to unaccompanied minors' past experiences of victimization and suffering to transform victimhood into a symbolic resource that can be used to obtain tangible benefits: free legal representation (chapter 4); legal status through asylum and SIJS (chapter 5); and aid from donors (chapter 6). How much humanitarian capital is needed to qualify—the "price," so to speak, of obtaining each of these tangible benefits—varies depending on the real and perceived scarcity of the good. An example of real scarcity is limited funding for free legal representation or the limited hours that legal clinic support staff have to assist hundreds of clients in need. Perceived scarcity depends on the supply of compassion itself in the asylum process. Anthropologist Didier Fassin argues that bureaucrats in the institutions that decide asylum claims act as if they must fairly distribute a scarce resource: refugee status.[42] Yet, the resource constraints in question are not material, like limited respirators in a hospital overwhelmed with COVID patients, but symbolic. Indeed, in both the French case that Fassin studies and the US context, there is no upper limit to how many asylum claims can be granted.[43] Of course, the value of refugee status is not symbolic at all for people who have fled their homes. It means protection from deportation back to danger, and, in the United States, a pathway to citizenship in just four years and access to welfare benefits.

Legal brokerage vis-à-vis all forms of legal status based on compassion entails an evaluation of humanitarian capital.[44] Yet, for each group of applicants, which experiences yield value is unique. For unaccompanied minors, those experiences that signal them as vulnerable, dependent children hold more value than others, giving rise to all sorts of paradoxes that I will discuss throughout the book. To obtain protection and recognition as refugees, unaccompanied minors must satisfy both legal definitions and formal eligibility criteria, as well as adjudicators' assumptions and cultural understandings of deserving refugeehood and childhood.

WHO COUNTS AS A REFUGEE?

Who counts as a refugee is a question of critical real-life importance for people on the move, as well as a debate that has attracted scholarly attention. Two sets of conceptual dichotomies have been used to define population movements: *economic* and *voluntary*, as pertains to migrants; and *political* and *forced*, as pertains to refugees. Each focusing on one group, international migration and refugee studies originated as separate fields of intellectual inquiry, a division of labor that hindered theoretical developments and reified existing dichotomies.[45] Scholars have since made strides to bridge these fields of study and have taken various approaches to problematize our conceptual dichotomies.

Some have critiqued the effectiveness of the distinction between *political* and *economic* to explain both macro-level push factors in sending countries and micro-level migration decision-making, arguing that these two forces overlap and compound one another so as to become analytically indistinguishable.[46] Others have pointed out that agency in migration decision-making is not binary (*forced* or *voluntary*). Rather, it ranges in degrees between reactive and proactive, with migration decisions occurring along a "continuum of compulsion."[47] In addition to compulsion, recent scholarship has highlighted how aspirations also play a role in motivating migration from countries characterized by widespread rights violations and lack of liberty.[48] Other scholars have gone further yet, arguing that the very distinction between migrants and refugees is an artificial form of "categorical fetishism" or even a dangerous legal fiction that can serve the malignant political goal of making "harsh border control measures more ethically palatable to the general public."[49]

In light of existing approaches, ranging from those that add nuance to conceptual dichotomies (political/economic; voluntary/forced) to the more iconoclastic that would do away with the migrant/refugee distinction altogether, I thought extensively about how to write about my research participants. As I sat across the desk from dozens of asylum-seeking youths during my research and volunteer work in legal clinics, I certainly observed the fact that real migratory experiences blur the political/economic distinction beyond serviceability and complicate simplistic notions of refugee migration as forced and hence completely devoid of agency. However, what struck me most was the realization that an asylum system ostensibly meant to protect those who fear returning to their homes fails so momentously at this goal. Because this process is so little understood, the widely held assumption among the general public and policymakers is that if so many asylum seekers are denied, this must mean that they are *not really* refugees and that their claims for protection are "bogus." This book seeks to debunk that assumption.

I position my research within the scholarship that adds nuance to our conceptual tools to define population movements but stops short of calling for doing away with the distinction between migrants and refugees altogether. Instead, I take a realist approach that rests on the premise that there are some elements that characterize refugee flows as a distinct type of international migration.[50] Political scientist Aristide Zolberg and colleagues argue that the key defining feature of refugee flows is violence.[51] They define the refugee as an individual who escapes from life-threatening violence in the home country. Threats to an individual's life are attacks not merely on one's biological existence—the risk of death—but also on one's social existence and the basic material conditions necessary to maintain it.

I use this definition, which is based on circumstances of migration, to refer to *de facto* refugees. Conversely, I term those who have been recognized through the bureaucratic selection process—the US asylum process—and who have successfully obtained the refugee label and the rights it confers: *de jure* refugees. I use *immigrant* as an umbrella term to describe all those who have crossed international borders and *asylum seeker* to describe those who intend to apply, or have applied, for refugee status. Political scientist Rebecca Hamlin has argued that the scholarly distinction between de facto and de jure refugees is well-intentioned but meaningless because, without formal legal status, there are no associated rights and protections.[52] In my view, making this distinction to critically examine practices of refugee status recognition in asylum systems is, instead, a powerful way to show when and how protective laws fall short of their promises. Pointing to such gaps is both one of the theoretical pre-rogatives of studies of the law in action and an advocacy strategy that can help expand protection to more people who flee their homes.

While non-refoulment protections from deportation are broadly appli-cable, the refugee definition is narrow by design and therefore inherently difficult to satisfy. With the 1980 Refugee Act, the United States intro-duced the UN definition into its domestic law. Refugees are persons out-side their country of origin and "unable or unwilling to return. . . . Owing to a well-founded fear of being persecuted for reasons of race, religion, nationality, membership in a particular social group, or political opinion." Refugees need protection from the international community because they have lost the protection of the state in their country of origin. The UN Refugee Convention of 1951 applied only to Europeans displaced because of World War II, but the geographic and temporal limitation was elimi-nated in the 1967 Protocol. This vastly expanded the protective scope of refugee law so it could apply universally, irrespective of country of origin.

Even so, the legal criterion of *persecution* remains narrow. First, it only applies to individuals who are personally singled out and targeted and not to victims of what is conceived as generalized violence.[53] Yet, para-doxically, as we will see in chapter 5, infantilizing US asylum case law is often also at odds with recognizing Central American youths who are di-rect targets as eligible for refugee status. Second, the persecution criterion does not extend protection to those who suffer as a result of structural violence, as it is manifested in exploitation, extreme poverty, and depriva-tion, even when these conditions are the result of governmental neglect or violation of human rights.[54] Yet, as I will demonstrate, structural violence and the acts of direct, interpersonal violence that cause individuals to flee Central America today are intertwined and co-constitutive. It is the most vulnerable in society—the poor, indigenous groups, women, children, and youths—who are most at risk.

Children and youths—but also other "nontraditional" de facto refugees—fit uncomfortably in the formal refugee category. By virtue of its historical underpinnings, refugee law privileges the experiences of male adults flee-ing the persecution of repressive states.[55] Feminist legal scholars and advo-cates have highlighted how the asylum system fails to protect women and have thus obtained significant gains for victims of gender-based violence, like female genital mutilation or intimate-partner violence.[56] Like gender, age and conditions tied to the life course are important dimensions that structure an individual's social position and exposure to violence. Yet US asylum law has yet to evolve to adequately recognize the experiences of children and youths. In the next chapter, I extend theories of international migration to explain why and how youths migrate from contexts of violence in Central America. Understanding how violence spurs youth migration has important real-world implications and can potentially transform practices of refugee recognition.

MIGRATION AND THE LIFE COURSE: REVISITING YOUTH MIGRATION AS A RITE OF PASSAGE

Central American unaccompanied minors concurrently find themselves in limbo between the legal categories of refugee and "illegal" immigrant and the social categories of child and adult. As a social position relative to adulthood, childhood can generally be characterized by lesser maturity and decision-making autonomy and by greater dependence on family for subsistence. However, understandings and experiences of childhood are both historically contingent and culturally constructed, with meanings varying significantly between developed and developing countries. The extent to which children are seen as dependent on adults also intersects with chronological age and with various dimensions of an individual's social position, such as gender, class, race, and ethnicity.[57] Throughout the book, I refer to my study participants as "youths" rather than "children," not only because they are teenagers who rarely see themselves as children, but also to highlight their "liminal" stage in the life course.[58] In crossing international borders, these youths bring with them their own understandings of childhood, as well as their personal dreams, goals, and aspirations for the transition to adulthood. I examine how the individual experiences and narratives of migrant youths complement or clash with legal and cultural understandings of childhood in the United States.

In Guatemala, Honduras, and El Salvador, children have very different experiences than do children in the United States. Educational opportunities are scarce in all three sending countries. The rates of out-of-school children are highest in Honduras where secondary schooling is not compulsory. Children there only spend 7.5 years in school on average, and 17 percent of primary school age children and 38 percent of adolescents are not in school. In El Salvador, the rates of out-of-school children and adolescents are 15 percent and 17 percent, respectively, and in Guatemala, they are 12 percent and 33 percent.[59] Overall, it is more common for children from the poorest families, for males, and for those living in rural areas to drop out of school to work at an early age.

Children in Central America engage in unpaid care work and work for pay, with both their families and employers. Children help take care of younger siblings and carry out household chores. They are employed in dangerous and exploitative jobs in agriculture, construction, and domestic work.[60] Guatemala has the highest rates of child labor in the region, where 16 percent of children ages five to fourteen either work full time or both work and study, followed by 9 percent in Honduras, and 7 percent in El Salvador.[61] Rural children from Guatemala also participate in agricultural work in neighboring Mexico, where minors account for over 13 percent of labor migrants.[62]

Anthropologist Lauren Heidbrink has argued that, for indigenous children in Guatemala who are members of expansive kin networks, contributing to household economies through their paid and unpaid labor is a key part of their identities.[63] Shared familial responsibilities give these youths a positive sense of belonging. Youths may bring these values with them to the United States, migrating with aspirations to support their families. Conversely, many other children in Central America grow up without one or both of their parents and are raised by other adults. Demographers estimate that, in the early 2000s, about 15 percent of children in El Salvador and Guatemala experienced parental absence due to migration, a number likely to have increased considerably since, as emigration has continued to grow.[64]

Scholars of the life course in the Global South argue that young people living in "postwar" countries that have failed in the transition to democracy, like Guatemala, El Salvador, and Honduras, inhabit a condition of perpetual waiting or "waithood."[65] These youths struggle to meet cultural expectations for the transition to adulthood in their home countries. They feel unable to change the broader political, social, and economic realities that impact their lives. The lack of coming-of-age opportunities in the

Table 1 Characteristics of unaccompanied minors in ORR custody, 2014–2019

		2014	2015	2016	2017	2018	2019
Gender	Male	66%	68%	67%	68%	71%	66%
	Female	34%	32%	33%	32%	29%	34%
Age	0–12	21%	17%	18%	17%	15%	16%
	13–14	16%	12%	12%	13%	12%	12%
	15–16	36%	38%	37%	37%	37%	37%
	17	27%	30%	31%	32%	35%	35%
Country of Origin	Honduras	34%	17%	21%	23%	26%	30%
	Guatemala	32%	45%	40%	45%	54%	45%
	El Salvador	29%	29%	34%	27%	12%	18%
	Other countries	5%	9%	5%	5%	7%	7%

SOURCE: Office of Refugee Resettlement (ORR), www.acf.hhs.gov/orr/about/ucs/facts-and-data.

developing world—through work, marriage and childrearing, civic participation, or higher education—has created a youth-specific "culture of migration."[66]

Past scholarship has conceptualized the migration of adolescents as a "rite of passage" to adulthood. By migrating to countries with more resources and opportunities, youths emancipate themselves from adult control, seek adventure, access jobs, and find ways to support family and gain prestige in their communities of origin.[67] These studies, however, were based solely on the experiences of male labor migrants and have not examined how youth migration differs by gender and in contexts characterized by violence. Unlike previous male-dominated flows of independent youth migration to the United States, roughly one-third of unaccompanied minors today are females (Table 1).[68] This calls for updating existing theories of independent youth migration to account for gendered dynamics. In chapters 2 and 6, I discuss how youths' migration experiences are patterned by gender in sending countries and the United States, respectively.

Like youths who migrate to seek adventure and work, de facto refugee youths migrate, not only to escape from violence and find safety from harm, but also to overcome waithood, seek coming-of-age opportunities, and pursue their aspirations. Unlike their "adventurous" peers, however,

unaccompanied minors' migration experiences are not necessarily emancipatory, nor do they guarantee a clear pathway to adulthood. Instead,
while they navigate infantilizing and victimizing asylum proceedings, unaccompanied minors undergo what I term a rite of reverse passage as they
adapt to their new homes. The ritual that marks the transition between
two stages of the life course is *reversed*: to elicit compassion and seek protection in their liminal state, these teenagers regress to childhood rather
than move forward to adulthood.

In the US context, ideas about which children deserve compassion in-
tersect with chronological age, as well as with gendered and racialized
constructions. Younger children are seen as more deserving of adult protection than teenagers. Girls are more readily seen as vulnerable victims
as compared to boys, who are stigmatized as deviant in the context of gendered processes of deportation and policing in communities of color. All
Central American youths, but particularly boys, risk being criminalized
as MS-13 gang members and, thus, being associated with the category of
persecutor, rather than persecuted, in the asylum process.

HOW IMMIGRANT YOUTHS ADAPT TO THE UNITED STATES: FROM ACCULTURATION TO LEGAL SOCIALIZATION

The case of unaccompanied minors provides a strategic opportunity to
insert the previously neglected role of the state in the scholarship on
immigrant children. Studies of immigrant assimilation have examined the
experiences of US citizen children of immigrants,[69] undocumented children who migrate with their parents at a young age,[70] and, more recently,
teenagers who migrate independently but remain outside of state systems because they are never apprehended and admitted as unaccompanied minors.[71] These studies have produced theories to explain how an
individual's stage in the life cycle at migration and family-level characteristics stratify assimilation outcomes like educational attainment and
socioeconomic mobility. Processes of acculturation have been identified
as one key mechanism that leads to positive assimilation outcomes. In
other words, youths are socialized to "Americanize" or acquire US cultural
values and English-language skills, becoming more similar to the "mainstream" native-born population.[72]

Unaccompanied minors' experiences in the United States differ from the conventional assimilation model in important ways.[73] In the assimilation model, acculturation and social learning are a consequence of the process of settlement, but they occur slowly over time, emerging from everyday interactions, which take place largely in inclusive institutions like K–12 public education. Conversely, from the moment when they first step foot on US soil, unaccompanied minors interact intensively with state bureaucrats and are socialized quickly as they navigate the different agencies of the maze-like US immigration system. Like all asylum seekers, unaccompanied minors face high informational barriers to pursue their claims for relief, which require specific knowledge of complex immigration laws that lay people typically do not possess. They also face linguistic barriers, which makes interactions with US bureaucracies even more challenging. To overcome these high barriers and pursue claims for legal status, unaccompanied minors are reliant on legal brokers who teach them about the law.

Taking these differences into account, I shift attention away from the processes of *acculturation* that have been the focus of past migration scholarship to, instead, propose the analytic lens of *legal socialization*, which I borrow from research in criminology. Legal socialization is the "process whereby people develop their relationship with the law via the acquisition of law-related values, attitudes, and reasoning capacities."[74] Because the law is a key institution that structures society and guides individual behavior, learning about the law is an important part of growing up in society. While legal socialization can occur throughout life, childhood and adolescence have been identified as key moments in this process.

The internalization of law-related values occurs through sustained social interactions in legal institutions and bureaucracies, as well as in other institutions based on rules and relationships of authority, like school and family. Individuals can develop positive or negative legal attitudes and perceptions of the fairness of authority figures. Research on US citizen adolescents and adults has found that frequent or negative interactions with the police and other punitive institutions causes individuals to become disenfranchised.[75] They develop legal attitudes that range from "legal cynicism"—the idea that the law is unfair and cannot help them—to an "oppositional consciousness"— the idea that rules are illegitimate and should be repudiated.[76]

Overall, immigrants tend to have higher levels of trust than citizens in the laws and institutions of the receiving country because they compare it with countries of origin where they suffered rights violations and lack of liberty.[77] Yet this gap decreases over time and across generations. Undocumented 1.5 generation children socialized in US schools from a young age learn that the privileges afforded to their US citizen peers are unavailable to them due to their legal status.[78] This sense of unfairness has led youths to become activists in the Dreamers social movement, contesting immigration laws and procedures to seek policy change and disrupt deportations.[79] Some groups of recently arrived undocumented adults can experience distrust of the state, which instead dissuades them from claiming rights. Immigrants who spend long periods of time in detention develop legal cynicism.[80] Those who live in the shadows, at risk of workplace raids and arrest, are fearful of the state.[81] While undocumented adults face exclusion and legal violence, the legal socialization of unaccompanied minors occurs in a mixed context of reception, characterized by laws that exclude and protect them. This book will describe how these youths develop understandings of the law and claim rights and belonging as they adapt to their new homes.

CENTRAL AMERICAN YOUTH MIGRATION IN HISTORICAL CONTEXT AND THE ORIGINS OF PROTECTIVE LAWS

The historical treatment of Central Americans by the US government has brought about a series of path-dependent processes that have both created the conditions that push youths to migrate alone from Central America today (see chapter 2) and have crucially shaped the legal context of reception that these youths encounter upon their arrival. This section explains how existing protections for children and asylum seekers were introduced in US immigration policy as a result of the historic tug of war between proponents of immigration restriction and advocates.

Salvadorans and Guatemalans started seeking asylum in the United States in the 1980s. They were fleeing civil war and the persecution of right-wing military regimes backed by US funding. Much like it does today, the United States already externalized migration control back then by financing Mexico to apprehend and deport Central American migrants transiting North.[82] Those who made it were not considered refugees. The Ronald

Reagan and George Bush administrations (1981–1993) granted only about 2 percent of Salvadoran and Guatemalan asylum claims.[83] This treatment was characteristic of the Cold War approach to refugee policy, where humanitarian admissions also served the purpose of pursuing geopolitical objectives, designating some countries as enemies and others as allies in the fight against communism.

In response, civil society mobilized in the Sanctuary Movement to demand that the US government provide a safe haven and recognition as refugees to Central Americans.[84] Advocates filed a class action lawsuit, *American Baptist Church (ABC) versus Thornburg*, that represented over five hundred thousand Guatemalan and Salvadoran asylum seekers.[85] In 1991, the resulting settlement agreement established that the US government had not fairly assessed their claims.[86] They would be allowed to reapply in the newly created US asylum office, staffed by a special corps of bureaucrats trained to assess eligibility for refugee status based on the wording of the UN definition. This historic advocacy work both led to the creation of the US asylum bureaucracy and established several legal aid organizations that are still fighting for the rights of asylum seekers and unaccompanied minors to this day, many of which are located in Los Angeles.

Unaccompanied minors were already part of the Central American refugee exodus of the 1980s, with approximately two thousand to five thousand children apprehended at the border each year during that period.[87] Unaccompanied minors were released to family to await the outcomes of their immigration proceedings until 1984, when the US government began to systematically detain immigrant children for the first time.[88] A Los Angeles–based advocacy organization challenged the new child detention policy by representing Jenny Lisette Flores, a fifteen-year-old from El Salvador who was detained in abysmal conditions in a California motel refashioned as a detention facility. A long legal battle ensued, resulting in the 1997 *Flores Settlement*, which established protections for all immigrant children in US detention facilities. The Flores Settlement requires the federal government to hold children in the "least restrictive setting"—licensed facilities that comply with child welfare standards—and to promptly release them from detention. In 2002, with the passage of the Homeland Security Act, which introduced the protected category of "unaccompanied alien child" into US immigration law, the Office of Refugee

Resettlement (ORR) became responsible for the detention of unaccompanied minors.[89]

Officially, the Flores Settlement applies to all children. In practice, however, these protections have been insufficiently implemented in the treatment of *accompanied* children. Both the Obama and Trump administrations detained children alongside their mothers in unlicensed family detention centers for longer than the maximum of twenty days permitted under the Flores Settlement. Advocates responded to these rights violations with several lawsuits, stopping attempts from both the Obama and Trump administrations to eliminate Flores or to limit its scope so it would protect only *unaccompanied* children.[90] During its tenure, the Trump administration separated over five thousand children from their parents at the border and placed them in facilities for unaccompanied minors. Since these children were placed in facilities compliant with child welfare standards, the Trump administration argued that it could detain their parents indefinitely or even deport them. Hundreds of families separated under this policy have yet to be reunited. Prior administrations had already considered family separations as means to circumvent the Flores Settlement, but none actually carried through with them, deeming the practice to be far too unethical and cruel.[91]

The most important piece of US legislation that protects unaccompanied minors today was passed in 2008: the Trafficking Victims Protection Reauthorization Act (TVPRA). Advocates for children's rights gained bipartisan support in Congress during the George W. Bush administration, convincing lawmakers to include protections for unaccompanied minors in a law intended for trafficking victims by arguing that persecuted children deserve the same protections as those who are trafficked.[92] The TVPRA introduced a host of protections. For one, it established that unaccompanied minors are exempt from credible fear screenings at the border, the interviews that adults must pass to be classified as asylum seekers and avoid immediate deportation. Unlike adults, unaccompanied minors are automatically admitted.

Importantly, this protection applies only to unaccompanied minors from noncontiguous countries, which means that Mexicans are excluded.[93] Officially, Mexican minors are screened by the Border Patrol to determine whether they are trafficking victims or have a credible fear of persecution before they are deported through an expedited process. In practice, however, these screenings have been denounced by advocates as inadequate. This explains why Mexican unaccompanied minors make up just 5 percent of youths placed in ORR custody, despite the fact that they comprise a large portion of arrivals and flee similar forms of violence and harm as Central Americans.[94] It is, of course, no coincidence that the most numerous nationality group of unaccompanied minors who migrated to the United States at the time when the 2008 TVPRA was approved was explicitly excluded from this provision (Figure 1). This was a means to limit the scope of this protective policy to keep overall levels of child migration low. Lawmakers did not anticipate that increased numbers of eligible Central Americans would arrive years later and benefit from this protection. Central Americans from El Salvador, Guatemala, and Honduras surpassed Mexicans in 2013, and they still make up the vast majority of unaccompanied minors arriving in the United States today. Following surges at the border during the Obama and Trump administrations, lawmakers tried to amend the TVPRA to do away with this protection, but they were ultimately unsuccessful.[95]

The TVPRA also introduced other protections for unaccompanied minors in the US asylum process, which otherwise discriminates between asylum seekers who are apprehended at the border and those who are not. The former group can apply for asylum only in a trial setting in immigration court, where they face cross-examination from a government attorney whose job is to argue for their deportation. The latter group first apply during one-on-one interviews at the USCIS asylum office; they are sent to immigration court to appeal only in case of a negative outcome.[96] Unlike apprehended adults, unaccompanied minors are given full due process.[97] They can first apply at the asylum office, an agency that grants asylum cases at higher rates than immigration court and that trains its officers in child-friendly interview modalities.

Another key protection for unaccompanied minors at the US asylum office was introduced procedurally through an internal memorandum circulated in 2013. The Kim Memo established that the asylum office should accept the initial determination of unaccompanied minor status— assigned, at the border, to minors apprehended without their parents or legal guardians—even *after* these youths reunify with their parents or turn eighteen. This is a crucial protection because most unaccompanied minors arrive in the United States as older teenagers—close to the legal threshold of adulthood—and, before the Kim Memo, they had "aged out" of their access to the asylum office. As we will see in chapter 5, the Trump administration undermined this protection, making it more difficult for the asylum office to take jurisdiction over unaccompanied minors' cases when they submit their asylum applications after their eighteenth birthday. Litigation seeking to safeguard this protection is ongoing as this book goes to press.[98]

During its time in office, the Trump administration introduced hundreds of executive actions targeting virtually all categories of immigrants.[99] Dozens of these were aimed specifically at unaccompanied minors and asylum seekers in a blitzkrieg that advocates described as "the death of asylum." In addition to the sheer volume of exclusionary measures, a qualitative change took place during the Trump era. When pursuing goals of immigration control, the US government no longer tried to signal even merely performative compliance with its legal commitments and humanitarian concerns, as it had done under the Obama and prior administrations.

The policy most exemplary of this anti-democratic turn was the so-called Migrant Protection Protocols (MPP). In violation of non-refoulement, MPP required asylum seekers who presented themselves at the US-Mexico border to apply for refugee status in tent courts in Mexico. There, obtaining access to attorneys was nearly impossible, grant rates were virtually zero, and asylum seekers faced severe danger and human rights violations.[100] Yet, tellingly, even in the particularly exclusionary Trump era, unaccompanied minors were exempted from MPP. It was only in 2020, with the COVID pandemic, that the Trump administration started to deny entry even to this protected category of children, in violation of the TVPRA. Using Title 42, an obscure public health provision, the Trump administration expelled all immigrants who arrived at the border, including unaccompanied minors, with no recourse or ability to seek asylum. Over thirteen thousand unaccompanied minors had been expelled when, in November 2020, advocates secured a temporary injunction exempting this population from Title 42 expulsions.[101] For over two years, unaccompanied minors were virtually the only group of asylum seekers admitted at the border. Indeed, during that time, Trump's policies had the effect of *producing* more unaccompanied child migration, as asylum-seeking families stuck in Mexico and desperate to save their children sent them to the US-Mexico border alone.[102]

Table 2   Summary of US laws and policies protecting unaccompanied minors

1990 Public Law No. 101-649	Introduces Special Immigrant Juvenile Status (SIJS) in response to pressures from child welfare advocates in Southern California. SIJS was initially narrowly designed to provide a path to legal status for undocumented children in foster care.
1997 Flores Settlement	Introduces protections for all immigrant children in detention facilities:
	- Children must be detained in the "least restrictive setting" and promptly released to a family member or other responsible adult. - Children can only be held in non-licensed facilities in emergency contexts and for a maximum of twenty days.
2002 Homeland Security Act	Introduces the unaccompanied minor category in US immigration law (formally, "unaccompanied alien child").
	Designates the Office of Refugee Resettlement as responsible for detaining unaccompanied minors.
2008 TVPRA	Strengthens protections for unaccompanied minors at the border by establishing that they can be held for no longer than seventy-two hours in CBP custody.
	Protects unaccompanied minors in the asylum process:
	- Exemption from credible fear screenings at the border (except Mexicans, who are screened through separate process). - Exemption from one-year filing deadline. - Guarantees access to the USCIS asylum office.
	Expands SIJS eligibility: from only children abandoned, abused, neglected by *both parents* to also children abandoned, etc. by *one parent* and reunifying with the other in the United States (the former group must apply before age twenty-one and the latter before age eighteen).
2013 Kim Memo	Protects access to the USCIS asylum office for youths categorized as unaccompanied minors at the border even after they turn eighteen or reunify with parents.

Under Biden, additional exemptions from Title 42 expulsions have been introduced, allowing certain vulnerable families and individuals, such as those with medical conditions, to enter the United States at the discretion of the Border Patrol. Following the Russian invasion, Ukrainians have also been allowed to enter the country. Several lawsuits are ongoing as this book goes to press, with the Biden administration seeking to end Title 42 and a host of Republican states trying to preserve the policy. Early in its tenure, the Biden administration also attempted to end MPP to restore access to the US asylum process, an effort likewise met with multiple conservative lawsuits. It took two years of litigation until the Supreme Court finally granted the administration permission to end MPP and restore access to asylum in June 2022. However, until Title 42 remains in effect, many individuals seeking protection will continue to be turned back at the border.[103]

As we will see, the Biden administration has intervened to roll back some of the draconian changes of the Trump era, returning the legal context of reception back to the Obama-era status quo in some regards but not others. Throughout the book, I discuss what changed from Obama to Trump, and how advocates responded to the Trump administration's exclusionary changes to continue to seek protection for their young clients. In chronicling these distinct political contexts, this book demonstrates the aspects of humanitarian laws that are resilient and shows which rights and protections are most at risk when the state privileges exclusion and immigration control.

THE MULTIAGENCY BUREAUCRATIC MAZE FOR UNACCOMPANIED MINORS

Because of all the policies described above and summarized in Table 2, unaccompanied minors navigate a unique, multistep trajectory through the multiple agencies of the maze-like US immigration bureaucracy (Figure 3, Figure 4). Most unaccompanied minors cross the US-Mexico border at the Rio Grande Valley in Texas, where they are either apprehended or turn themselves in to Customs and Border Protection (CBP).[104] Within seventy-two hours of apprehension, unaccompanied minors are transferred to ORR detention facilities, where they spend between one and four months on average.[105]

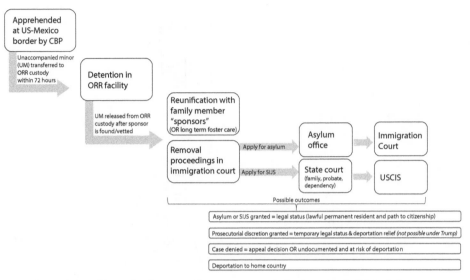

Fig. 3. The multistep legal process for unaccompanied minors in the United States. (Chart by author)

To comply with the Flores Settlement, ORR releases unaccompanied minors to individuals who serve as their "sponsors." At this stage, the legal label "unaccompanied" is effectively a misnomer since the vast majority of youths are released to the care of family members: their parent(s), in 60 percent of cases, and other family members, in 31 percent of cases.[106] Since minors, by definition, lack legal capacity, their adult family member "sponsors" play an important role in supporting them, not just in their everyday lives, but also as they navigate US immigration proceedings. However, most of these adults are undocumented immigrants, which can make it challenging for them to support youths' immigration cases. After their release, youths are placed in removal proceedings in immigration court, and they request deportation relief by applying for asylum and/or SIJS (Figure 2; Table 3).

There are different potential outcomes to the legal process that I examine in this book. These outcomes have life-changing implications for youths. In the best-case scenario, youths win their asylum or SIJS cases; they are protected and on the path to permanent residency and US citizenship. Alternatively, their immigration cases may be closed, or youths may be granted temporary deportation relief.[107] On the other hand, youths'

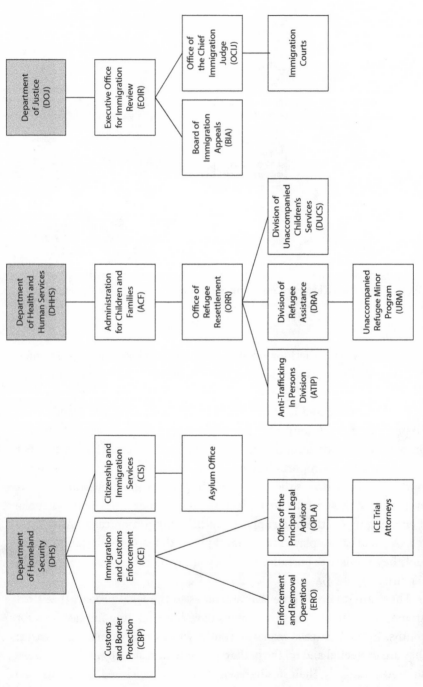

Fig. 4. Federal agencies that process unaccompanied minors. (Byrne and Miller 2012)

Table 3   Total number of SIJS applications submitted
to USCIS, 2010–2020

2010	1,646
2011	2,226
2012	2,969
2013	3,996
2014	5,815
2015	11,528
2016	19,574
2017	22,161
2018	21,917
2019	20,721
2020	18,711

SOURCE: Number of I-360 Petitions for SIJS by Fiscal Year
(https://www.uscis.gov/sites/default/files/document/reports/
I360_sij_performancedata_fy2022_qtr1.pdf)

cases may be denied. They can either appeal these decisions—an onerous process involving additional financial and emotional costs—or remain
undocumented and living in the shadows. The worst-case scenario is that
youths are deported back to their home countries, where their lives are in
danger. While we have insufficient data on the fates of those who lose their
asylum cases, one Human Rights Watch report documented 138 cases of
Salvadorans, including unaccompanied minors, who were killed in recent
years after the US government deported them.[108]

LOS ANGELES AS A RESEARCH SITE

Los Angeles was an ideal location to conduct this study for several reasons. First, it is the main destination for unaccompanied minors in the
United States. Between 2014 and 2019, nearly twenty thousand unaccompanied minors were released from ORR custody to sponsors residing
in Los Angeles and the other nine counties that fall under the jurisdiction of the LA Immigration Court.[109] Second, Los Angeles is a relatively
immigrant-friendly context as compared to other parts of the country.

The Los Angeles asylum office has a reputation for being staffed by liberal and young officers, and it granted the cases of unaccompanied minors at higher rates than the national average during the years this research took place.[110] Compared to other parts of the country, Southern California State courts are also more favorable to SIJS applicants.[111]

Third, due to the availability of federal-, state-, and county-level funding, and to the existence of a network of advocates dating back to the Sanctuary Movement of the 1980s, Los Angeles is relatively well served by legal aid organizations. Many attorneys specialize in working with unaccompanied minors. Indeed, between 2014 and 2017, 70–79 percent of unaccompanied minors whose cases were pending before the Los Angeles immigration court were represented compared to 60–69 percent nationwide.[112] Even so, since the United States does not provide government-funded access to counsel to all immigrant children in removal proceedings, demand for free and affordable legal services far exceeded the supply even in Los Angeles (see chapter 4).

Overall, the relatively favorable Los Angeles environment and its consolidated network of legal aid organizations made this study feasible, despite the inherent difficulties in accessing this hard-to-reach population of immigrant youths for research purposes. It also allowed me to better observe, not only the exclusionary forces that have been the focus of past studies on undocumented and asylum-seeking adults, but also the protective forces at work in the immigration system, which may have been obscured in a more anti-immigrant part of the country.

STRUCTURE OF THE BOOK

The book is structured to guide the reader along the pathways that unaccompanied minors take from their countries of origin through the multiagency bureaucratic maze that awaits them in the United States (Figure 4). Chapter 2 is set in El Salvador, Guatemala, and Honduras. I discuss how multiple forms of violence rooted in broader historical and structural processes, and patterned in age-specific and gendered ways, prompt youth migration from the region today. Chapter 3 describes youths' initial institutional encounters and the quick start of their legal socialization upon their arrival in the United States, during apprehension at the border, detention in ORR facilities, and the state-mediated process of release from custody and reunification with family members. Chapter 4 describes how unaccompanied minors obtain free or affordable legal representation. I explain how legal aid organizations manage the limited resources at their disposal by using different strategies to select clients, some of which, in turn, have implications in structuring unequal access to protection. Chapter 5 examines how legal brokers help youths apply for asylum and SIJS. I expose the mismatches between the migration experiences of de facto refugee youths and the narrow, formalistic legal definitions of the refugee and the abandoned, abused, or neglected child. I discuss how attorneys frame youths' experiences of victimization and escape from violence to fit the legal molds available to them and the multiple challenges that arise in the process. Chapter 6 widens the analytic lens beyond the legal process to explore other dimensions of Central American unaccompanied minors' lives as adolescents on the brink of adulthood navigating school, work, and conflict during reunification with family after long periods of separation. Chapter 7 synthesizes the study contributions and makes policy recommendations that would enable the United States to better fulfil its legal and ethical responsibility to protect vulnerable young people who migrate on their own.

2 Central American Youths Escape from Violence

From the safety of a nondescript Los Angeles coffee shop, Carla told me the story of how she and her older brother escaped from the violence they faced in El Salvador. The youngest of three siblings, Carla was the second to flee, at the age of sixteen. She did so with the help of her parents, undocumented immigrants who had both migrated to the United States by the time she was just seven years old. After MS-13 gang members killed Carla's uncle, her mother began to receive threatening phone calls: "They called her from jail and told her they would kill my brother, send him to her in pieces. They said they knew where to find him, where he studied." Carla's parents decided to pay a coyote to help their seventeen-year-old son reach the United States first. They believed that, of their three children, he was most at risk because he had received a direct death threat, and the gang members threatening him knew his whereabouts.

Carla explained how gendered violence shaped the risks that she and her brother faced in their everyday lives as teenagers in El Salvador, even before the situation escalated with their uncle's assassination: "He was most at risk because he is a boy. Gang members hit boys, beat them up. They abuse girls and sometimes hit them too. I had a friend in El Salvador. She was walking to school with her brother when gang members beat

36

him up and [sexually] abused her. That was our fear. I thought, 'what if that happens to me too?' because I walked to school too." To extract her from these dangers, Carla's parents next paid a coyote to bring her to the United States, where she had been living for over a year when I interviewed her. At the time, Carla's sister, a young woman aged twenty-one, was still in El Salvador. Since she was older and no longer attended school, the family considered her to be less at risk, choosing to invest their scarce resources in the migration of their two younger children first. Even so, Carla's sister was living in fear and largely secluded at home, waiting for her own chance to migrate, when her parents could save enough money for the trip.

The year Carla fled, in 2015, El Salvador was ranked the world's most violent country not at war. The truce between the two rival gangs or *maras*—MS-13 and Barrio 18—fell apart, and the homicide rate peaked at 103 per 100,000, or twenty-one times higher than the US average.[1] With a wisdom beyond her years, Carla reflected on the constraints on Central American youths' life chances and their ability to choose to migrate: "Sometimes young people don't have the opportunity to come here [to the United States], so they decide it's better to join [the gangs] so nothing will happen to them. I think they would like to come here instead too, but they can't." What Carla had, and others lacked, were resources that enabled her to overcome significant structural constraints and migrate to safety in the United States. Carla's parents lived in Los Angeles. They could afford the smuggling services indispensable to circumvent restrictive US immigration policies, which have made mobility increasingly costly and dangerous for Central Americans.

This chapter argues that Central American unaccompanied minors are de facto refugees, in other words, individuals who escape life-threatening violence. Contrary to conventional wisdom, which assumes that refugees—and the children among them in particular—are passive victims, I demonstrate that refugee youths have migratory agency. When Central American youths and their families make migration decisions in contexts of violence, they exercise agency through the strategic management of risk and mobilization of resources to overcome the constraints imposed on them by US immigration policies. Restrictive US policy relegates most Central Americans like Carla's parents to states of "illegality" and prohibits them from legally reunifying their children or even traveling to visit them.[2] As a result, the only way for families to reunite is for children to undertake costly unauthorized journeys to the United States. Central American families' migration decisions are thus informed by both the need to extract youths from danger and the underlying desire of families to be together.

Two sets of conceptual dichotomies have been used to describe migratory phenomena: economic and voluntary, as associated with immigrants; or political and forced, as associated with refugees. Scholars have since critiqued the inadequacy of the *economic* versus *political* distinction for understanding both macro-level push factors in sending countries and individuals' motivations to migrate. In practice, these two forces overlap and are analytically indistinguishable.[3] However, we still have not advanced beyond the second conceptual dichotomy: *voluntary* (immigrants) versus *forced* (refugees). Much has been theorized about the migration decision-making of so-called "voluntary" immigrants. New Economics of Labor Migration (NELM) scholars argue that families diversify risk in their income sources and pursue socioeconomic mobility by investing in the migration of one of their members, awaiting future rewards from remittances.[4] Migrant networks theorists have pointed to the role that the information and resources—circulating from immigrants in the receiving country to potential emigrants in sending countries—play in facilitating migration by lowering its costs.[5] Conversely, by thinking about refugee migration as *forced*—and hence devoid of agency—existing scholarship has ignored the question of how individuals make migration decisions in contexts of violence.

This chapter tackles that question. I link macro-level sending context dynamics to the micro-level migration decisions of Central American de facto refugee youths. Heeding recent calls to apply theories of international migration to understand refugee flows, I leverage migrant networks theory and NELM's analysis of family-level risk management.[6] I extend the latter to examine risks associated with violence rather than economic risks. The first part of the chapter describes how these risks in Central America are patterned along the dimensions of age and gender, as reflected in the criminal victimization of minors, the forcible gang recruitment of teenage boys, and gendered exposure to violence in and outside the home. These patterns of violence are rooted in broader structures and institutions and in a history shaped by decades of US intervention in Central America aimed at protecting its own economic and geopolitical interests. In other words, the United States has played a role in, and bears responsibility for, creating the conditions that push unaccompanied minors to flee their homes today.

The second part of the chapter delves into how micro-level migration decisions take place in this context. As the legal label suggests, some *unaccompanied* minors indeed migrate entirely on their own and without notifying caretakers. However, in most cases, youth migration from Central America is instead a family-level risk-management strategy. Parents and relatives, based in the United States and the home country, help youths manage risk and facilitate their migration to different degrees, depending on their resource availability and on how much they know about how violence is affecting their children's lives. Families strategize migration decisions by evaluating the "cost of staying" in the home country, as determined by risks of different types and degrees that youths face because of their exposure to gendered and age-specific patterns of violence.[7] As Carla's story shows, when families have limited resources to pay smuggling fees and more than one child faces danger, they make risk assessments to determine which child should migrate first.

When migration cannot be planned and funded quickly, youths may go into hiding, sometimes for prolonged periods of time. These youths inhabit what Susan Coutin calls the "space of non-existence," where potential refugees are biologically alive, but their legal and social personhood are erased.[8] For teenagers, whose stage in the life cycle is defined by the transition from childhood to adulthood, inhabiting this space means that their life-course transitions are put on hold. The inability to plan for or imagine a future can itself have violent and enduring traumatic effects. Like youths for whom migration is a rite of passage to adulthood, de facto refugee youths migrate, not only to seek safety from harm, but also to find a home where they can grow and pursue full lives. To find the lasting protection they need to live and grow, they seek asylum in the United States. Yet, while their experiences in El Salvador, Guatemala, and Honduras make these youths de facto refugees, this does not ensure that they will be recognized as such and granted refugee status. As we will see in later chapters, the US asylum system fails to recognize youths' agency and how age and stage in the life course shape migration decisions in contexts of violence.

CONTEXTUALIZING VIOLENCE AND CONDITIONS IN THE NORTHERN COUNTRIES OF CENTRAL AMERICA

If we measure the pervasiveness of violence in society by homicide rates, El Salvador, Guatemala, and Honduras rank among the most dangerous countries in the world. Quantitative studies have found links between the frequency of instances of criminal victimization and increased propensity to report intentions to migrate among adults.[9] Short-term increases in regional homicide rates are also associated with higher volumes of out-migration of unaccompanied minors from those same regions.[10] A survey conducted with transit migrants in Mexico by Doctors Without Borders found that over two-thirds of adults emigrating from El Salvador, Guatemala, and Honduras experienced the murder, disappearance, or kidnapping of a relative.[11] Others experienced direct assaults on themselves or their families (20.8%), extortion (14.9%), threats (14.3%), forcible gang recruitment (10.5%), and confinement (5.5%). An analysis of forensic medical evaluations of asylum-seeking children found that they had experienced direct physical violence (78%), threats of violence or death (71%), forcible gang recruitment (24%), sexual violence (18%), and witnessed violent acts (59%) prior to their flight; this violence was inflicted by family in 47 percent of cases and by gangs in 60 percent of cases.[12] But what historical processes and structural forces lie behind these numbers? What are the causes of violence, and how do institutions sustain it?

In the northern countries of Central America (Figure 5), social movements that pursued goals of democratization and wealth redistribution have long been met with militarized political repression. This authoritarian state response produced forced displacement dating as far back as the 1930s in the case of Salvadorans, who first fled to neighboring Honduras, where landless peasants had previously engaged in seasonal migration to work in plantations owned by foreign companies.[13] State violence peaked during the civil wars: at least seventy thousand were killed and

Fig. 5. Map of Central American sending countries. (Map by cartographer William Nelson)

millions displaced from El Salvador between 1979 and 1992, and at least two hundred thousand were killed—80 percent of whom were of Mayan origin—and about one million were displaced from Guatemala between 1960 and 1996.[14] US intervention leading up to, during, and after these conflicts has been well documented. In the 1980s, the United States provided military funding to the right-wing dictatorships that were persecuting both left-wing insurgents and common citizens in El Salvador and Guatemala. Honduras was used as a training ground for the US-funded Contras fighting the communist Sandinista government in neighboring Nicaragua. Although Honduras did not face a civil war, the Contras caused disruption along its border with Nicaragua. State repression grew as small leftist guerrilla groups emerged, with political disappearances and murders becoming increasingly common.[15]

Many fled to the United States during this period, mostly from El Salvador and Guatemala. In the context of the Cold War, the United States used asylum as a geopolitical tool, denying refugee status to Salvadorans and Guatemalans who fled the very conflicts it supported. Lacking legal status and financial stability, Salvadorans raised undocumented children in poor neighborhoods of cities like Los Angeles, where the MS-13 (Mara Salvatrucha) street gang was born, initially as a means for youths to protect themselves from ethnic conflict.[16] The widespread incarceration of gang members during the war on drugs in the 1990s caused these informal youth cliques to "graduate" into more violent criminal organizations. As gang members were targeted for deportation, US gang culture was introduced in Central America. Between 1994 and 1997, over ten thousand Salvadorans, Guatemalans, and Hondurans with criminal records were deported.[17]

These young men were forced back to states undermined by decades of foreign intervention, where the disarmament process was largely unsuccessful after the peace accords were signed in the 1990s. Weapons were readily available in a society with large numbers of unemployed men who formerly fought on both sides of the war, an institutional culture of violence within the security forces, and justice systems that enabled widespread impunity.[18] The aftermath of the civil wars produced "criminogenic" conditions: through a process of mimicry of state violence, common criminals began to use strategies to victimize others that resembled those used by the state to punish dissidents. The most marginalized thus began to inflict violence on their family members, peers, and neighbors. The *maras* have since been able to draw from a large recruitment pool of youth because El Salvador, Guatemala, and Honduras are demographically young countries, where economic hardship is widespread, and educational opportunities and government programs to advance the social integration of youths are limited. In all three countries, governments have used military force to respond to the proliferation of gangs. These "mano dura" (heavy hand) policies have done little to protect citizens from harm. Instead, these policies endangered the shift to a new civilian police force and favored a return to the military-dominant security of the wartime era.[19]

Indeed, scholars have refused the very idea of a "postwar" era in the northern countries of Central America. Decades of state violence and psychological warfare waged against common citizens have had enduring effects, causing widespread fear and distrust of state institutions, as well as the normalization of violence in society. Normalization expresses itself as a "numbing effect" among people who have long witnessed brutally violent acts and in the form of symbolic violence, as existing inequalities and injustices become so internalized that they seem commonplace.[20] Today, political violence and criminal violence have become indistinguishable as both state and nonstate actors terrorize the population through crime, corruption, gang violence, lynching, and paramilitarism.[21]

The blurring of criminal and political violence in Central America is more broadly reflective of a changing world where cross-border displacement is fueled less by authoritarian regimes and more by states that fail to guarantee basic human rights, leaving their citizens to face severe danger and deprivation.[22] As we will see in chapter 5, this blurriness between political (state) and criminal (private) actors raises important challenges for Central Americans attempting to obtain recognition as refugees in the United States today. Arguing that children victimized by non-state persecutors, such as gangs or family members, satisfy the refugee definition is a contentious legal struggle, which became increasingly challenging as new restrictive asylum case law was introduced under Trump. Yet criminal violence in Central America is effectively sustained by structures and institutions. So-called "private" actors commit violent acts with impunity in the context of corrupt judicial systems and police forces.

Domestic violence is a clear example. It takes place in the context of institutionalized discrimination, unequal power relations between men and women, and gender ideologies that devalue women's lives and legitimize punishments when women deviate from normative gender role expectations.[23] Justice systems in El Salvador, Guatemala, and Honduras have historically had inconsequential punishments for crimes against women. More recently, protections for victims of domestic violence and sexual abuse have come to exist in the law. However, these provisions are seldom enforced by the police, and only small percentages of cases are prosecuted.[24] In fact, in the past twenty years, feminicide rates have increased in the northern countries of Central America, becoming the highest in all of Latin America and among the worst in the world.[25] Between 18 percent and 26 percent of women and girls have experienced physical or sexual intimate partner violence at least once during their lifetimes.[26] In 2019, three-quarters of the acts of sexual violence reported in El Salvador were committed against girls under age seventeen. In practice, women and girls are ignored when they report crimes, which allows male perpetrators to victimize them with impunity. Like women, children and youths (girls and boys) fall victim to domestic violence. They similarly have little recourse when they are victimized by their family members because local institutions to report child abuse and extract children from violent homes are largely ineffective.[27]

In her book *Enduring Violence*, Cecilia Menjívar argues that structural violence—institutionalized inequalities of wealth, status, rights, and power—interact with and sustain seemingly individualized forms of interpersonal violence.[28] El Salvador, Guatemala, and Honduras have some of the most unequal wealth distributions in the world. Socioeconomic inequalities rooted in Spanish colonialism have been exacerbated by decades of subsequent developmental reforms, which have privileged the interests of foreign companies and a small, allied ruling class, and by more recent neoliberal policies, like the Central American Free Trade Agreement with the United States. These economic policies have been pursued hand in hand with the political repression of labor and indigenous organizers, making economic and political migration drivers difficult to disentangle, already for past refugee flows.[29]

Suffering has always been disproportionately distributed among the most disadvantaged members of society in El Salvador, Honduras, and Guatemala. It is precisely individuals at the bottom of the social hierarchy—the poor, women, children and youth, indigenous groups— who are most at risk of being victimized by gangs or family members today. The vast majority of the stories that I describe in this book are of youths from working-class, poor, or indigenous families. Many of these families were sustained by remittances from the United States or dependent on the labor of all family members, including children, for survival. Rather than individual tragedies or private matters, the crimes and victimization suffered by vulnerable youths must be understood in the context of a long history of state violence, which has devalued the lives of the poor and disadvantaged in the northern countries of Central America. The pervasive failure of sending states to uphold the human rights of their citizens keeps this violence unchecked.

VIOLENCE PATTERNED BY AGE AND GENDER:
RISK EXPOSURE AND THE COST OF STAYING

As a result of the historical and structural forces described above, violence in Central America is patterned along the dimensions of age and gender. These patterns shape the types and degree of risk that youths are exposed to today. Instances of victimization accumulate to make the perceived cost of staying in the home country higher for youths, prompting their migration decisions.

Victimization by gangs particularly affects young people in El Salvador, Honduras, and Guatemala. Criminologists agree that young men ages fifteen to twenty-four not only commit most street crime, but they also primarily victimize peers in the same age group.[30] Forcible recruitment into MS-13 and Barrio 18 is an extremely dangerous affair because the *maras* distinguish themselves by using brutal violence during initiation, subjecting youths to manipulation, humiliation, beatings, and death threats. My respondents recounted how their friends and family were killed because they had refused to join the gangs. It is no coincidence that most Central American unaccompanied minors migrate to the United States as teenagers ages fifteen to seventeen.[31] Becoming teenagers exposes youths to forcible recruitment and victimization at the hands of the *maras*. Between 2011 and 2017, roughly 8 percent of the entire demographic of seventeen-year-olds emigrated from these three countries.[32]

Schools were often sites of gang activity and recruitment. Commutes to school through rival gang territories exposed youths to dangerous interactions with gang members. As a result, youths often stopped going to school months, or even years, prior to their migration. Cadmael, a Guatemalan Maya youth, was sixteen years-old when school became too dangerous for him to attend. Gang members began trying to recruit him by telling him that joining was his only option because people "like him [read: indigenous people] need to disappear" and "never get good jobs." They threatened to kill him if he refused to join. When gang members severely beat him up after school one day, Cadmael decided to leave the country. His mother was initially reticent to let him leave because she knew all too well that the journey to the United States was dangerous. Cadmael eventually persuaded her that the risks of staying in Guatemala outweighed those of the journey. He planned to join his father who had migrated to Los Angeles when he was a small child because there was no work in their town for Mayan men. Indigenous groups suffer deep-seated discrimination from the Spanish-descendent population and structural violence not only in Guatemala but also in Honduras and El Salvador. The conditions that pushed his father to migrate years earlier had been further exacerbated by direct interpersonal violence, putting Cadmael's life at risk.

Following Zolberg and colleagues, in thinking about the de facto refugee as an individual who escapes life threatening-violence, I conceptualize life not merely as biological existence but also as social existence and the basic material and organizational conditions necessary to maintain it.[33] For Cadmael, the beatings and threats he had endured might well escalate, resulting in his death. Conditions in Guatemala also posed an existential threat to him because of his age and indigenous background. Cadmael wanted to study to "make something of [him]self" and become an engineer. He marveled at feats like the Golden Gate Bridge and told me that he wanted to build bridges himself one day. As a Maya youth in a Ladino-majority town in Guatemala, however, school had always been a place where he had been bullied and discriminated against by his peers and teachers alike.[34] School had now also become a place where he was in danger. He had no prospects of finishing high school, attending college, or obtaining work in his home country. How was he to envision a future for himself there?

With his decision to migrate, Cadmael had hoped that, in addition to finding refuge from harm in the United States, he would be able to pursue a full social existence in his new home. Yet Cadmael would have a difficult journey ahead to pursue his goals and aspirations to continue his studies. Having lost two years of schooling between the violence he suffered in Guatemala, the journey, and his detention in the Office of Refugee Resettlement (ORR) shelter, he was extremely disadvantaged as a student in the United States. By the time he was released from government custody, he was nearing his eighteenth birthday. He was therefore unable to enroll in high school in Los Angeles, and he had to attend adult school instead. There, he was taking English classes instead of working toward high school completion. He indeed worked in construction, alongside his father, but as a day laborer, not an engineer. Cadmael's case was denied at the asylum office, and this crucially threatened his ability to pursue a full social existence in his new home. The last time we spoke, he was planning to appeal the decision in immigration court. Cadmael was a de facto refugee who escaped from violence. Yet he was relegated to a state of legal limbo with just a work permit while his asylum case was being reassessed, with no guarantee of a positive outcome.

Reflecting broader patterns of gendered violence, while teenage boys like Cadmael were more at risk of forcible recruitment into gang activities, teenage girls living in gang-controlled areas were at risk of experiencing sexual violence at the hands of gang members. Alicia fled from El Salvador at age sixteen after being stalked by a gang member who forcefully tried to touch her whenever she left the house where she lived with her grandmother. One day, the gang member threatened to kidnap her if she did not become his "girlfriend." Alicia and her family knew that these were not empty threats. Years earlier, Alicia's cousin had also been approached by a gang member who wanted her to be his "girlfriend." After she refused, she and her sister were murdered in retaliation. As Alicia recounted, "The gangs killed them both; they cut their heads off and stabbed them over forty times."

Alicia and her family determined that the cost of staying in El Salvador was too high. Alicia's older sister used all her savings to help quickly organize her trip to the United States, where she would join their mother. Conceptualizing migration decision-making as a family-level risk-management strategy made following an assessment of violence in the home country, we might consider that Alicia fled somewhat preemptively. The family made this future risk calculus based on the gang's brutal assassination of Alicia's cousins years earlier. While this does not discount her experience as a de facto refugee, attorneys may struggle with such cases because they provide less lived experiences of suffering that can be used to consolidate humanitarian capital in youths' asylum claims. Like Cadmael, Alicia lost her asylum case. While Alicia did not know why her case was denied, it may have been due to the preemptive nature of her flight, organized before she could fall victim to sexual violence or death.[35] Asylum seekers face a frightening catch-22 as asylum officers and immigration judges decide whether to grant their cases. They must flee early enough to survive yet stay long enough to experience what will be considered a sufficient *amount* of harm to merit refugee status.

Of course, there is no way of knowing what would have happened to Alicia had she stayed. The story of sixteen-year-old Hector from Guatemala, who was able to save his life against all odds, is emblematic of the sheer luck often involved in making it out of violent contexts alive. Gang members had targeted Hector and his two best friends for recruitment. After enduring abuse and beatings, the boys received an ultimatum: if they did not join, the gang would kill them. The situation quickly escalated. Hector's two friends were murdered on two subsequent days. The mother of one the boys had paid for a coyote to smuggle out her son, but it was too late. The boy was murdered the night before he was scheduled to leave. The mother of the boy contacted Hector and urged him to use the passage that she had paid for to save his life. Too afraid to tell his grandmother in Guatemala or his mother in the United States, Hector left immediately with the coyote. He showed up at the US-Mexico border months later, when his family thought he was dead. While youths and their families attempt to assess risk in order to make migration decisions, accurately doing so in a context of violence is based largely on luck. Yet the timing of escape has key implications for youths' chances of success in the US asylum process, as we will see in chapter 5.

Other girls who did not flee preemptively like Alicia did experience sexual violence. Fifteen-year-old Esperanza was raped repeatedly by a gang member in her own home in El Salvador, where she lived alone with her eleven-year-old brother. When Esperanza's parents migrated to the United States, the siblings had initially lived with family members. However, the adults entrusted with their care were physically abusive and neglectful. They did not use the remittances Esperanza's parents sent them to feed the siblings properly or buy them clothing. Because of this, Esperanza's parents decided that their children would be better off living on their own. They did not predict that this living arrangement would place Esperanza at risk. For months, Esperanza was too scared to tell anyone about the sexual abuse she was enduring because the gang member had threatened her life and that of her brother. Esperanza only worked up the courage to tell her mother months later when she became pregnant. As soon as they found out, her parents found a way to bring both siblings to the United States immediately, borrowing money from a relative to pay the coyote, one strategy that families use to quickly plan youth migration.

Unlike Alicia, Esperanza's asylum case, which was based on multiple instances of rape that eventually led to her pregnancy, was granted.

To be sure, teenagers are not the only ones at risk in Central America. Sometimes, youths were not targeted directly by gangs but were still at risk because their family members were targeted. This was the case for victims of extortion. Based on asylum seekers' accounts, the *maras* seemed to be strategic in targeting families they thought could pay extortion fees. They targeted families who owned businesses. Owning a small chicken farm was enough to subject one boy's family in El Salvador to extortion and threats. Gangs also targeted those with migrant relatives in the United States, since they assumed that they would be receiving remittances. One Salvadoran father explained that it was shortly after he migrated to the United States that his wife and three daughters were targeted for extortion, even though he was able to send them very little money. After receiving several threatening notes and calls, the family eventually decided to use the money they could spare to send two of their children—the youngest, who was thirteen, and the oldest, who had a baby of her own—to join their father. Without sufficient resources for the entire family to make the trip, the mother and middle daughter stayed behind.

Those who witnessed violent crimes were likewise exposed to grave danger. Highlighting the ways in which political and criminal violence interact and become blurred in Central America, youths and adults may be victimized by so-called private actors, but their lives are at risk because the police are either corrupt and unwilling to prosecute their victimizers or fearful of suffering repercussions if they do so. Alejandro's story is a case in point. Alejandro witnessed the murder of his best friend, fifteen-year-old Daniel, whose commute through rival gang territories was enough to signal him as a potential informant. This was a death sentence. Alejandro recounted the day MS-13 shot Daniel before his eyes, "I told him to wait for me to get help, but he asked me not to leave him alone. He was afraid they would come back. He asked me to stay with him. I took him in my arms, and he died like that."

At first, Alejandro was wary of cooperating with the police in the investigation of Daniel's murder because he feared retaliation. But the police approached him several times and promised that they would arrest the gang members and protect him. Yet, after only two months, the police released the gang members from jail, supposedly because they lacked sufficient evidence against them. Alejandro's testimony, which had put him in so much danger, had seemingly been discounted. Alejandro thus commented on the broken promise of the Salvadoran justice system, "That's what happens with the police; they set them free. They said they would protect me, but I never once saw a police car outside my house." When I met him at a legal clinic in Los Angeles, Alejandro showed me the copy of his testimony that the police had collected. He was referred to with a code to protect his identity as a witness. Despite his young age, Alejandro knew very well that he was protected on paper but not in practice. He fled to save his life after he learned that the gang members had been released.

As we will see in chapter 5, the *types* of suffering that youths faced in their home countries prior to migration are key in determining the outcomes of their asylum cases, which oftentimes play out in contradictory ways. Despite the very real danger victims of gang violence face in Central America, their lived experiences often fail to satisfy the refugee definition, as it is narrowly interpreted in the United States. Youths' experiences of forcible recruitment by gangs—like Cadmael's—are especially prone to being discounted as the wrong type of suffering, one that is not considered meritorious of relief under existing US asylum case law. Importantly, the approach taken by the United States contradicts the position of the United Nations High Commissioner for Refugees, which instead considers that all forced recruitment by violent groups amounts to persecution.[36] Unlike interactions with gangs, which highlight the agency of both teenagers who resist recruitment and those who become involved, experiences of abuse in the home reify culturally specific Western notions of children as vulnerable because they are dependent on adults. The latter are more likely to satisfy child-specific interpretations of the refugee definition in the United States and to result in an asylum grant. What's more, having experienced abuse at the hands of caretakers can also qualify youths for relief through Special Immigrant Juvenile Status (SIJS).

Child abuse certainly is another driver of youth migration from Central America. As we saw in Esperanza's case, when parents leave their children behind to migrate to the United States, the adult family members entrusted with their care are sometimes abusive. Youths living with their parents in the home country may also suffer domestic violence. While both boys and girls were at risk of child abuse, gender norms could compound these risks for girls. According to patriarchal family structures and understandings of gender roles, girls were expected to participate in household labor and care work. These expectations were sometimes enforced by caretakers through physical punishment. Youths subjected to abuse within the home were also at greater risk of violence outside because of their unstable home environments. Indeed, some youths who fled after their lives were threatened by gangs had previously endured years of victimization at home. Yet it was the latter type of suffering that would position their asylum cases as more likely to win.

Central American unaccompanied minors also migrated to leave conditions of deprivation and economic hardship. In particular, indigenous youths from certain parts of Guatemala—where the homicide rates are lower than in Honduras and El Salvador—told me that they left for two reasons, "to help my family and because of the violence." As noted in chapter 1, experiences of economic deprivation and structural violence are excluded from the legal criterion of persecution. When poor people seek asylum in the Global North, they are more readily perceived as economic migrants and criminalized as "bogus" refugees. Yet these youths' migration decisions also ranged from more to less voluntary on a "continuum of compulsion."[37] For them, migrating to the United States was concurrently a preventative strategy to avoid falling victim to violence in the future, a response to the lack of material and organizational conditions necessary to maintain their social existence, and a proactive strategy to contribute to the survival and well-being of their families. As we have seen, in the northern countries of Central America, violence is patterned along various dimensions of social position, in particular age and gender, yielding cumulative risks that raise the costs of staying in the home country for young people.

TRANSNATIONAL FAMILY COMPOSITION AND THE MIGRATION OF THE FIRST GENERATION

Decades of restrictive US immigration and asylum policy have shaped Central American transnational family structures and the migration of the first

Table 4 Transnational family composition at the time of youth's migration

Youth lived with	Joined mother in US	Joined father in US	Joined both parents in US	Joined other family in US	Had no family in US
Other family in sending country	43	5	7	3	2
Mother in sending country	—	6	—	9	1
Both parents in sending country	—	—	—	23	1

* N = 100 cases (includes formal interviews and subset of legal clinic observations with full family information).

generation, with important implications for youth mobility from Central America today. Virtually all youths who are eventually categorized as unaccompanied minors have family members in the United States at the time of their migration. Only four youths I met over the course of my research had no family at all in the United States at the time of their migration, while 54 percent of youths migrated to join one parent, 7 percent joined both, and 35 percent joined other relatives (Table 4). The most common transnational family composition (43%) among my study participants was that of youths who lived with nonparent relatives in their home countries and migrated to join their mothers in the United States. Some of these mothers had migrated to flee abusive relationships. Others were the main breadwinners of their families, and they had migrated to support their children. This pattern is not surprising, given the high rates of female labor market participation in El Salvador, Guatemala, and Honduras, and the feminization of Central American migration dating back decades.[38]

The second most common type of family composition (32%) was that of youths who lived with their mothers or with both parents in the home country, and who migrated to join other family members in the United States. In most cases, youths had never met or barely knew these relatives. Notably, on both sides of the border, many youths lived with nonparent caretakers, and few lived in households where fathers were present. In their home countries, only about a quarter of youths lived in a household with both parents, while the rest either lived with only their mothers or with nonparent caretakers, usually their grandmothers or aunts. The composition of these transnational families reflects the broader family structures prevalent among socioeconomically disadvantaged families in the northern countries of Central America. Free unions and out-of-wedlock children are common, as well as female-led, multigenerational households and care arrangements.[39] These family-level characteristics are important for both youths' exposure to violence in the home country and migration decision-making dynamics.

Using two examples, I will discuss the intergenerational migration patterns of Central American families in cases when children migrated alone to join one or both of their parents in the United States (61%). In each of these two families, the parents of unaccompanied minors had themselves migrated to escape from violence and could thus be considered de facto refugees. Yet they were denied recognition, legal status, and family reunification rights in the United States. In reading the stories that follow, keep in mind this counterfactual: had the US government recognized the first generation of Central Americans as refugees, as it did for example with the Vietnamese—recognizing its ethical responsibility toward those displaced as a result of US military intervention in Vietnam and resettling them in large numbers—these families would not have experienced separation, their children could have legally joined them in the United States, and they would not have been exposed to violence in their home countries.[40]

Jose and Rafael were two Salvadoran siblings who migrated at ages seventeen and sixteen. They joined their parents, who had been living in Los Angeles for over ten years. Their father, Pedro, migrated from El Salvador for the first time during the civil war, after being targeted by the government due to his involvement with the guerrillas. Pedro was among the 98 percent of asylum seekers denied refugee status by the Reagan administration. He hired an attorney to appeal the decision but was unsuccessful, and he remained an undocumented immigrant. After the peace accords were signed in 1992, Pedro returned to El Salvador, where he fathered his children. His boys were toddlers when Pedro decided to go back to the United States to work and support his family. The following year, however, violence struck the family once again. Jose and Rafael's mother, Juana, started receiving death threats after she witnessed a murder. She fled to the United States, where, despite having escaped from violence, she never applied for asylum, perhaps due to Pedro's unsuccessful attempt years before. She remained an undocumented immigrant as well.

Jose and Rafael stayed in El Salvador in the home of abusive grandparents. The lack of protection at home left them more exposed to violence outside when they reached the risky age of adolescence. Jose was dating a girl in his high school, where there was a heavy gang presence. When they split up, and she started dating a gang member, Jose and his family were targeted. Jose was intimidated, followed home from school, assaulted, and threatened by gang members on multiple occasions. His best friend, who had been recruited by the gang, was murdered. Jose's grandmother received threatening phone calls and extortion requests. These multiple instances of criminal victimization compounded the cost of staying in El Salvador for Jose and Rafael.

Playing the part of both abuser and savior, the boys' grandmother called Pedro and Juana to tell them that it was no longer safe for their sons to live in El Salvador. She asked for help and resources to plan their migration. As undocumented immigrants or, perhaps more accurately, unrecognized refugees, Pedro and Juana had no means to legally reunify their children, leaving them no other option but to rely on a coyote to help them reach safety in the United States. Like both their parents had done in the past, Jose and Rafael escaped from violence, positioning them as de facto refugees. Unlike their parents, however, the brothers faced better odds in a US context of reception positively impacted by years of advocacy work that expanded the scope of asylum protections for unaccompanied minors. Both of their asylum cases were granted.

The next story is that of Kevin—a fourteen-year-old unaccompanied minor—and his mother, Maria, who migrated from Guatemala to escape domestic violence when Kevin was just a baby. Kevin's father was sexually and physically abusive. He threatened to kill Maria if she ever reported him to the police. It was Maria's mother who convinced her to leave her two small children in her care so she could migrate to the United States and save her life. Despite the danger she had been in, Maria could not overcome the feeling that she had abandoned her children. She recounted struggling with that guilt over ten years later, "It was with pain in my soul that I had to come to this country. I never thought I would. People talked about it, but I was happy with my kids and my job. We had food, and we could survive. I think no woman wants to leave her children."

I asked Maria if she knew about asylum and had ever thought to apply. She explained, "No, I was ignorant, I didn't know there were laws for women here." Unbeknownst to Maria, around the time she arrived in the United States, in the early 2000s, other women who had escaped domestic violence like her were engaged in lengthy legal battles that would expand the scope of US asylum protections for women. After two victories for individual claimants from Guatemala and Mexico (Matter of R-A- and Matter of L-R-), in 2014, the Board of Immigration Appeals issued precedent-setting case law, Matter of A-R-C-G-, which officially recognized asylum claims based on domestic violence. This belatedly brought US asylum law up to par with existing protections for women in countries like Canada.[41] This expansion of the US interpretation of the refugee definition would benefit several unaccompanied minors during my research (see chapter 5). Unsurprisingly unaware of the complex legal struggles that were favorably altering the legal context in the country that provided her physical refuge from harm, Maria escaped from violence but lacked recognition as a de jure refugee. Such recognition would have given her freedom from the preoccupation that still loomed large over her life: that her deportation would be a death sentence at the hands of her abusive ex.

Crucially, it would have also given her the right to legally reunify her children. As an undocumented immigrant, Maria worked hard to support her children in Guatemala. Yet, from afar, she had little means to protect her son Kevin from the danger he would face upon reaching adolescence. Kevin's grandmother was a loving caretaker. However, following a common pattern in these transnational families, she was elderly by the time Kevin was targeted for forced recruitment. She was unable to protect Kevin from dangers outside the home. Gendered violence once again shaped exposure to risk in the sending country, prompting migration in this family. When Kevin turned thirteen, his father—an incarcerated gang member—started to contact him from prison to try to involve him in gang activities, a sinister rite of passage through which young boys become men. Conversely, Kevin's older sister was never singled out to this end because of the gendered ways in which gangs target youths.

Kevin had previously had little contact with his father. He did not know that his father had abused his mother, causing her to flee, nor why he had been incarcerated for most of his childhood. Hoping to reestablish a relationship with this man about whom the adults in his life had told him so little, Kevin naively accepted when his father asked him for a "small favor." He thus unwittingly became involved in lower-level gang activities as a courier, picking up extortion money from his neighbors. He started to realize something was wrong when he noticed a new fear in his neighbors' eyes. As the realization of what he was doing became concrete, Kevin grew increasingly desperate. This desperation was reflected in the self-harm behaviors and enduring trauma that he and his mother would later tell me about. Kevin did not feel that he could confide in his elderly grandmother for fear of putting her life at risk, nor in his mother, with whom he had lost all familiarity because he had not seen her in ten years. Without support from his unknowing caretakers, Kevin organized his own escape at the age of fourteen. He told me, "I didn't recognize myself anymore. I thought, if I keep this up, I'll eventually die."

What are the implications of these intergenerational migration patterns for youth migration from Central America today? The parents of unaccompanied minors overwhelmingly lack legal status in the United States. Even when violence played a role in the migration of the first generation, as we saw for Maria, Pedro, and Juana, these de facto refugees were never recognized as de jure refugees. Refugee status would have enabled parents to legally reunify their children. With no family reunification rights, undocumented immigrants and unrecognized refugees are separated from their families for extended periods of time. Parents miss out on most of their children's formative years. The toll of separation weighs heavily on families, yielding emotional distance. Youths like Kevin, Jose, and Rafael often feel estranged from their parents and experience feelings of abandonment, particularly when they do not know why their parents migrated to the United States without them. Children are left in the home country with caretakers who are sometimes abusive and other times loving. In the former cases, violence within the home can push youths to migrate, and it can also make them more vulnerable to violence outside the home, making them targets of choice for gangs. In the latter cases, loving caretakers, often grandparents, can become too elderly or ill to care for youths, similarly exacerbating their vulnerability to violence outside the home.

In the context of the constraints on mobility produced by decades of restrictive US immigration policy, the only means for Central American families to reunite and manage the risks associated with violence in the home country is for children to migrate to the United States outside of legal channels. In the next section, I show how youths and their families exercise agency in migration decision-making to overcome these constraints by strategically assessing and managing risk and mobilizing information and resources flowing through migrant networks.

MIGRATION DECISION-MAKING AS A FAMILY-LEVEL RISK-MANAGEMENT STRATEGY

The vast majority of Central American unaccompanied minors have family in the United States, and migrant networks provide crucial resources that facilitate youth migration. Migrant networks theory notes that contacts with immigrants in the receiving country in the form of both "weak" (friends and extended family) and "strong" (immediate family) ties lower the costs of migration. These ties provide resources to fund migration and information about the migratory process and life in the receiving country.[42] I found that strong ties to parents in the United States were especially important to provide resources that eased the constraints on youth migration from Central America. I also found that the flow of information in migrant networks was crucial to facilitate youth migration, not just from the receiving to the sending country, but in *both directions*.

To be able to help plan migration, family members in the United States had to be aware of the violence that youths faced. However, as we saw in the case of Kevin, youths were not always willing to share this information. Youths who had long been separated from their parents did not always feel close enough to them to tell them about the risks they faced. Others feared discussing such delicate topics over the phone because they felt their every move was being scrutinized and any misstep could put them and their families in even greater danger. Parents in the United States, like Pedro and Juana, might also be unaware of their children's suffering at the hands of abusive caretakers because children sometimes feared that abusive situations could worsen for them if caretakers found out that they had told their parents.

Depending on how much they knew about the risks their children faced, families were involved in facilitating youth migration to the United

States to varying degrees. At one extreme were children who were not consulted, and were even surprised, by migration decisions made on their behalf. Their caretakers on both sides of the border thought that it was safer to get them out of the country quickly, with as few people knowing as possible, so they would not risk being detected. This type of arrangement was uncommon but more frequent in the cases of younger children who, unsurprisingly, had less decision-making autonomy from the adults in the family. More often, if adults deemed that the level of danger was low enough to allow time for this, they involved their children by negotiating these decisions or at least discussing them over the phone. At the other extreme were youths like Sofia, who took matters into their own hands and migrated without notifying their family members in the United States or in the home country.

Sofia lived with both her parents in Guatemala. Her older brother had migrated years before and was living in Los Angeles, but Sofia had lost touch with him. Sofia's father was severely abusive. The dangerous situation Sofia faced at home was exacerbated when gang members started trying to recruit her at age thirteen. They beat her and threatened to kill her and her family if she did not join the gang. These beatings led Sofia to be hospitalized with a broken leg. She told me, "I have a scar, and it will never go away, not even in my heart, because it was so terrible what happened." With no support at home in Guatemala, and no contact with her brother who lived in the United States, Sofia left without telling anyone as soon as she could walk again. She brought her backpack and schoolbooks with her when she left her house so nobody would suspect that she was leaving the country. She left without knowing where she was headed, working and begging for money along the journey, asking other migrants for directions. It took her over a year to reach safety and reunite with her brother in Los Angeles. She was able to locate him only after she was detained in an ORR shelter. Her brother was surprised to learn that he would have to take in his younger sibling who had arrived in the United States alone and without warning. Compared to youths whose parent(s) lived in the United States, youths like Sofia who had nonparent relatives there were generally less likely to be in contact with them. These nonparent family members were hence less likely to be privy to information about youths' safety and well-being in the home country. As a result, youths like Sofia had less access to the resources and information flowing in migrant networks that could ease the constraints on their migration.

In most cases, family members' involvement in youth migration fell somewhere between the two extremes of the child passively extracted from harm and the one who essentially ran away from home. Migration decision-making and planning involved collaboration between youth and family. When parents and relatives had information about the risks their children were exposed to, they usually participated in migration planning by providing resources and helping youths assess and manage the risks associated with violence in the home country. As we saw in the case of Carla and her brother at the start of the chapter, the dynamics of how families managed risk and strategized migration in contexts of violence were most apparent in cases where more than one child was in danger, and family members could not afford to pay for a coyote to smuggle out all the children at once. These families had to make decisions about which child was most at risk and should migrate first.

While the preexisting desire for family reunification sometimes meant that parents had been able to plan and save resources to finance migration ahead of time, violence quickly accelerated migratory decision-making and planning. The case of Victor and his three older siblings illustrates how these two forces—the need to manage risks associated with violence in the home country and the desire of families separated by borders to reunite—interact to shape migration decision-making. When Victor was four years old, his father abandoned the family. Victor's mother, Lucia, migrated to the United States to provide for her children as the breadwinner of the household, leaving them in the care of their maternal grandmother in El Salvador. Lucia's dream was to live with her children in the United States. She had planned to bring one child at a time by gradually putting together savings for each journey, as her wages allowed. Victor explained, "My mom decided she would do it like that because she didn't have enough money to bring us all at once." In 2013, Lucia decided to bring her eldest child to the United States first, her daughter, who was eighteen years old at the time and was pregnant. Lucia wanted her daughter to have her baby in the United States, where she could help her.

Soon after Lucia brought her daughter, their hometown in El Salvador became more dangerous. In 2014, Lucia's second-eldest child was singled out by gang members who extorted and beat him, while attempting to recruit him. Lucia's mother participated in the family's risk assessment and migration planning by calling Lucia to tell her what was happening. Lucia used her savings and paid for her second-eldest child's passage to the United States, with a coyote. The family's risk-determination strategy was, unsurprisingly, to extract from danger the youth who had been the direct target of threats first. After he left, however, the gang shifted their recruitment efforts to Lucia's third-eldest child, also a boy. This was a common pattern in the stories I heard. Siblings would be targeted, in turn, from eldest to youngest. Those who stayed behind when their older siblings fled were at risk of retaliation from gang members.

The following year, in 2015, Lucia had saved enough money to pay for her third-eldest child to migrate to safety in the United States. He was seventeen years old at the time. Thus, he happened to arrive in the United States as an unaccompanied minor, unlike his older brother who had turned eighteen just before his arrival at the US-Mexico border and was thus processed as an adult. The different treatment of asylum-seeking unaccompanied minors and adults in the United States was apparent in the case of these two siblings, who had such a small age difference. The seventeen-year-old, who was categorized as an unaccompanied minor, and thus benefitted from special protections, had already won his asylum case when I interviewed Victor in 2017. The eighteen-year-old, who was processed as an adult, had also applied for asylum. Yet about three years after his arrival, he was still in legal limbo and waiting for his day in immigration court, where he would face far worse odds of being granted asylum.

Seeing his three siblings leave one by one in subsequent years, Victor rationalized that he would have to wait until 2016 for his own turn to migrate to the United States to join his family. In the meantime, however, the risks had become exacerbated, compounding the costs of staying in El Salvador for Victor. Gang members approached his house various times to look for his two older brothers. Without involving Victor, who was just thirteen years old at the time, in the decision, his mother and grandmother planned his escape and effectively surprised him. Just one month after his seventeen-year-old brother left, Victor told me that he overheard the news that he was to leave the next day, "I was eating breakfast when the coyote called my grandmother. I overheard him saying that I needed to be ready to leave because he would come the next day. She told me, 'Stay home, don't go to school.' I asked her, 'Why don't you want me to go?'" At first, Victor's grandmother did not want to tell him. Maybe it was too painful for her to admit that her favorite grandson, whom she affectionately called her "little clown" because he always made her laugh, would leave her. They would likely never see each other again. Victor experienced leaving his grandmother behind with sadness; he felt as if he had lost one mother to find another as he joined Lucia in the United States. Like his seventeen-year-old brother, Victor arrived in the United States as an unaccompanied minor and won his asylum case.

The story of Victor and his siblings illustrates how families assess risk to plan migration by identifying which youth finds him or herself in the most danger. In this case, it was the youth who was directly targeted by the gang because he was the oldest. Other families made decisions similarly based on risk assessments. For instance, some chose to extract boys from gang violence before girls because the boys had been targeted for recruitment and were thus deemed to be most at risk. In the context of domestic violence within the home, families sometimes made the opposite gendered assessment, extracting girls rather than boys because they were thought to be at greater risk than their brothers. In the case of Victor's family, the underlying desire for family reunification allowed his mother, Lucia, to save money and plan, but escalating threats accelerated migration decision-making, prompting the family to assess an increased level of risk. Victor did not know how his mother had come up with the money to pay the coyote so quickly. Perhaps, like other parents who shared their stories with me, she might have requested a loan from a family member or an employer.

Families attempted to assess and manage home country risks, but these assessments were inherently imperfect because, as we saw in the case of Hector's chance escape after the murder of his two best friends, violence often strikes in sudden and unpredictable ways. The time to plan migration and save money for transit was a luxury that youths and their families often did not have. One way to manage risk and cope with violence, while trying to buy time to plan and save money for migration, was for youths to go into hiding. This was what fifteen-year-old Brayan from Honduras did. Brayan had endured years of abuse from his alcoholic father, who beat him and often kicked him out to sleep on the streets. The danger he was in at home was exacerbated when gang members started trying to recruit him. Brayan ran away from home. He lived in hiding at his cousin's house for over a year. That was how long it took for Brayan's cousin to locate Brayan's brother in the United States and organize and finance his trip.

Brayan told me that, while he was in hiding, he had been so depressed when he thought about his future that he cut himself because the physical pain distracted him. He showed me his forearms, which were lined with small white scars. The self-harm behaviors that Brayan described were not unique. Other youths had coped with fear and desperation in similar ways. The experience of waiting in violent contexts, coupled with the fear and uncertainty about whether they would survive, had enduring traumatic effects on youths. Youths who cope with violence by going into hiding inhabit a "space of non-existence."[43] They are biologically alive. Yet it is as if they do not exist because their legal and social personhood are erased. For Brayan, staying alive in Honduras depended on complete isolation from the outside world. Brayan's social existence was erased as he went into hiding and ceased to be a son, a student, and a young worker. He and others like him are clearly de facto refugees.

For teenagers—who are in a liminal stage in the life cycle, between childhood and adulthood—such erasures make it impossible to envision and plan a future in their home countries. As Brayan described, this was a deeply painful condition. De facto refugee youths migrate to seek both safety and a chance to continue their coming-of-age. Like youths for whom migration is a rite of passage to adulthood, migrant networks also shape the aspirations of these young people and provide them hope for the future. For Brayan, dreaming of someday joining his older brother in the United States was a fantasy that gave him respite and helped him endure years of abuse at the hands of his father. His brother ultimately lived up to Brayan's expectations. When he found out what Brayan was going through in Honduras, he comforted him over the phone and promised to support him, so he could be safe and continue his education in the United States. True to his word, he put together the funds to make Brayan's extraction from danger possible. He later paid Brayan's asylum application fees and provided for him while he attended high school in Los Angeles.

MIGRANT NETWORKS AND THE MIGRATION INDUSTRY: PROVIDING RESOURCES FOR COSTLY TRIPS

In the context of severe constraints on mobility to the United States, the migration industry and migrant networks interact to facilitate youth migration. The migration industry allows Central Americans to circumvent what David Fitzgerald calls the "architecture of repulsion."[44] Rich democracies in the Global North use an intricate combination of geographic and physical barriers, draconian policies, visa restrictions on air travel, and bilateral agreements with transit countries to keep out undesired migrants from the Global South. These countries also thus block access to asylum for those who find themselves in danger. Scholars agree that restrictive immigration control measures like these create the conditions for a thriving migration industry and opportunities for entrepreneurial brokers like coyotes to provide their services.[45]

The journey to the United States has become increasingly costly and risky as the US government externalizes migration control by providing funding to the Mexican and Guatemalan governments to apprehend, detain, and deport migrants transiting through their territories. By 2015, Mexico was deporting more Central Americans than the United States.[46] The United States also pressured Mexico and Central American governments to limit the mobility of minors traveling without parents in other ways. For example, since 2014, minors have been required to have a visa to enter Mexico and written parental permission to cross any Central American border unaccompanied. This policy has had the effect of making the *authorized* independent migration of minors in the region all but impossible.[47] Indeed, two Honduran youths I interviewed who were traveling without a coyote told me that they had to bribe officers at the border with Guatemala to be allowed out of Honduras. One youth had to do this despite having a written note from his father granting him permission to travel with his aunt who accompanied him to the border crossing point. Trapping minors in their countries of origin where they are being persecuted is a form of exit control that undermines the fundamental basis of the international refugee regime: an individual's right to seek asylum.

Research has demonstrated that less experienced migrants are more reliant on smugglers to make the journey.[48] It is thus not surprising that unaccompanied minors, many of whom had never even left the towns where they were born, needed the help of adults—both in their informal networks and in the migration industry—to make the journey to the United States. In some cases, when adult family members were traveling North, they brought children and teenagers with them. Some of my study participants had aunts or grandmothers who accompanied them during part, or all, of the journey. If these youths made it to the border with these adult caretakers, they would then be separated from them, categorized as unaccompanied minors, and detained separately.[49] Being categorized as unaccompanied minors gives youths comparative advantages in the asylum process. Yet these separations were nonetheless frightening and confusing for youths who did not know where their relatives were being taken and whether they would ever see them again. When no adults could make the journey, groups of minors sometimes traveled together, and teenagers were entrusted with caring for younger siblings or relatives, a responsibility they took very seriously.

Smuggling services were even more important when the help of older relatives could not be secured. Seventy-eight percent of the youths I interviewed and most youths I met through my ethnography in legal clinics had traveled to the United States with a smuggler. Youths usually relied on family members to connect them with coyotes and to pay for smuggling services. Precisely due to their stage in the life cycle, most youths were still dependent, to some extent, on adults. They rarely had personal savings at their disposal because they were still in school. Those who were working did so for limited hours and in exploitative jobs. When it came to preparing youths' asylum applications, it was important not to include detailed information about who had paid for smuggling services. This information could otherwise later be used against undocumented relatives who had helped youths escape from violence if they ever sought to legalize their own status in the United States. Acts of familial love and solidarity are thus weaponized in the US asylum system, ignoring the reality that unaccompanied minors have no option but to flee with coyotes precisely because US policies make it impossible for them to obtain valid travel visas.

Unauthorized trips to the United States were extremely expensive, ranging from $3,000 to $10,000 per person. Youths and their family members recounted that coyotes offered a two-tiered service: a more expensive one that supposedly allowed immigrants to avoid apprehension; and a less expensive one for those who were "crossed over" in points with heavy Border Patrol presence, where they would likely be apprehended.[50] According to one mother, for a trip from Guatemala in 2016, the former service cost $6,000 and the latter $3,000. Brokers in the migration industry might be fashioning their services to capitalize on provisions that allow unaccompanied minors to be admitted to the United States. However, for family members, the decision of which service to pick was usually merely financial.

One Salvadoran mother recounted that, when she had time to plan and save for the migration of two of her children, she paid $7,250 for each of them to join her in Los Angeles, "The coyote delivered them to me in eight days. They weren't caught by immigration, and they had been well taken care of." When her younger son faced immediate danger years later, she paid $5,000 for him to be taken only as far as the border because she could not afford the more expensive option. She had not planned to bring this child to the United States. Because she did not anticipate the risk he would be in, she only had $2,000 in savings when the need to urgently extract him from violence arose. She had to ask for two loans to make up the rest of the money quickly, one from a money lender and another from her employer. She was unaware of the protections for unaccompanied minors in the United States, but she hoped that her child would be admitted. She was surprised that her son's apprehension by the Border Patrol turned out to be what she characterized as "a benefit" because he was able to get free legal representation and win his SIJS case (he qualified because he had been abandoned by his father). Conversely, his older siblings who were never apprehended, had never interacted with the US immigration bureaucracy. They were thus unaware that they too might have qualified for this form of relief, until they were too old to apply.

While the adults involved in facilitating youth migration knew a lot about the risks of the journey and the options provided by the migration industry, they knew far less about asylum and US immigration laws protecting unaccompanied minors. In most cases, youths themselves had only incorrect or no knowledge of US immigration laws prior to migration. As we will see in the next chapter, the legal socialization, not just of newly arrived youths, but also of their undocumented family members who had previously lived in the shadows, started upon youths' arrival, as they were made to navigate the US immigration process.

USING INTERNATIONAL MIGRATION THEORIES TO EXPLAIN YOUTH MIGRATION FROM CONTEXTS OF VIOLENCE

This chapter has explained how Central American youths and their families make migration decisions in sending contexts characterized by violence. Age, gender, and other dimensions of social position interact to shape the risks that youths face in El Salvador, Guatemala, and Honduras. Girls and boys are vulnerable to child abuse at the hands of their caretakers. When youths are abused at home or receive little support for other reasons, such as when caretakers become elderly or ill, they are more vulnerable to violence outside the home. Because gang members target their peers—the young and marginalized who lack opportunities to work and pursue an education—the age of adolescence exposes youths to the violent reality of forcible gang recruitment. Both boys and girls may be recruited into gang activities, but this is more likely to be a risk for boys, while girls risk sexual violence at the hands of gang members. Youths' family members may also be targeted by gang members for extortion. Witnesses of crimes of all ages risk their lives. These risks and instances of victimization accumulate to raise the perceived cost of staying in the home country, prompting migration decisions.

US immigration policies make it increasingly challenging for asylum seekers to reach its sovereign soil. These same policies deprive undocumented and de facto refugee parents of the right to legally reunify children left behind. In this context, migrant networks are crucial in giving young people choices and enabling them to exercise migratory agency to escape from violence. Family members on both sides of the border help youths assess and manage risks. They provide information and resources that are indispensable to allow teenagers, who are usually inexperienced in travel and lack personal savings, to secure the smuggling services needed to travel to the United States. For family members to be able to help assess risk and support youth migration, it was necessary for information to flow through migrant networks, not just from the receiving to the sending country, but in *both directions*. Parents were more likely than nonparent relatives in the US to possess information about how violence was affecting their children's lives.

Overall, family members living in the United States provided more resources to fund youth migration than family members in the sending country. Among US-based family, parents provided more resources than nonparent relatives. Yet living without legal status in the United States meant that family members often worked exploitative jobs. They did not always have savings available on short notice when the sudden need to migrate arose. In these cases, families had to take out loans and prioritize which child to extract from danger first by making imperfect risk assessments. Youths who were unable to tap into the resources and information provided by migrant networks told me tales of escape based on equal measures of self-reliance and sheer luck. I could discern as much from the many stories I heard about classmates, friends, neighbors, and family members who had *not* been lucky enough to survive.

I have argued that Central American unaccompanied minors who migrate in response to life-threatening violence are de facto refugees. Nonetheless, as the next chapters will show, these youths must navigate a complex bureaucratic maze and arduous legal struggles, with no guarantee of being formally recognized as de jure refugees. In the exercise of translation of human suffering that takes place in the US asylum process, only some lived experiences that occurred in the sending country are considered of value. Others are dismissed as the wrong types of suffering because they clash with narrowly defined legal and cultural understandings of deserving childhood and refugeehood. The timing of youths' escape is also key. The decisions that loving Central American families made to extract their children from harm go on to carry unexpected weight in how their asylum cases are assessed, playing out in paradoxical ways.

3 Enter the Bureaucratic Maze

THE LEGAL SOCIALIZATION
OF UNACCOMPANIED MINORS BEGINS

The coyote told me—well, actually, I guess he sort of
abandoned us. But he did tell me, 'OK, I'm going to leave
you here—like, in the mountains—and you should just keep
walking for like an hour, until you get to a street where they
[US immigration authorities] can see you, and they will
catch you.' . . . We walked for a while, and I asked my
friends, is this the US or Mexico? We decided to keep
walking in one direction. I thought, if I'm lucky, that's the
US, and US immigration [authorities] will catch us. If it's
Mexican immigration [authorities], they will send us back.
But one of the two things has to happen. We are in the
middle of the desert. We don't know where we are. . . . We
eventually got to the road, and we saw a sign in English. . . .
Then a car passed, and the Border Patrol agent started
speaking to us in English. We couldn't really understand,
but I think he asked us if we had weapons. We said no. He
told us to get in the car. . . . I thought they might send me
to my family, or I might go to jail. I didn't know. I had never
been caught by immigration before.

In these words, Fernando recollected the day he first stepped foot on US
soil. He was just fifteen years old at the time. He had left his mother behind
in Guatemala, and he was traveling north with a coyote and a group of
boys. He remembered that day well, even four years later, when he told me
his story. However, he could not recall the exact moment of his crossing.

The border separating the United States and Mexico was invisible to his eyes. He only knew that he had made it when it was an English-speaking Border Patrol officer, and not a Spanish-speaking one from the Mexican immigration authorities, who stopped him. Fernando felt lucky to have reached the United States, but he did not know what would happen next. The coyote had explained nothing. His family members who migrated to the United States before him did not share information about US immigration law that would have prepared him for the journey. Two opposite scenarios ran through Fernando's mind. Would he soon join his uncle in Florida? Would he end up in a detention facility?

Like Fernando, most unaccompanied minors have only partial, incorrect, or no information about US immigration laws prior to their migration (see Table 5 below). Yet their legal socialization starts quickly upon their arrival. Compared to teenagers who migrate independently but are never apprehended, thus remaining outside of state systems, and to undocumented adults who live in the shadows for years, youths who are apprehended at the border and admitted as unaccompanied minors are subjected to receiving state scrutiny from the moment they first enter the United States.[1] As they navigate the bureaucratic maze, unaccompanied minors interact intensively with state bureaucrats and legal brokers. Youths thus develop commonsense understandings of the law and ideas about their position in US society, or what socio-legal scholars refer to as "legal consciousness."[2] These understandings are important because they inform whether and how individuals claim rights vis-à-vis the state. As we will see, unaccompanied minors' legal consciousness is characterized by contradictory elements that mirror the legal context that receives them: feelings of both stigma and deservingness; fear and trust in the receiving state; and both misinformation and knowledge about US laws.

This chapter first discusses what youths know about US asylum law and protections for unaccompanied minors *before* migrating.[3] I next examine youths' legal socialization in the first three junctures of the bureaucratic maze: (1) apprehension by Customs and Border Protection (CBP) at the US-Mexico border; (2) detention in Office of Refugee Resettlement (ORR) facilities; (3) placement in foster care or release to family member "sponsors" who take on an immigration control role delegated to them by the state. Finally, I anticipate the factors that will shape youths' perceptions of the fairness of the US asylum system. The next chapters will trace how youths' legal socialization continues as they interact with legal brokers to apply for asylum and Special Immigrant Juvenile Status (SIJS).

The bureaucrats working in each agency that processes unaccompanied minors are trained to implement distinct mandates that reflect different combinations of the forces of *exclusion* and *protection* in the contradictory legal context of reception. At the border, youths interact with CBP, an agency with the mandate of *policing state sovereignty* to keep out undesired immigrants from the Global South. This mandate is inherently at odds with protections that allow unaccompanied minors to be admitted under the Trafficking Victims Protection Reauthorization Act (TVPRA). Youths experienced rights violations at the border as CBP agents attempted to deny their TVPRA protections.

Unaccompanied minors are next detained in ORR facilities, which have *dual mandates of care and control*: to care for them because they are children, and to control them because they are immigrants.[4] The state continues to exercise control over youths after they are released from ORR custody to their, mostly undocumented, immigrant family members, who carry out a mandate of *delegated care and control*. Paradoxically, the state simultaneously constructs the "illegality" of family members, while also entrusting them to monitor youths' compliance with immigration law, for instance, by making sure they show up to immigration court.[5] As youths interact with loving and well-meaning family members, and with ORR social workers who care for and control them, they internalize normative notions about deserving citizenship and desirable teen and migrant behavior. Upon release to family, youths are also influenced by the misinformation about US laws and fear of the state that circulate in immigrant communities. Conversely, youths' interactions with legal brokers will attenuate fear, fostering their trust in the state and the perception that the United States is a country where "children are protected." The outcomes of youths' asylum cases can later bolster or undermine this trust.

This chapter contributes to scholarship on how immigrants experience and understand the effects of the law on their lives. Sociologists Cecilia Menjivar and Leisy Abrego argue that immigration enforcement laws and policies constitute "legal violence," allowing states to exclude and inflict harm and suffering on noncitizens.[6] These laws also have powerful discursive effects, exerting "symbolic violence," the imposition of dominant categories of thought on subordinate groups who not only internalize existing unequal social hierarchies but also unintentionally contribute to their perpetuation.[7] Immigration enforcement laws help consolidate immigrants' marginalized positions, legitimizing inequalities between citizens, "illegal" immigrants, and the categories that fall in between. As a result, undocumented adults are fearful of the state and perceive that they have no rights to claim.[8] Given the legal context of reception characterized by protective laws that exempt unaccompanied minors from aspects of immigration enforcement targeting adults at the border, in detention, and in the asylum process, this chapter asks: To what extent do protective policies attenuate exclusion and legal violence? How do interactions with state agents, and during a family reunification process mediated by the state, shape unaccompanied minors' understandings of the law?

I argue that protections for unaccompanied minors attenuate legal violence in some junctures of the bureaucratic maze more than others. Exclusion is strongest at the border and progressively weaker as youths advance through the maze. Through their interactions in these spaces, unaccompanied minors learn about the law and their rights and obligations. They also internalize normative messages about deserving youth citizenship and about the behaviors expected of "good" kids, "good" immigrants, and "real" refugees. These notions become so entwined that youths can seldom tell apart information about their actual legal obligations from the normative "advice" they receive from state and nonstate actors. Discourses about deserving citizenship are construed in opposition to stigmatized identities that are widespread in the United States: the "bogus" refugee, the deviant Latinx teen, the "bad" immigrant.[9]

According to Goffman, stigmatized identities are attributed to categories of individuals through social interaction, at three different levels: social identity (i.e., how society sees you); personal identity (i.e., who you are and what people know about you); and felt identity (i.e., how you think about yourself).[10] It was striking to see how much my respondents had internalized stigmas about the social identity of immigrants, asylum seekers, and Latinx youths during their interactions with different actors in the US immigration system. Youths reproduced these stigmas during their interviews with me as they presented their personal identity. It became clear that even this protected group of immigrant children is not exempt from the symbolic violence of immigration law. Unaccompanied minors retain trust in the state and are hence able to claim rights and belonging. Yet, as they perform their own deservingness, they reproduce stigmas about their co-ethnics.

PRE-MIGRATION KNOWLEDGE ABOUT US PROTECTIONS FOR UNACCOMPANIED MINORS

Attorney General Jeff Sessions described Central American unaccompanied minors as "wolves in sheep's clothing," threatening and potentially gang-affiliated teenagers deviously cheating their way into the country by taking advantage of so-called "loopholes."[11] This comment was characteristic of the Trump-era rhetoric about the previously agreed-upon laws that protect unaccompanied minors at the US-Mexico border and in the asylum process. In stark contrast to this portrayal, I found that most unaccompanied minors had only vague, incorrect, or no knowledge of US immigration laws prior to their migration. The vast majority of youths did not even know what asylum was, let alone assume they would be granted it. Only a minority were aware of TVPRA protections for unaccompanied minors at the US-Mexico border, which would allow them to be admitted without first having to undergo credible fear interviews like asylum-seeking adults. Table 5 summarizes what my youth interviewees knew about this protection at the border, which is a crucial one because it enables them to enter the United States, where they may find at least a temporary place of refuge from the harm and violence that pushed them out of their home countries.

Youths like Fernando, whose quote opens the chapter, did not know anything about what would happen to them at the US-Mexico border. Left alone in the desert with no idea where he was, Fernando had little option but to keep walking and hope for the best. Youths who had limited contact with their US-based family members prior to migration were the least likely to know anything about protections for unaccompanied minors at the border. Most feared that they would be deported. Some hoped to avoid apprehension and slip into the country undetected.

Other unaccompanied minors, and their US-based family members, possessed the vague notion, sometimes acquired from coyotes, that they

Table 5 Pre-migration knowledge about protections for unaccompanied minors at the border

No Information about US Protections, n = 22 (49%)

Some Vague and/or Inaccurate Understanding, n = 18 (40%)

Learned from coyote	8
Learned from family	7
Learned in home country from peers	3

High Understanding with Accurate Information, n = 5 (11%)

Learned from coyote	1
Learned from family	3
Learned in home country from peers	1

Data from N = 45 formal interviews with unaccompanied minors. Some respondents acquired information from more than one source. To simplify, I categorized them under the source highlighted most during interviews.

would be "let in" because they were *menores* (minors). However, they did not understand the process that would follow, nor did they have high hopes that they would be able to "fix their papers" (obtain legal status). While coyotes played an information provision role, they seemed to be doing so by providing partial information as they opportunistically promoted their services. One boy recounted that the coyote had explained that, if he turned himself in to the Border Patrol, it would be "easier to find his mom." This is a partial truth because unaccompanied minors who are detained are next usually transferred to ORR, which indeed works to reunite them with family. However, this information is also misleading. These messages make the process seem straightforward, obscuring potential obstacles at the border, where CBP officers may attempt to deny unaccompanied minors the right to be admitted, as well as the long legal battles that youths face in removal proceedings that I describe in the next chapters.

Predictably, families were more knowledgeable about protections at the border when they had already sponsored other children through the process for unaccompanied minors or knew others who had done so. In these cases, more information flowed through migrant networks to shape youths' pre-migration understandings of the law. For instance, sixteen-year-old Yesenia's parents frequented a church in Los Angeles where more than one congregant had recently sponsored an unaccompanied minor, obtaining their release from ORR custody. Yesenia had cancer. In El Salvador, she was denied medical care, abused by her family, and bullied in school. Her parents were anxious for her to be by their side, where she could finally access the care she needed to survive. Yesenia recounted, "My mom knew, that's why I came to the border like that, looking for immigration [authorities], because otherwise, it's harder, more expensive."

Youths almost never knew what asylum was prior to migration. Danny, who migrated at age fifteen from Honduras, was the exception to this rule. Despite migrating entirely alone, without warning his family in Honduras, and even though he was not in contact with his uncle in the United States, Danny was especially savvy. He had a far more developed understanding of the law prior to migration than other youths. Because he grew up in what he described as a "political family," Danny knew that unaccompanied minors are admitted at the US-Mexico border and that he could apply for asylum because he feared for his life in Honduras.

Danny's experience is quite revealing in disrupting the "loopholes" rhetoric popularized during the Trump administration. As we will see, knowing about one's rights, not only does not equate to scheming to take advantage of "loopholes," but it also does not necessarily guarantee access to those rights. Given unaccompanied minors' unequal power relationship with the state, they remain vulnerable to exclusion. This is especially true before youths secure the services of legal brokers, whose intermediation is crucial to enable them to access the protections that exist in the law. In each agency of the bureaucratic maze that processes unaccompanied minors, protection competes not only with exclusion and legal violence but also with rights violations or illegal violence.

POLICING STATE SOVEREIGNTY: SOCIALIZATION DURING INTERACTIONS AT THE US–MEXICO BORDER

Like other immigrants who are apprehended, the agency that unaccompanied minors first interact with when they arrive in the United States is Customs and Border Protection (CBP). Most unaccompanied minors cross the US-Mexico border at the Rio Grande Valley in Texas and are apprehended by the Border Patrol, part of CBP. Less commonly, unaccompanied minors present themselves at an official port of entry and are processed by the Office of Field Operations, also part of CBP. Crossing the border at these official sites was already difficult toward the end of the Obama administration. Port of entry staff started implementing so-called metering practices, creating waitlists that made asylum seekers wait to enter the United States for weeks or even months. In 2018, capitalizing on the fact that metering was obstructing admissions at ports of entry, the Trump administration introduced a policy that made all immigrants who crossed the border *between* ports of entry ineligible for asylum. This policy violated US legal commitments, and it was successfully blocked by advocates through impact litigation.[12]

Of all the agencies that unaccompanied minors navigate, the US-Mexico border, with its cage-like holding facilities, is the institutional space where the force of exclusion is the strongest. CBP officers are trained to implement the mandate of policing state sovereignty to keep out undesired immigrants from the Global South. This mandate is at odds with TVPRA protections for unaccompanied minors, as well as with the non-refoulment rights of asylum seekers of all ages. Under the TVPRA, unaccompanied minors are exempted from a significant hurdle that adult asylum seekers must overcome before they are admitted: the credible fear interview. Being exempted means one less chance for CBP agents to exercise exclusionary discretion, since they are the ones who decide whether to refer adults to interviews with asylum officers or to immediately deport them.[13] What's more, the Trump administration raised the bar that asylum officers used to determine whether migrants have a credible fear of returning to their home countries: from a 10 percent chance of being harmed to "more likely than not" or an over 50 percent chance. As it became extremely difficult to pass credible fear screenings and gain admission to the United States during the Trump years, the TVPRA protection exempting unaccompanied minors from this initial barrier became even more crucial.

Whether they had no knowledge of the law like Fernando, were savvy like Danny, or fell someplace in between, only a minority of unaccompanied minors sought to avoid apprehension. Most youths recounted actively seeking out Border Patrol agents, including Cecilia, a fifteen-year-old asylum seeker from El Salvador who was "crossed over" by a coyote in a heavily patrolled part of the border. Cecilia told me that she searched for hours for the Border Patrol. Traveling through a strange new landscape without trusted adults or a guide, she grew increasingly frightened as time passed. She said, "There are people who don't want to be caught, and they find them in a couple minutes. I had to walk until it was dark!"

The act of willingly declaring their presence to CBP reflects the trust these young migrants place in the receiving state, hoping that they will be protected. However, once youths are apprehended, their trust is immediately met with suspicion. CBP officers commonly accused youths of lying about their age. This accusation carries significant implications: misclassifying minors as adults is a means to deny their entry rights. This happened to Alicia, whom we met in the last chapter. Recall that Alicia fled from El Salvador after a gang member tried to force her to be his "girlfriend," and her cousins had been brutally murdered after being targeted in similar ways. She told me:

> The officer didn't believe my name or age. I was sixteen, and he thought I was, like, twenty-one. He asked me for my fingerprints and said, "you're going to sign and leave. You know that if you're lying, we can put you in prison for years?" I said, "I'm not going to sign because I have rights to stay here." I told him I didn't want to go back to my country, and he said, "I don't care why you came here, just give me your identifying information." It was really ugly because they were angry, and they treated people as if they were not people, just because they were from immigration, and they had their uniforms. Many people signed but I didn't because I wasn't going to let them intimidate me.

Alicia arrived without any documentation to prove that she was a minor, thus posing a challenge to CBP's mandate of policing state sovereignty. Yet, when I interviewed Alicia at age eighteen, she still looked younger than her years. I was skeptical that her appearance two years earlier would have given the officer reason to think that she was an adult. Alicia challenged CBP's mistrust and questioning of her identity by affirming her rights, despite describing that she felt dehumanized—treated as if she were "not a person"—by officers who accused her of fraudulently trying to pass as a minor. By claiming that he was not interested in Alicia's account of escape from violence, which would have also clearly flagged her as a rights-holding asylum seeker, but only in her identifying information, the CBP officer positioned Alicia solely as an alien body to be registered and monitored by the state.

Not only did CBP inflict legal violence on Alicia by questioning her age, but the officer also violated her rights by attempting to coerce her into signing a deportation order. Alicia was able to resist intimidation and rights violations at the border because she knew about her right to be admitted as an unaccompanied minor. The coyote had told Alicia what would happen once she arrived at the border. She had packed her birth certificate to be prepared but lost it during the journey. If Alicia had not been aware of her rights, she could have more easily been deported. However, even immigrants who knew their rights were at risk. Indeed, many youths recounted stories of illegal deportations of family members who had escaped from violence. Despite not benefitting from TVPRA protections, adults who express a fear of return should, at the very least, be granted access to credible fear screenings and likely also admitted as asylum seekers. Alicia's older sister, who arrived at the border as an adult less than a year after her, was among those illegally deported. She expressed her fear of returning to El Salvador and even had police reports demonstrating that her family had been threatened. Yet CBP still coerced her into signing a deportation order. For Alicia's sister, knowing her rights was no protection from exclusionary forces at the border.

In contrast to Alicia, most unaccompanied minors I met during my research did arrive at the border with their birth certificates. This is the main form of identification for minors in El Salvador, Guatemala, and Honduras, where it is not possible for those under age twenty-one to obtain a passport without the written consent of both parents. Seventeen-year-old Manuel from Guatemala was carrying his birth certificate when he was apprehended, but he was also faced with officers who did not believe that he was a minor. I met Manuel at a legal clinic where I was helping fill out his asylum application. There, he showed me the birth certificate that he had shown the officers. This looked exactly like many others I had seen, making it unclear why its authenticity would be questioned if not simply to deny his rights.

One of the agents didn't believe I was seventeen. He said I was eighteen, and that I was lying. They put me in this small room, by myself, which was like a punishment so that I would tell the truth. It was cold; they didn't give me water or anything to eat. I felt hungry when they took me out to ask me again. I always told them I was seventeen. It was the whole truth.

Manuel had no prior knowledge about US protections for unaccompanied minors at the border. Thus, unlike Alicia, his reaction was not so much an affirmation of the rights that (he did not know) were denied to him but, rather, an affirmation of his identity, even in the face of punishment that violates legal standards for the detention of minors under the Flores Settlement. Eventually, CBP processed Manuel as a minor, but it was unclear to him what had made them change their minds. Importantly, he remained deeply marked by the suspicion he had been treated with. When I asked Manuel if he would change anything about the immigration system during another conversation months later, I was expecting a response about the treatment he received from institutions like CBP, which I knew had been punitive. Instead, I was surprised when Manuel replied by positioning himself in the role of the immigration bureaucrat and reproducing the "bogus refugee" stigma: "Other [people] sell a different story each time, different to what they lived, and they let them stay. But I prefer to say the truth, stick to my word, not like those who spend time inventing lies to pass as a different person. I don't like that about certain people."

Rather than contest stigmatized identities, unaccompanied minors manage them by engaging in distancing mechanisms, a strategy that is also used by other subordinate social groups.[14] As they claim rights and belonging, youths present their personal identity in opposition to the stigmas associated with their peers, co-ethnics, and other asylum seekers. In this case, Manuel distanced himself from the stigma associated with protected categories in US immigration law—asylum seekers, unaccompanied minors—to perform his own worthiness as a truth teller, unlike others who supposedly take advantage of humanitarian immigration laws in fraudulent ways.

During their very first interactions with the state, unaccompanied minors face CBP, an agency that exerts state power coercively while policing sovereign borders. As bureaucrats trained to implement this mandate, CBP officers tried to deny unaccompanied minors' entry rights and imposed dominant categories of thought that discredit their credibility. While youths reacted and gained admission either by using the law to claim their rights or by asserting their true identities, they also learned a lasting lesson: that they are seen as untrustworthy in the United States. As we will see, credibility and the importance of telling the truth is emphasized from the moment of apprehension and during virtually each stage of the asylum process, which makes youths acutely aware of the "bogus refugee" stigma. Like Manuel, youths internalized the stigmatizing discourses imposed on them, and they unwittingly legitimized the state's exclusionary practices by reproducing such tropes.

The examples above highlight that CBP does not solely inflict *legal violence* while screening unaccompanied minors to determine whether they are, in fact, under age eighteen. Rather, CBP also inflicts *illegal violence*. The American Civil Liberties Union (ACLU) documented hundreds of instances of rights violations at the border, suing CBP for its noncompliance with the TVPRA and the Flores Settlement.[15] While the media only brought to the public's attention the cages where children are inhumanely detained at the border when family separations made the news in 2018, the treatment of minors at the border has been consistently dismal, during both the Obama and Trump administrations.

Savvy fifteen-year-old Danny arrived in the United States during the Obama administration at the height of the 2014 "crisis."[16] He was detained in extremely poor conditions, which violate Flores protections for minors, and for eight days, which is far more than the maximum of seventy-two hours allowed under the TVPRA. Danny suffered these rights violations despite the fact that he knew about his rights as an unaccompanied minor and asylum seeker. He thus described the agonizing time he spent in the cells that immigrants call the *"hieleras"* (iceboxes) because of the extremely cold air conditioning, which itself appears to be a punishment of sorts.

> I didn't think that they would treat minors like that in this country. It was the worst experience I could have imagined. . . . I didn't know if it was day or night. . . . We almost never ate or slept. . . . All they gave us was a cold sandwich or some weird fruit from time to time. . . . There was one bathroom for twenty children, all crammed in the same room. There were children as young as two with us. They weren't even our family, and we had to take care of them. We took off our shirts and gave them to the children so they could

stand the cold, because they cried so much. . . . I met children who stayed there one, two, three days, a lot had been there eight. One kid was there fourteen days. He was pale, tired, and you could see he hadn't been eating well. He cried so much when he got out.

Like Danny, virtually all youths described being subjected to inhumane treatment at the border: they were verbally abused, intimidated, and deprived of food and sleep. Youths remembered being fed inedible and semi-frozen sandwiches and burritos. The trauma they had endured at the border expressed itself in their lasting antipathy for or even inability to eat these foods. I discovered this when I attended an event for unaccompanied minors where a sandwich buffet was left almost entirely intact because it reminded attendees of the food at the border.

As soon as they step foot on US soil, hopeful and trusting youths are met with dehumanizing treatment and suspicion. This sends unaccompanied minors a clear message in the very first institutional space they navigate: that even they—a protected category—are undesired immigrants in the United States. The US-Mexico border, patrolled by CBP, is undoubtedly the part of the bureaucratic maze where the force of exclusion is the strongest. Nonetheless, Mexican unaccompanied minors, who are excluded from TVPRA protections at the border, fare far worse than Central Americans (see chapter 1). Between 2013 and 2019, about a fourth of unaccompanied minors arriving at the border were from Mexico (Figure 1). Yet, in the same period, Mexicans made up less than 5 percent of minors referred to ORR (Table 1). The vast majority of Mexican unaccompanied minors are immediately expelled through a quick process euphemistically called "voluntary return," after undergoing preliminary screenings with CBP officers. These screenings should serve to identify and admit vulnerable Mexican youths, but they are conducted inadequately by bureaucrats in an agency that is mandated to exclude. These trends highlight that, even in the most hostile of immigration agencies, the mediating effects of protective laws for vulnerable groups cannot be denied. Laws like the TVPRA limit the ability of bureaucrats in a state agency focused on enforcement to exercise exclusionary discretion. Unsurprisingly, I seldom met Mexican unaccompanied minors in the legal clinics where I did my research, since they face this significant additional barrier at the border before they can gain entry and access protection.

DUAL MANDATES OF CARE AND CONTROL: SOCIALIZATION DURING CUSTODY IN ORR

From the border, unaccompanied minors are transferred to the custody of the Office of Refugee Resettlement (ORR). Through subcontracts with mostly nonprofit organizations, ORR detains youths in facilities called "shelters" that are located all over the country (Figure 6). These shelters are supposedly child-friendly sites where only unaccompanied minors are detained. Advocates have indeed documented conditions in shelters to be comparatively better than in both adult and family detention centers.[17] Based on their ethnographic research in ORR facilities, anthropologists Susan Terrio and Lauren Heidbrink have characterized ORR as an agency with *dual mandates of care* (for children) *and control* (of immigrants).[18]

Youths' characterizations of their experiences in ORR shelters reflected these dual mandates. Some youths described shelters as "exasperating," "sad," "like being an orphan," or "like being a prisoner," reflecting the control mandate. Reflecting ORR's care mandate, however, youths also, and oftentimes simultaneously, recounted receiving important services, such as therapy that helped them begin to overcome the traumatic experiences that they had faced in the home country and during the journey. Some youths expressed what they saw as staff members' genuine concern for their well-being, with one boy going so far as to claim, "I was in love with that place. All of them were super good people." Of course, after escaping violence and deprivation, risking dangerous journeys, and enduring inhumane treatment at the border, it is not difficult to understand why shelters seemed like a safe haven to many youths by comparison.

Andres, who migrated at age seventeen from Guatemala, aptly captured the inherent tension of ORR's dual mandates during his interview by describing the shelter to be "like a fancy prison." Andres laughed, visibly pleased to see that his joke had landed well with me, his captive audience. He elaborated, "Everything is clean, they treat you with respect, and you can study. So, it's like being in prison, but in style! . . . I thought that if I spent four or five months there, I was going to become fat. . . . We played soccer once in a while, but usually all we did was go to class, eat lunch, eat dinner, clean up, and go to sleep." In his joking way, Andres pointed out the most important feature of shelters for unaccompanied minors in the United States: children are not allowed to leave.

Fig. 6. Map of ORR facilities that detain unaccompanied minors. (GAO 2020, https://www.gao.gov/products/gao-20-609)

Notably, this is unlike other countries in Europe that house, rather than detain, unaccompanied minors in facilities where conditions are often deficient but, nonetheless, youths can enter and exit freely during the day.[19] One ORR shelter that I was able to visit had a summer camp–like layout with newly furnished bungalows with two beds in each room. Yet it also featured visible prisonlike elements: wire mesh in the windows, a high cement wall surrounding the facility, parts of which were lined with barbed wire, and a locked entry gate. Seventeen-year-old Gael from El Salvador recounted that staff members in the shelter where he was detained essentially threatened youths, telling them that if they approached the wire fence around the shelter, it would electrocute them. If they succeeded in jumping over the fence, he said, "the police would come after us, arrest us, and we would be deported immediately."

ORR subcontracts the management of its shelters to nonprofits that run three types of facilities of varying security levels.[20] The most "child-

friendly" are foster care–type arrangements. Some of my respondents resided for short periods of time in the homes of Spanish-speaking families,
and they had fond memories of kind caretakers taking them on Sunday
field trips to see the sites in New York City. In the middle, the most common type of shelter where unaccompanied minors are detained is the
"fancy prison" that Andres described, the type of facility I visited. Youths
had access to schooling and recreational opportunities, and their needs
were met, but it was clear that it was a prison, as they could not leave.
While youths like Andres characterized detention in these spaces as being
"treated well," lawsuits and media reports have documented inhumane
practices occurring in these types of shelters, such as children being coerced into taking psychotropic medication against their will or pregnant
girls being denied access to abortions.[21] At the punitive side of the spectrum are secure facilities for youths categorized as security threats and
large "emergency" facilities, which have not been certified as compliant
with child welfare standards.

The US government has argued that "emergency" facilities are necessary to deal with sudden increases in arrivals of unaccompanied minors.
These facilities were used during both the Obama and Trump administrations, but one huge Trump-era tent shelter in Homestead Florida received
much negative media attention due to the rights violations and inhumane
conditions documented there.[22] Homestead was run by a for-profit prison
company and could detain over two thousand youths at a time. Johnathan
and Darwin, two Salvadoran siblings I met during my ethnographic fieldwork, spent a total of fifty-four days at Hampstead, an experience they
recounted in exclusively negative terms: "The heat was unbearable. One
day, the air conditioning broke, and a bunch of girls fainted. One kid had
been there so long that he actually saw them put up the tents."

My respondents' disparate descriptions of the conditions they encountered in ORR, to some extent, reflected these three different types
of facilities. Some youths had also moved between facilities, and they
compared their experiences in each kind. Virtually all the youths I spoke
to brought up the almost mythical figure of the "kid who had been [in
ORR] so long," sometimes for six months, a year, or more. At times, this
seemed to be a real child who was staying in the shelter at the same time
as my respondents. Other times, it was just a rumor, a cautionary tale that

anxious youths shared among themselves, fearful that they would never be reunited with their families or that they would be sent back to their home countries.

The structure of daily life in ORR shelters was characterized by many rules and a tight schedule, which from my respondents' descriptions seemed militaristic. Cecilia described the strict rules in the shelter where she was detained, which was a middle-ground type of facility: "The girls couldn't brush each other's hair or give each other hugs; those things made them [the shelter staff] angry. . . . Girls could brush each other's hair only once a week, on beauty day. In our room, we couldn't do it. They said these were the laws of that place, and we needed to respect them"

Rules such as these seemed to be meant not so much to protect youths as to teach them compliance with authority and discipline. In Spanish, Cecilia called the rules enforced inside ORR facilities *leyes*, which translates to "laws," rather than "rules." This word choice highlights her awareness of the importance of compliance. Indeed, the stakes of noncompliance with shelter rules are high. Compliant youths are rewarded with recreational opportunities, food, shorter periods of detention, and transfer to less restrictive facilities. Youths who do not comply are detained for longer and moved to more restrictive facilities.[23] For some youths, noncompliance is harshly punished: a report by investigative journalists found that, between 2014 and 2020, at least eighty-six children were transferred to the custody of local law enforcement after allegations of fights, property damage, or mental health crises. Many were charged with misdemeanors, and at least ten minors were tried and charged as adults.[24]

As ORR staff taught immigrant youths to respect the "laws" of the facility, they prepared them to comply with the laws of the country, by going to court and being traceable by the government. Indeed, ORR shelters are key spaces where the legal socialization of unaccompanied minors takes place. Yet shelter staff seemed to be teaching youths far more about the desirable behaviors expected from future citizens and "good" teenagers than about their rights and obligations under US law. In at least some ORR shelters, unaccompanied minors have access to "know your rights" presentations like the ones that nonprofits give in immigration court, which I describe in the next chapter. During those presentations, unaccompanied minors learn about their rights and obligations as immigrants in removal proceedings and about asylum, SIJS, and other pathways to legal status that they may qualify for. However, most of the youths I interviewed had no recollection of attending these presentations in ORR. A few recalled being told that they would "have an immigration case" and should find an attorney, but they did not learn about their rights. This meant that youths either did not receive this information in ORR or, even if they did, they did not retain the information they may have been given about protections that could benefit them. This is telling, given how much youths *did* retain the normative messages about "good" behavior transmitted through their conversations with shelter staff. For instance, fourteen-year-old Cesar from El Salvador thus recounted his interactions with his ORR social worker: "[The social worker] told me, 'everything will be fine here son. You won't have any problems here, unless you look for problems.' And he always asked me how I was doing, whether I was behaving badly, things like that."

Cesar's account reflects how ORR staff is trained to implement the dual mandates of care and control as they interact with the immigrant youths in their custody. The social worker exercised the care mandate as he reassured Cesar of his future life in the United States and asked about his current well-being. At the same time, he exercised the control mandate, as he monitored Cesar's conduct, designating him as responsible for avoiding "deviant" youth behaviors. Indeed, Cesar, who fled from El Salvador after gang members tried to forcibly recruit him, was worried about encountering gangs in the United States. As his social worker reassured him, he also taught him a lesson, noting that, if anything bad happened to him in the United States, it would be his own fault for "look[ing] for problems." These institutional encounters teach newly arrived immigrant youth about how they are expected to behave, both while in the shelter and after their release.

Alicia told me that her social worker warned her of the dangers that she could face after her release from ORR because "there is a lot of diversity in this country and a lot of fun as well." This comment stuck with Alicia, and it reflects the racialized notions that ORR staff express and transmit to unaccompanied minors, in this case, using coded language to label minority youths as dangerous "others" who engage in suspect, potentially illicit activities. Through seemingly benevolent advice, ostensibly offered to protect youths, ORR staff actively policed membership boundaries by transmitting normative notions of appropriate behavior and deserving citizenship that reify stigmas attached to immigrants and minority groups.

Melvin, who migrated at age seventeen from Honduras, also recounted the advice that he received from ORR staff about the importance of good behavior after release. Melvin expected that his compliance with these behavioral norms would be rewarded with acceptance and legal status: "They told me that the most important thing was to behave well, to show the government we're good people who came here for a good life. That we're not coming, like many others, to hurt people. I don't know why they hurt innocent people like that." During our interview, Melvin reproduced the stigmatizing discourses used by ORR staff. He leveraged these to claim his own belonging as someone who came to the United States for a better life, in opposition to "many" other immigrants who "hurt innocent people."

What surprised me during my interviews was how often youths brought up these discourses without prompting. For example, I asked Dominic, a Guatemalan unaccompanied minor who had left the shelter three years earlier, what I thought was a fairly neutral question, "Who do you live with?" As he replied, Dominic felt the need to let me know that he was staying away from the "problem behaviors" that unaccompanied minors are repeatedly warned about by social workers, their attorneys, and others. This was particularly important since he was sharing an apartment in Los Angeles with his teenage friends from his hometown in Guatemala. He said, "I live with my friends, but they are chill. They don't drink or smoke. Sometimes, if we get bored at home, we go play [soccer]."

Of course, in an increasingly hostile receiving context characterized by racialized notions of Latinx youths as deviant and the criminalization of Central American youths as suspected gang members, Dominic's demeanor is understandable. Yet, as youths like Melvin and Dominic manage stigmas—the "bad" Latinx kid, the "bad" immigrant—discursively through distancing mechanisms, they inevitably reproduce discourses that disenfranchise others in their same social category. This reflects the symbolic violence that is imposed even on this group of ostensibly protected humanitarian claimants. What's more, my research also revealed that, after being released from custody, many unaccompanied minors, especially boys, went beyond discursive strategies and changed their behaviors. They curtailed their mobility, doing little besides going back and forth from home to school or work. They avoided staying out late to avoid police surveillance and being perceived as "bad kids."

The normative notions about desirable behavior that youths learn by interacting with ORR and CBP staff—and later with their family members—become so entwined with their knowledge of the law that youths usually cannot tell laws, rules, and advice apart. Yet all this coalesced information combines to form the legal consciousness of unaccompanied minors, which is characterized by feelings of both stigmatization and deservingness, and both misinformation and information about the law.

While ORR staff members may indeed be well meaning, as certain youths described, this juncture of the bureaucratic maze is nonetheless a perilous one. Spending longer periods of time detained in ORR exacerbates unaccompanied minors' liminality in the United States. Youths who are detained in ORR generally do not have access to attorneys, and they might turn eighteen and age out of eligibility for some humanitarian protections for minors by the time they are released. Turning eighteen while in ORR custody before a sponsor is identified and approved is a risk for many youths since about a third of unaccompanied minors arrive in the United States at age seventeen. During the Obama administration, youths who turned eighteen were usually released on their own, even if a sponsor had not been identified. Conversely, the Trump administration made it routine policy to transfer unaccompanied minors from ORR to adult detention facilities on the day of their eighteenth birthday. Being transferred to an adult detention center meant being stripped of unaccompanied minor status and its associated protections and being fast-tracked for deportation. A series of advocacy victories following a class action lawsuit, *Garcia Ramirez et. al. v. ICE*, eventually put an end to this practice, protecting unaccompanied minors who turn eighteen in ORR custody from being placed in adult detention.

LONG-TERM FOSTER CARE: CONTINUED LIMBO WHILE IN THE CARE AND CONTROL OF THE STATE

When a family-member sponsor cannot be identified, children may be placed in long term foster care. Less than four percent of children in ORR custody are referred to long term foster care programs, where they reside in the homes of families rather than in group facilities.[25] Fernando was one of them. As it turns out, his dilemma at the border had been warranted: he ended up neither in a detention center nor with his uncle in Florida. The ORR social worker determined that Fernando's uncle was ineligible to sponsor him because "he had some sort of problem with the law." The social worker asked then-fifteen-year-old Fernando if he wanted to stay in the United States with a foster family. Fernando agreed. He was eager to leave the ORR shelter, where he had spent six months, and he did not want to return to Guatemala. Fernando was placed in foster care in California, far from Florida, where his uncle and several immigrants from his hometown lived. While "unaccompanied" is effectively a misnomer for most of the youths behind the category, this label aptly describes those in long-term foster care.

Fernando recounted his experience in foster care in negative terms. He moved around a lot and lived with three different families. This made it hard to settle in, and he missed several months of school. Fernando resented all the rules imposed in the foster home, where his behavior was closely monitored, he was forced to go to church, and he was not allowed to have a cell phone. Most importantly, Fernando resented having to go to high school. His aspiration had been to work, so he could be independent and support his mother in Guatemala, an unacceptable objective for a minor in the care of the state. For youths like Fernando, long-term foster care meant exacerbating and prolonging the experience of heightened state scrutiny that all unaccompanied minors experience, most acutely, while they are detained at the border and in ORR custody. Fernando found long-term foster care infantilizing. He emphasized the claustrophobic nature of this arrangement—the control and constraints on his desired coming-of-age trajectory—over the care and resources he was able to access, like a free immigration attorney, housing, food, and clothes.

DELEGATED CARE AND CONTROL: SOCIALIZATION DURING STATE-MEDIATED REUNIFICATION WITH FAMILY

To comply with the Flores Settlement, ORR usually releases unaccompanied minors to sponsors, who in 60 percent of cases are youths' parents, and in 31 percent of cases are other relatives, like aunts and uncles, cousins, older siblings, and grandparents.[26] Being released to family was a great relief for youths who had endured years of family separation, violence in their home countries, dangerous journeys, and, at times, lengthy and inhumane periods of detention while fearing deportation. ORR delegates to family members its mandate to both care for and control youths. To obtain custody of their children, family members sign a formal contract with the state called a "sponsor care agreement," where they commit to financially support the minor; sign her up for school; and provide for her physical and mental health (care functions); as well as ensure the minor shows up for appointments with the immigration bureaucracy and even complies with a removal order if she were to lose her case (control functions).

Family members were sometimes wary of interacting with state institutions like ORR to request custody of their children because virtually all of them were undocumented or had only temporary forms of legal status. The legal consciousness of these adult immigrants, long accustomed to living in the shadows, was therefore characterized by fear of the state rather than trust.[27] For example, Lisette, an undocumented Guatemalan immigrant, told me that she had feared declaring her presence to the state to take custody of her fifteen-year-old son.

LISETTE: I was worried because I have two children here, and [other immigrants] had told me that I can't take him out [of ORR]. I wondered what would happen to me with my children. I was scared for them, and I told the social worker my situation, everything.

CHIARA: Was the social worker nice? Did he try to reassure you?

LISETTE: Yes, he did; the social worker helped me.

The main breadwinner of a transnational family, Lisette felt torn between her obligations to her teenage children in Guatemala and her US-citizen children, who were just toddlers. Since was undocumented, she was afraid that claiming her recently arrived son would put her at risk of deportation. However, she ultimately overcame her fear and confided in the ORR social worker, who gave her the confidence necessary to request her son's custody. Through interactions such as these, the state positions itself between youths and their families, gaining the trust of adult undocumented immigrants before delegating its care and control functions to them.

Paradoxically, the same legal regime that constructs Lisette's "illegality" also designated her as an agent of immigration control, responsible for her son's compliance with the law. The legal process for unaccompanied minors positions immigrant parents and other family as either brokers in their children's access to humanitarian protections (when cases are approved) or complicit in their deportation, the most severe form of exclusion and legal violence (when cases are denied). In this context, undocumented sponsors' interests of self-preservation—by evading attention that could signal their presence to immigration authorities—conflict with the interests of the youths in their care who must interact with state agencies to apply for humanitarian relief. These competing interests create important dilemmas for immigrant families, as we will see in chapter 4.

Lisette took custody of her son during the Obama administration. If she had done so under Trump, her fears of declaring her presence to the state would have been warranted. A new policy introduced in 2018 required potential sponsors and all the other immigrants living in the household where the unaccompanied minor would be released to be fingerprinted and vetted before they obtained custody of youths. This policy had the effect of putting undocumented potential sponsors and their families at increased risk of being apprehended and deported. Indeed, in just the first five months of implementation, 170 undocumented potential sponsors were arrested, the vast majority of whom had no criminal record.[28] As word spread in the immigrant community that coming forth to claim unaccompanied minors was dangerous, fewer relatives came forward to request custody of their children. This, in turn, prolonged the amount of time that youths spent detained in ORR. The population of unaccompanied minors eventually grew to exceed, by far, the availability of beds in shelters. To remedy the unsustainable situation created by the Executive branch, Congress intervened to strike down the fingerprinting policy in 2019. Notably, this was one of the few immigration-related pieces of legislation passed by Congress, which has otherwise been deadlocked on the issue during the past decade.

Upon obtaining custody of unaccompanied minors, sponsors took their care and control responsibilities very seriously. Several youths were subject to quite strict surveillance at home to ensure their compliance with behavioral models of "good" rather than deviant youth. While undocumented immigrant families commonly control their children to protect them, in the case of unaccompanied minors, this control is formally mandated by the state through the ORR-sponsor contract. The stakes involved are also considerably higher because unaccompanied minors are highly visible in removal proceedings, where noncompliance with laws and behavioral norms could mean case denial and swift deportation. Alicia thus described how ORR staff encouraged her mother's control during phone calls before her release:

ALICIA: [The social worker] told my mom that she should always check on me: who was at home with me, who I was going out with, who my friends were. . . . My mom calls me all the time, to see if I got to school, if I ate lunch, when I get out of school.

CHIARA: Do you mind that she calls you very often?

ALICIA: No, because she pays attention to me, something that didn't happen in El Salvador. My mom is so kind; she gives me too much; she takes care of me; she's really protective of me. I always say that she's just like the social worker said she should be.

Alicia noted that her mother called her constantly to check on her. Indeed, as I sat with Alicia at Starbucks for two hours, we paused the interview twice because her mother had called. Alicia was eighteen when I interviewed her. Legally speaking, she was an adult. She was also an adolescent who might wish to exercise greater independence from her parent as a marker of her coming-of-age. Therefore, I was surprised at her answer when I asked her if she minded receiving all those phone calls from her mother. After years of separation, Alicia perceived her mother's control as a means to catch up for the lost time when she was not able to receive her care. It was a source of joy to have a mother who was attentively following the social worker's instructions for monitoring her appropriate behavior. In this way, Alicia actively reinterpreted the state's motivation for her mother's control—keeping a potentially deviant teenage immigrant in check—by perceiving it as an act of love. Of course, not all the youths I met were happy about complying with their family's control, or they only begrudgingly accepted it. As I will discuss in chapter 6, a gendered pattern emerged in youths' experiences of family reunification: boys more commonly perceived family involvement in their lives in a negative light, as control or surveillance, while girls like Alicia more commonly perceived it as an act of love.

Upon release to their—mostly undocumented—immigrant family members, youths were influenced by the fear of the state and misinformation about US laws that circulated in their migrant networks. The influence of their caretakers contributed to shaping youths' legal consciousness, which is characterized by both fear of and trust in the state and by a combination of misinformation and information about the law. When I asked Jesus, who migrated from Honduras at age sixteen, who helped him most since he arrived in the United States, his response reflected the role that his mother Marcela played in his legal socialization: "My mom has helped me, in many ways. . . . She told me that I shouldn't do bad things because, here, laws are very strict, with just one thing that you do, they can deport you. She tells me that I shouldn't misbehave with this country."

An undocumented immigrant who had lived in the United States for over ten years, Marcela acted as an intermediary between her recently arrived immigrant son and the state, carrying out her delegated control function. She also transmitted her fear of the state. Indeed, Jesus, who had already been awarded the significant protections of refugee status, nonetheless demonstrated fear and acute awareness of the law and state power. He brought up the advice that he received from his mother and in ORR multiple times during our interview. This advice included an admonishment that US immigration laws are strict and that, if he misbehaved, he could be deported. Reflecting his internalization of his mother's fear, Jesus described the state in a way that resembles an unforgiving parent who will not pardon any mistakes.

At the same time as they expressed fear, after being released from ORR custody, youths also felt secure. They now finally found themselves in a country that, at the very least, offered them a temporary place of refuge from the harm and violence that had put their lives at risk. Accordingly, youths commented on feeling "at peace," protected, and having more opportunities in the United States, as compared to their home countries. As we will see in chapters 4 and 5, youths' interactions with legal brokers while applying for asylum and SIJS crucially contributed to fostering their trust in the state. When assembling applications for relief, legal brokers juxtaposed the "bad"/lawless home country and the "good"/lawful host country, probing youths to compare their relative safety and rights in each context. Legal brokers also taught youths about their rights and about protections for unaccompanied minors in US immigration law. These messages gave youths some sense of immediate protection, as well as hope that they would obtain future long-term stability through legal status. Interacting with legal brokers thus allowed youths to retain trust in the state despite their family's fears. Youths expressed this trust by characterizing the United States as a country where "laws protect children."

Danny's experience navigating the different junctures of the multi-agency bureaucratic maze and interacting with his sponsors reflects the combination of trust and fear, misinformation and information, which characterizes unaccompanied minors' legal consciousness.

> I talked to my aunt about how I was going to get out of [ORR]. . . . She got a lawyer because other immigrants were saying that you needed to be a resident to take out a minor. . . . My friends were taken out by uncles, cousins, friends, the ones who had papers. . . . While I was there, waiting for so long, I thought they weren't going to be able to take me out. . . . My uncle said, "I have TPS [Temporary Protected Status].[29] I'm not a resident, I can't take you out." My aunt said, "I'll do it." Her husband, who is a citizen, said, "I'll support you too." So, they put the papers in, with the lawyer, and, the truth is, they didn't ask them for their documents [immigration status], they just let me out.

As he moved through the various sites of the US immigration bureaucracy, the seemingly contradictory elements of Danny's legal consciousness were configured as he oscillated between trust in and fear of the state. He first expressed knowledge of his rights and trust in the receiving state by voluntarily turning himself in at the border. As we saw in the previous section, in CBP custody, Danny was given good reason to fear the state and to doubt the United States' commitment to protecting immigrant children. Once in ORR custody—during the Obama administration, when undocumented sponsors could indeed claim unaccompanied minors without risk—Danny was influenced by the misinformation circulating in his migrant networks. His family members thought that only citizens and permanent residents could take custody of their children from ORR, and Danny feared that he would be detained indefinitely.

Yet, upon release, Danny once again placed his trust in the state when he decided to appear in immigration court when summoned for his removal proceedings. Danny made this decision despite having been exposed to misinformation from other migrants in his networks who had been deported or had returned to Honduras. Those individuals had advised Danny's relatives to tell him to abscond because he would eventually be deported in any case. Instead, Danny decided to pursue an asylum application. Indeed, absconding is very uncommon among unaccompanied minors; 95 percent of youths who have legal representation show up for their immigration proceedings.[30] Danny's trust in the state paid off: his asylum case was granted, and he was a permanent resident when I met him.

HOW CASE OUTCOMES INFORM LEGAL CONSCIOUSNESS AND TRUST

Danny had a far more developed pre-migration understanding of the law than most other youths, as he already knew what asylum was before arriving in the United States. Once there, like other unaccompanied minors, he interacted with attorneys who advanced his legal socialization by teaching him more about asylum, a process that I describe in detail in chapters 4 and 5. When I asked Danny to tell me about his interview at the asylum office, he said, "I told my story, which, by the way, was true. They still asked for proof, and I turned it in. I think that helped a lot, since I had proof, and my story was real, not fake."

Reflecting his understanding of the law, Danny rightly identified proof as one factor that enabled him to win his asylum case. Yet, like other unaccompanied minors who won their asylum cases, he identified truth-telling, rather than credibility—the officer's perception of the veracity of his account—as the most important reason why he won. Youths assumed that asylum officers who make credibility determinations could ascertain whether their stories were true, an assumption with little grounding in scientific evidence that instead shows that individuals are not skilled at detecting lies.[31] Notably, despite being quite critical of his treatment at the border, Danny did not challenge the stigma of the "bogus refugee." Rather, he reproduced and distanced himself from it. In a context characterized by suspicion and limited asylum approval rates, Danny thus positioned himself as a truth-teller, a deserving exception to the supposed norm.

Youths who navigated the system successfully and whose asylum cases were granted, like Danny, experienced heightened feelings of trust in the state. They viewed the asylum system as protective and inherently just. They believed their cases had been awarded because they deserved it and because they told the truth. As we will see in the next two chapters, however, the reality is far more complex. Multiple, sometimes arbitrary, factors shape how a case progresses through the asylum system and whether it is likely to be granted. In contrast, youths whose asylum cases were denied felt stigmatized and experienced diminished trust in the state. One example was Hector, the sixteen-year-old we met in chapter 2, who described a dehumanizing interaction with the asylum officer who interviewed him:

HECTOR: I told [the asylum officer] that I fled my country because they were going to kill me, and he said something else. He was very intimidating when he asked questions. He tried to confuse me. He talked to me like he was angry, like he didn't want to see me sitting there in front of him. He said he didn't care what happened to my friends, he only cared about what happened to me.

CHIARA: How did it make you feel when he said that?

HECTOR: It made me feel bad because those friends, I loved them like brothers. We had known each other since we were little.

Based on Hector's account, it appears that the asylum officer coercively discredited him by producing the very contradictions—"He said something else. . . . He tried to confuse me"—that make asylum cases especially vulnerable to denial. Unlike Danny, Hector was critical of the asylum process, and he did not feel at ease disclosing sensitive information to the hostile officer. Hector felt dehumanized when the officer said that he did not care about his friends who were murdered by the gang members who were trying to forcibly recruit them. This made Hector feel as if his suffering—losing his best friends at such a young age—did not matter. The officer's behavior sounded adversarial to me, an approach that seemed to disregard asylum office guidelines for child-friendly interviews (see chapter 5). What's more, the officer dismissed events that were relevant to Hector's asylum claim. The asylum officer used his discretion to deny Hector's case and exclude him, a manifestation of legal violence in the US asylum process.

These negative experiences make youths like Hector feel disenfranchised and distrusting of the legal process; they are acutely aware of their position in the group considered unworthy of humanitarian protections.[32] When I met Hector, his attorney had advised that he apply for SIJS to seek relief from deportation and the certain death he felt awaited him in Guatemala. However, after his experience at the asylum office, Hector felt little optimism about the outcome. While, like all youths, he had dreams for the future, he put them on hold while his case was pending:

CHIARA: When you imagine a future here in the US, what is that future like?
HECTOR: Finishing high school, going to college, having a good job, helping my family.
CHIARA: What would you like to study?
HECTOR: To become a lawyer. An immigration lawyer, to help people like me.
CHIARA: Do you have a specific college in mind?
HECTOR: No. Since they denied my case, I stopped making plans. I have no hope about anyone or anything, I don't want to anymore. I'm just waiting now, to see what they tell me.

Hector experienced the legal violence of the denial of refugee recognition so acutely that this effectively froze his coming-of-age. He could only contemplate his life goals to obtain higher education, work, and help his family (all markers of adulthood) in abstract, when I asked him to *imagine* his future. When I asked him a specific question about *planning* for that future, he told me that he could not because he had lost hope. While Danny was finishing high school and making plans to apply to college, Hector felt stuck and helpless. In chapter 6, I describe in more detail how unaccompanied minors' liminal legal position exacerbates their liminal social position, suspended between childhood and adulthood.

When protection is granted, trust is enhanced, and youths like Danny perceive their rights and position in US society in more positive ways. When protection is denied, youths like Hector feel disenfranchised. That youths' trust in state institutions and perception of the fairness of the asylum process were informed by how their own cases were assessed is perhaps unsurprising. Yet this perception goes against the grain of the scholarly evidence about the inherently indeterminate and capricious nature of the US asylum system. While this institution is indeed meant to be protective, it has been characterized as a "refugee roulette" where case outcomes are determined by a narrowly interpreted refugee definition, subjectively perceived merits, the personal inclinations of adjudicators, and a good degree of chance.[33]

Keep this in mind when reading the next two chapters that describe how lawyers strategically co-construct with youths what they hope to be successful asylum cases: as de facto refugees who escaped from violence, Danny and Hector fled similar conditions and the same degree of acute, life-threatening risk. They both made it out alive out of sheer luck: Hector thanks to his friend's mother who had already paid the coyote's fare when her son was killed and urged Hector to make the journey himself; Danny because he was friends with a coyote, who quickly smuggled him out for free as a personal favor. Both Danny and Hector fled dire and immediate threats: criminal actors were looking for both boys to kill them; their persecutors had proven themselves extremely dangerous by murdering their friends, other teenagers like them. Both boys had access to an attorney. In fact, they were represented by the same legal aid organization. Both boys took their chances in the refugee roulette. Only Danny was protected.

UNACCOMPANIED MINORS' CONTRADICTORY UNDERSTANDINGS OF THE LAW

Unaccompanied minors are quickly socialized, as they interact intensively with multiple state agencies from the moment when they first step foot in the United States. This process of legal socialization shapes how youths understand the law and their relationship with the state. The legal consciousness of unaccompanied minors is characterized by three elements: (1) a combination of fear in the state's enforcement branch and trust in its protective institutions; (2) concurrent feelings of deservingness/rights and stigmatization/subordination; (3) both information and misinformation about US laws. While these elements seem contradictory, in fact, they mirror the "ambivalent" legal context that receives them, characterized by exclusion and protection.[34]

While they are socialized through interactions with immigration bureaucrats in sites of detention—and with family members delegated to act as agents of immigration control—unaccompanied minors internalize the stigmas tied to their subordinate social group. Youths receive normative "advice" about the behaviors expected of deserving young citizens, which they conflate with information about their actual legal obligations. These messages become so entwined that unaccompanied minors usually cannot tell laws, rules, and advice apart.

Like other members of subordinate social groups, unaccompanied minors manage the stigma imposed on them through distancing mechanisms.[35] They present their personal identities in opposition to stigmatized identities: as truth-tellers and worthy humanitarian claimants, as opposed to "bogus" refugees who cheat the system; as well-behaved children, as opposed to criminal, possibly gang affiliated, Latinx youths or "bad" immigrants. As they reproduce these discourses, youths unwittingly lend legitimacy to such tropes, evidence of the symbolic violence imposed even on this protected group of immigrant children as they are socialized in US institutions. Indeed, youths' trajectories through the bureaucratic maze, which culminate in their applications for legal status on humanitarian grounds, are disempowering experiences overall.

Unaccompanied minors are especially at risk of exclusion at the border, where they suffer rights violations and legal violence. They inhabit a liminal and precarious state while detained in ORR with limited access to attorneys and at risk of aging out of eligibility for state services and immigration relief. Conversely, once they are released, youths are better positioned to access the protections that exist in US humanitarian immigration laws. The next chapters describe how youths obtain legal representation (chapter 4) and then claim membership rights vis-à-vis the state with the help of immigration attorneys by applying for asylum and SIJS (chapter 5).

Whereas state actors are focused mainly on ensuring their traceability and compliance, unaccompanied minors start to acquire more information about their rights when they interact with legal brokers. The intermediation that attorneys and other advocates carry out is indispensable for youths to be able to claim rights and request deportation relief and legal status. As unaccompanied minors interact with legal brokers, their legal socialization continues in important ways. Youths learn how to navigate another series of bureaucracies: immigration court, the asylum office, other USCIS offices, and, for SIJS, state-level family, probate, and dependency courts. As we will see, some youths are better positioned than others to learn about and understand how complex US immigration laws apply to their individual circumstances. For youths to be formally recognized as refugees in the US asylum process, they must not only have experienced the right types and amount of suffering in their home countries, but they must also learn to describe their experiences in the language of the law.

While the asylum process is rife with indeterminacy, as the tragic example of the disparate treatment of Danny and Hector shows, legal brokers adopt a variety of strategies to mitigate risk and maneuver in the system to obtain favorable outcomes for their young clients. Thanks to this support, some unaccompanied minors are indeed able to obtain protection and legal status. Protection from deportation back to insecurity and danger in the home country is invaluable. Yet, as we will see, the price to obtain it can be high, particularly when youths are made to compete for the scarce good of free legal representation and for compassion in shrinking supply.

4 Access to Legal Representation

REPRESENTING ELIGIBLE YOUTHS
OR CHOOSING THE "COMPELLING" CASE

One morning in 2018, the juvenile docket of the Los Angeles immigration court—a purportedly "child-friendly" space where immigration judges hear only the cases of unaccompanied minors—was characteristically packed. The smaller size of the courtroom, one of the key differences with the adult dockets, was meant to make this institutional space feel less intimidating. Yet, without exception, youths described immigration court as a scary place. The main thing the smaller courtroom seemed to accomplish was to make seating scarce. Families typically cramped both the benches and hallways while court was in session. That morning, fourteen youths were sitting in the benches, alongside several adults. Most were the family-member "sponsors" who had agreed to be responsible for youths and make sure that they showed up to court. Others could be identified by their suits and briefcases as the immigration attorneys representing the few youths who already had legal representation. Before the judge entered the courtroom to hear the cases on the docket, a lawyer from a local non-profit started off the daily legal orientation presentation, in Spanish, by asking, "Do any of you know what it means to be in removal proceedings?"

After a moment of silence, one of the adults in the courtroom suggested, "They send you back to your country?" Nodding in agreement, the lawyer explained, "Basically, the government says young people can't stay, or maybe they could stay if they qualify." She then introduced the different bureaucrats who would take part in this life-altering decision by pointing out who sits where in the courtroom. At the central stand, the immigration judge sits in the middle, the interpreter to the right, and the clerk to the left. At one end of the courtroom is the desk where the Department of Homeland Security (DHS) trial attorney sits. The lawyer explained, "Don't be afraid of the judge. The judge works for the Department of Justice, not for immigration. . . . The trial attorney is the one arguing that you should be expelled." Next, she pointed to the table at the other end of the courtroom, which had two large sets of headphones on it. She explained that this is where the minor sits, alongside his or her attorney and sponsor, listening to the proceedings through the interpreter's translation.

Apprehended at the border, unaccompanied minors are *pushed* into the immigration system as soon as they step foot on US soil, making them highly visible to the state. From border holding facilities, youths are transferred to ORR custody, where they are detained until an eligible family-member "sponsor" can be identified. Upon release to family, unaccompanied minors receive a letter that initiates their removal proceedings, summoning them to immigration court.[1] Removal proceedings are the bureaucratic process through which the state sorts individual immigrants into different legal categories and outcomes: they will either be subject to deportation or considered eligible for, and deserving of, different forms of legal status. As the legal broker above explained, the DHS trial attorney defends the exclusionary immigration control interests of the state during these proceedings by arguing for the deportation of the immigrant. Unaccompanied minors and adults alike are allowed to remain in the United States only if they demonstrate that they qualify for exemption from deportation and legal status.

It is at this juncture of the bureaucratic maze that most unaccompanied minors learn that they may qualify for humanitarian paths to legal status—mainly, asylum and Special Immigrant Juvenile Status (SIJS)—and that, to access these protections, it is indispensable that they obtain legal representation. While unaccompanied minors submit their asylum and SIJS applications to different agencies of the maze-like US immigration bureaucracy—usually Citizenship and Immigration Services (USCIS), which includes the asylum office (see chapter 5)—they must nonetheless appear in immigration court periodically to update the judge about what forms of relief they are applying for and whether any decisions have been made on their case. During the Obama administration, immigration judges had the discretion to administratively close the cases of youths who had applied for asylum and SIJS and whose applications were pending, which meant that youths no longer had to attend court regularly. Conversely, the Trump administration stripped judges of this discretionary power. This meant that youths or their sponsors had to return every few months to the intimidating, and potentially risky space of immigration court, which exacerbated their liminality and "deportability."[2]

The first part of this chapter describes how legal brokers explain the complex provisions of immigration law during free legal orientation presentations that take place in the "child-friendly" juvenile dockets of immigration court and in legal clinics. I discuss how legal brokers carry out one key aspect of their jobs: legal translation.[3] They explain the eligibility criteria of humanitarian forms of relief in simple ways so that they are understandable to young immigrants who have limited years of schooling and almost no accurate knowledge about US immigration laws and bureaucracies. They also teach youths about their rights and obligations and how they should behave while attending immigration court. In "translating" the contradictory legal context of reception, legal brokers inevitably reproduce messages that reflect both the protective and exclusionary forces at work in the US immigration system. Interactions with legal brokers during these free courses are key moments for the legal socialization of unaccompanied minors. Yet vast information gaps persist. No number of such courses would be sufficient for unaccompanied minors to be able to successfully represent themselves in removal proceedings.

The second part of this chapter discusses how youths find an immigration attorney to represent their case. Legal representation drastically increases unaccompanied minors' chances of being allowed to remain in the United States, from 15 percent to 73 percent.[4] Yet the US government does not guarantee free legal representation to immigrants in removal proceedings. Even advocates' attempts to argue that all immigrant *children* should have the right to government-funded legal representation have failed.[5] Nevertheless, the creation of the "unaccompanied minor" category—and corresponding protections in US immigration law—combined with the existence of funding for the legal representation of this population at the L.A. County, California, and federal levels, has fostered the development of a professional field of legal brokers specialized in working with unaccompanied minors. Thanks to this funding, and to the existence of a network of legal advocates dating back to the Sanctuary Movement of the 1980s, Los Angeles is relatively rich in nonprofit legal service providers. Indeed, 75 percent of unaccompanied minors were represented in Los Angeles on average during the years this research took place, as compared to a national average of 66 percent.[6] While the Obama administration increased federal funding for the legal representation of unaccompanied minors following increased arrivals in 2014, the Trump administration decreased it. To fill the gaps left by Trump-era cuts, the State of California and L.A. County increased their own funding for legal aid organizations that represent immigrants.

Even in the relatively favorable Los Angeles context, however, unaccompanied minors' demand for free legal services has always exceeded the supply. Because family members have just paid hefty sums to coyotes to extract youths from life-threatening danger in the home country, often on very short notice (see chapter 2), paying thousands of dollars for a private attorney is a luxury very few can afford. With limited funds and high demand, nonprofit legal service providers must find ways to manage and allocate the finite resources at their disposal. These organizations use two types of models to decide which clients to represent. The first is the *triage model*, where lawyers select cases both most likely to be successful (i.e., "strong cases") and most "compelling," an evaluation that reflects a US-centric system of values and expectations about childhood, refugeehood, and agency. The second is the *quasi-universal representation model*, where the client is either assigned or able to choose the organization that represents them, and the eligibility bar for taking cases is low. In other words, cases must be eligible but not necessarily "strong." Legal brokers determine whether cases are "strong" or "weak" based on an evaluation of what I call the immigrant's humanitarian capital, a form of symbolic capital that is activated relationally during attorney–potential client interviews. By recognizing instances of suffering, and assigning differential value to each, legal brokers manage risk in an inherently indeterminate legal process and anticipate whether adjudicators will likely grant the case.

Past studies have examined the role of legal brokers in the immigration context. Some scholars have argued that legal brokers play not just an intermediation role but also an advocacy role by challenging and expanding eligibility categories to promote undocumented immigrants' access to legal status beyond policy makers' intentions.[7] Others have argued that legal brokers limit undocumented immigrants' access to legal status and perpetuate a humanitarian system of admissions that is inherently compatible with restrictive immigration control.[8] Based on her ethnographic fieldwork in a legal clinic that helped battered women apply for US citizenship, Roberta Villalon identifies client selection as a key part of the legal process where biases may be introduced, and attorneys can create additional barriers for immigrants' access to relief.[9] By comparing two distinct client selection models used by nonprofit legal clinics, I demonstrate how some organizational practices but not others undermine young migrants' chances of obtaining the legal representation that is indispensable to pursue applications for humanitarian relief.

I argue that the triage model exacerbates the limited compassion of the humanitarian immigration system, where only the most severe cases of suffering and victimization, which have the most humanitarian capital, are considered deserving of legal status. The underlying assumption of the triage model is that it is better to invest scarce resources in representing youths who actually have a chance of winning their case, as opposed to "wasting" resources on those whose cases will likely be denied regardless. In practice, however, attorneys make these evaluations based on far too limited information and only a very partial picture of youths' lived experiences in the home country. In the context of limited resources, an organizational model based on triage makes it more difficult to access legal representation, and hence to apply for relief, for older teenagers and those whose lived experiences of suffering do not conform to subjective evaluations of deservingness and to narrow interpretations of the legal categories of refugee and abandoned, abused, or neglected child. I also discuss how each organizational model, in turn, shapes lawyering strategies, either enabling legal brokers to challenge existing categories to expand access to protection or constraining them to reproduce the existing bounds of the restrictive humanitarian system.

IMMIGRATION LAW FOR KIDS 101

During legal orientation presentations, legal brokers introduced youths and their families to their rights and obligations under US immigration law, explained what types of relief from deportation unaccompanied minors are commonly eligible for, and provided advice on how to find an attorney. As we saw in the last chapter, for most youths, this was their introduction to US immigration law. While ORR shelters are supposed to provide similar presentations, notably, few youths remembered learning about the law and their rights in that space.

Legal orientation presentations first focused on the obligations of unaccompanied minors and their family member sponsors vis-à-vis the state. The importance of showing up to immigration court was particularly emphasized. This obligation is part of the contract that sponsors sign with ORR to obtain custody of their children. The onus of going to court is placed on the adult sponsor rather than the minor. While immigration judges often waived the presence of minors after they attended court for the first time, if sponsors missed court, the minor could receive a deportation order. This requirement was a source of preoccupation for sponsors, the vast majority of whom were undocumented. These anxieties became exacerbated during the Trump era, as spaces that were previously assumed to be safe became potential targets for immigration raids.

Soon after Trump was elected, Kevin's mother Maria, whom we met in chapter 2, suddenly became fearful of accompanying her son to court. Maria was a confident, cheerful, and talkative woman who, despite being undocumented and thus, by definition, vulnerable to deportation, initially seemed comfortable with her life in the United States. Displaying a new preoccupation at the prospect of her first appointment in court under the newly elected president, Maria asked her son's attorney, "Can't I send a family member with him?" She knew Kevin could be ordered deported if she did not show up. However, she was also worried that going to court might result in her own deportation to Guatemala—where her life was under threat by her abusive ex—and her separation, not just from Kevin, but also from her US-born children. Maria was especially anxious since she had a "record" with immigration. She had been ordered deported in absentia years before because she had not shown up to immigration court since she did not know at the time that she was eligible to apply for asylum.[10] Kevin's lawyer offered little in terms of reassurance, telling Maria that she could only miss court if she had "a good excuse, like if you're really sick."

Attorneys who represent unaccompanied minors cannot give legal advice to their parents and relatives. Oftentimes, the interests of these two parties are at odds. In this case, protecting the son meant exposing the mother. Thus, instead of providing legal advice, attorneys limited themselves to acknowledging the catch-22 situation that parents found themselves in. That day, the lawyer told Maria, "ICE has been to court, so I can't tell you that you'll be fine. But if the judge said so, you have to go." Later in the Trump presidency, when the initial surge of anxiety in the immigrant community became somewhat subdued as they grew accustomed to living in the new "normal" of heightened uncertainty and risk, legal brokers might also provide imperfect reassurances that sponsors would be fine. For example, "We always go to court, and we have never seen anything happen." In other cases, instead of providing reassurance, legal brokers pressured parents into complying with phrases like, "If the minor doesn't show up, and he gets a deportation when they come looking for him, it can put the whole family at risk if they don't have papers."

The last message seemed to play into adult caretakers' fears, positioning legal brokers, not just as intermediaries in access to legal status, but also as actors who effectively help impose state power by making immigrants acutely aware of state scrutiny and the expansive reach of immigration enforcement. Legal brokers thus encouraged compliance with immigration law and with the expectations of the state. This was a common thread during my research. As intermediaries of the contradictory context of reception—concurrently characterized by punitive enforcement and by protective laws—legal brokers, to some extent, inevitably reproduced exclusionary forces. They did so despite their personal ideologies and professional motivations, which were to protect vulnerable youths and advance social justice battles to make the United States more inclusive for immigrants.

The next topic that legal orientation presentations discussed was courtroom etiquette. In other words, how youths and their family members were expected to behave when attending court. Immigrants were told to speak clearly, not have side conversations, to be punctual and not "arrive running or all sweaty," and to never eat, drink, or chew gum in court. In sum, legal brokers told immigrants to adopt a demeanor of respect for the adjudicators in this institutional space who would exercise so much power over their lives and decide whether they would be allowed to stay in the United States. These presentations were among the first of many times that youths would hear recommendations about how to dress in these spaces, including this advice that I heard repeated over and over during my fieldwork, "Dress as if you are going to church."

During one presentation in a legal clinic in Los Angeles, a volunteer showed a room full of teenagers a PowerPoint slide with a picture of a young, light-skinned boy, who looked about eight years old, wearing khaki pants and a blue polo shirt. The volunteer suggested that this boy was a model for how to dress appropriately, while clothing such as low-cut shirts, ripped jeans, shorts, and baseball caps should be avoided. The subtext was that those items signaled deviant or sexually provocative youth behavior. Clothing choices should instead convey an image of a "good," well-behaved, conservative young citizen, who is as childlike as possible. In providing these recommendations, legal brokers forewarned youths about the assumptions they believed adjudicators would make about them, as teenagers in a liminal state between childhood and adulthood, and as Latinx youths who are criminalized in the US context. Legal brokers were well aware that aesthetic and performative considerations factor into the subjective element inherent in the discretionary decisions of asylum officers and judges who decide whether to grant cases.[11]

On a different slide, the PowerPoint presentation featured a cartoon image of Pinocchio. Pointing to the screen, the volunteer asked the audience, "Why do we have Pinocchio here?" She paused, and there was silence in the room. "Because it's very important that you tell the truth. The judges have been doing their jobs for a long time, and they are going to know if you lie to them, and everything is being recorded." The importance of telling the truth was stressed not only during these presentations but in several spaces: at the US-Mexico border, where Border Patrol officers question unaccompanied minors' age; on the retainers that youths sign to hire their immigration lawyers; during meetings with legal brokers when their asylum and SIJS testimonies are prepared; at the asylum office; and in immigration court. Legal brokers warned youths not to lie by mistake by trying to "guess" the answer to the judge's question because this could produce inconsistencies in the record that may later be interpreted as a lack of credibility. The continuous reiteration of this message led youths to internalize the idea that state bureaucrats perceive them as suspicious actors, who are assumed to be lying unless proven otherwise.

Next, presentations shifted focus to the rights and protections afforded to unaccompanied minors under US immigration law. Legal brokers used short stories as examples of circumstances that might qualify youths for each type of humanitarian relief. This intuitive strategy allowed youths to learn what forms of relief they might be eligible for and to begin thinking about the work that lawyers do, in other words, matching their lived experiences with the formal requisites of legal categories. By explaining the complex and evolving provisions of immigration law, legal brokers played an important role in the legal socialization of newly arrived immigrant youths. During legal orientation presentations, they first discussed the two forms of relief that unaccompanied minors are most commonly eligible for—asylum and SIJS—followed by those that fewer youths qualify for—the T-visa and U-visa. Tellingly, legal brokers mentioned family reunification only in passing at the end of presentations, to emphasize that Central American unaccompanied minors were generally *not* eligible to be reunified by their (mostly undocumented) parents and relatives. That this last message was a standard part of legal orientation presentations reflects the historical denial of refugee recognition to past generations of Central Americans and the enduring curtailed paths to legal status for these immigrants in the United States (see chapter 2).

Following the order used in presentations, I now turn to highlighting how legal brokers translated eligibility criteria for each relevant humanitarian category in US immigration law. For *asylum*, one legal broker explained eligibility in these simple terms:

> We hear a lot about asylum but, perhaps, this is the most complicated. To qualify, I need to be afraid because I was harmed, or I would be harmed if I return to my country. . . . Careful! The reason for the harm is important! It needs to be a protected reason. For example, if you are indigenous, if you have a specific religion, if you are suffering because you are someone's son, because of your sexual orientation, because you are part of a political family.

The legal broker first outlined a key concept in asylum law: fear of return to the home country. This concept was intuitive for youths because it connected directly with their subjective understandings of their experiences of escape from violence. However, the legal intermediary also cautioned that qualifying for asylum would be far more "complicated." She explained that fear of return, by itself, is not sufficient to qualify. Instead, the reason why youths are afraid—the *types* of suffering they endured prior to their escape—must fit under one of the five protected grounds in the refugee definition. The legal broker exemplified these eligibility grounds as follows: (1) race ("if you are indigenous"); (2) religion ("if you have a specific religion"); (3) political opinion ("if you are part of a political family"); (4) membership in a particular social group ("if you are suffering because you are someone's son," "because of your sexual orientation"); and (5) nationality (no example).

Central American asylum seekers, both youths and adults, are by far most likely to apply for asylum under the ambiguous particular social group (PSG) grounds. The idea of the PSG is especially difficult to translate because its definition is constantly evolving through US asylum case law, which determines what experiences are eligible. As we will see in chapter 5, the two PSGs that attorneys considered "strong" for unaccompanied minors' asylum claims were family membership and child abuse. These two types of suffering reinforce notions of childhood as a time of passive dependency on adults. The legal broker explained the family PSG ("if you are suffering because you are someone's son") in more depth by using a fictional story: "Carlota's family suffers violence from the *mara roja* [fictional 'red gang']. They threaten them and say that they will kill them if they don't pay an extortion fee. The family reports the threats, but the police do nothing. The mara burns Carlota's house down, and her mom and sister die. What does Carlota qualify for?"

The fictional Carlota was harmed because her family was targeted, and she continues to be at risk because she is a member of this family. At the time of this presentation, in 2018, a case like this based on family membership was likely to succeed at the asylum office.[12] Providing information like this, on PSGs likely to succeed, in all introductory presentations was helpful as a practical strategy to teach youths about the law. Yet it also inevitably reified existing child-specific interpretations of US asylum law, which ignore youth agency and instead reward the passive victim. The child is dependent on her family, even when it comes to the cause of the persecution she suffers. While it is true that some youths are at risk because their family members are targeted, as we saw in chapter 2, many others are instead personally targeted by the *maras* precisely due to their age. In the example above, the legal intermediary paints a picture of Carlota as a child with no agency or protagonism in the story, the most salient characteristic being that she suffered indirectly because her mother and sister were harmed.

Legal brokers next explained eligibility for *Special Immigrant Juvenile Status* (SIJS), which they referred to, in Spanish, as "*la visa juvenil*" (the youth visa). SIJS provides a path to citizenship for unmarried immigrant children under age twenty-one who have been abandoned, abused, or neglected by *both* parents, when returning to the home country is not in the child's best interests. Children abandoned, abused, or neglected by *one parent* (who are in the care of the other parent in the United States) are also eligible but must apply before age eighteen. The SIJS application is a complex process that involves two different sets of bureaucracies: (1) the state-level family, dependency, or probate courts that usually make decisions pertaining to all children, irrespective of immigration status, in matters such as divorce, parental custody, state custody, and guardianship; (2) USCIS, a federal-level immigration agency. SIJS is also unique in that it combines state-level (in this case, California) child welfare laws—which provide legal definitions of parental abandonment, abuse, or neglect—with federal immigration law.

Without going into the intricacies of all the steps involved in applying for SIJS (see chapter 5), legal brokers used fictional examples to translate its three eligibility criteria: abandonment, abuse, and neglect. With these stories, legal brokers described a series of home-country scenarios and prompted Central American youths and their family members to rethink what a "normal" childhood should look like. One legal broker explained neglect by using an example of child labor and irresponsible parenting: "Juanito left school when he was nine. We have a little kid like this [makes a gesture of a short child's height], working in the fields in dangerous conditions, with a machete, cutting himself. When he gets home, his dad is drunk. . . . I know in some countries it's common for minors to work but, here in the United States, it's illegal." Another fictional story reflected the abandonment and abuse categories: "Carlos's mom died when he was little [abandonment]. His dad drank a lot of alcohol and did not work. He hit Carlos when he got drunk [abuse]. In Carlos's country it's normal for parents to hit their kids, and the police do nothing. What does he qualify for?"

A man who was listening to the presentation that day replied to the question. He offered asylum as an answer, explaining, "because he's scared of going back." Reflecting his understanding of the fear-of-return concept introduced earlier in the presentation, this man thought that fictional Carlos qualifies for asylum because he fears returning to the country where he was abused. However, the legal broker corrected the man by asking, "But is there a reason for the persecution?" The group of immigrants listening to the presentation answered, "No," in chorus. The legal broker explained that this would be a "stronger" SIJS case because fictional Carlos was abused by his dad and because his mom died, which can be considered abandonment under California law. This conversation took place in 2018, soon after Attorney General Jeff Sessions issued a decision (Matter of A-B-) that overturned hard-won asylum case law in place since 2014 (Matter of A-R-C-G-) to disqualify domestic violence as a valid reason to seek asylum. If the presentation had taken place just weeks earlier, the man's answer would have been correct. Before Matter of A-B-, attorneys had considered experiences of child abuse as the "best" type of suffering for unaccompanied minors' asylum cases.

This example reflects how an asylum system that was already indeterminate to begin with became increasingly volatile under Trump. Legal brokers now had to accurately transmit complex information about changes in the interpretation of legal categories and quickly evolving case law. It was challenging even for attorneys to keep up with the Trump administration's constant policy changes, which were introduced at an exhausting speed. In this context, legal orientation presentations provided more ambiguous explanations of the law. After the Matter of A-B- decision, a legal broker discussed child abuse and asylum eligibility in these terms, "This is complicated because the law used to allow one to qualify [for asylum] based on domestic violence. We are optimistic that this might still work. So, if anything like this happened to you, make sure to tell your attorney." Constantly evolving legal definitions made the already complex issue of asylum eligibility immensely more difficult for immigrant youths to grasp, undermining the extent to which they could learn and retain accurate information about the law.

Next, the T-visa for trafficking victims and U-visa for crime victims were discussed in legal orientation presentations, but only briefly since Central American unaccompanied minors were generally less likely to qualify for these forms of relief. Legal brokers explained the *T-visa* through examples like: "If you were forced to come to the United States based on threats or lies and forced to work or have sex" and "Sometimes coyotes force young people to transport drugs." In the presentations I observed, no youths ever thought they were eligible for the T-visa or requested additional information about this type of relief. At the time of writing, the T-visa is still an underused path to humanitarian legal status for immigrants of all ages. According to my attorney interviewees, applying for the T-visa is difficult due to the challenges involved in satisfying the trafficking definition, which requires part of the trafficking to have occurred in the United States.

The fictional examples that legal brokers used to describe *U-Visa* eligibility followed a format such as this: "What happens sometimes is that young people haven't suffered as victims of a crime [in the United States] but their parents or older siblings have. So, if Juanito's mom was a victim of domestic violence, and she's bleeding, and she goes to the police . . . then she qualifies and Juanito qualifies too." Like the example of fictional asylum seeker Carlota above, once again, the youth is not the protagonist of the story. Instead, Juanito qualifies for the U-Visa as a derivative on his mother's application. Interestingly, during the course of my fieldwork, I never met any recently arrived unaccompanied minors who qualified for the U-Visa through parents who had been victimized. Conversely, I met five unaccompanied minors who were eligible for the U-Visa because they had *themselves* been victims of a crime in the United States.[13] These were teenage boys who had been mugged or assaulted with a weapon in dangerous neighborhoods or had been aggressively bullied by local gangs in their schools in Los Angeles. While the example of Carlota reflects the child-specific biases of existing US asylum case law, it was unclear to me why the legal broker would choose this adult-centric story in the case of the U-Visa while talking to a room full of teenagers just as likely to be victims of crime as adults. When legal brokers subscribe to the infantilizing logic of a legal system that fails to recognize the agency of migrant youth, they risk reproducing messages that paint youths as deserving of protection only as passive dependents even when eligibility for the legal category in question does not require any childlike traits.

FINDING AN ATTORNEY: SUPPLY AND DEMAND OF LEGAL SERVICES

Legal orientation presentations ended with advice on how to find an attorney. During one presentation in the Los Angeles immigration court, a paralegal asked for a show of hands to see how many unaccompanied minors did not yet have an attorney representing their case. Most youths raised their hands. The paralegal handed out two sheets of paper, a list of legal service providers based in Los Angeles and a green form. She explained,

> Those of you who do not have an attorney, the judge will ask you if you want an extension [to prepare your case]. Say yes. This can be a long or short amount of time. It depends on the judge. If the judge tells you to come back to court in three months, do not wait until the last day to look for an attorney. Try this afternoon! You should try to call at least one attorney every day.

Lifting up the green form so everyone in the courtroom could see it, she added, "This is a tool we've created that the judges accept. Each time you call a lawyer, write it down on this form, so you can show the judge. So, if the judge tells you to come back to court in one month, how many lawyers should you have tried to call?" A woman sitting in the benches—one of the minor's sponsors—replied, "Two or three at most." Like a teacher running out of patience, the paralegal corrected her, "No! Thirty lawyers. You should try calling a different lawyer each day. There are resources in Los Angeles, but it's not easy! You have to make an effort."

Legal brokers created the green form to help youths and their caretakers successfully ask the immigration judge for more time to find an attorney to prepare their case.[14] The judges on the juvenile dockets had agreed to accept the form as evidence that immigrants were trying to contact different attorneys and hence deserved more time. The green form allowed immigrants without legal training or assistance to make their efforts tangible in the realm of immigration law, where "papereality" serves to lend legitimacy to what immigrants say and do.[15] Asking family member sponsors to spend time each day adding names to the green form was a means to encourage them to secure legal representation for the children in their care. Yet it also reflected the new salience that the law suddenly took in the everyday lives of undocumented immigrants who had previously hid from the immigration bureaucracy. These individuals were now being told to completely shift their mindset to act as brokers in their children's applications for humanitarian relief. The arrival of unaccompanied minors inevitably pushed undocumented adult caretakers out of the shadows, making them visible to the state.

The urgency that legal brokers transmitted during these presentations was not unwarranted. Demand for free legal services exceeded supply even in the relatively favorable Los Angeles context with its well-consolidated organizational landscape of legal service providers. As the main destination for unaccompanied minors in the United States, demand was always high. During the course of my fieldwork, the backlog in the Los Angeles immigration court increased from under fifty-one thousand pending cases in 2015 to over eighty thousand in 2019.[16] About half of these cases involved unaccompanied minors and adults from the northern countries of Central America. The local legal aid organizations that provided free legal representation almost always had long wait lists to take on new cases. Finding legal representation, while avoiding falling victim to fraud and malpractice, could therefore be challenging. To further complicate matters, misinformation and rumors about which lawyers should be considered competent and trustworthy circulated in immigrant communities. For example, it was rumored that free legal services were not high quality and that, if attorneys were being paid, they would pay more attention to the case and obtain relief more quickly. Indeed, legal orientation presentations addressed this rumor directly. One legal broker thus reassured immigrants that lawyers working at nonprofits "do have a salary, we just don't charge anything to our clients, or we charge a small amount."

In immigration court, legal brokers handed out a list of *abogados de confianza* (lawyers you can trust). Both legal brokers and immigration judges encouraged immigrants to ask attorneys to show them their Bar license cards. This was to make sure that they were not hiring *notarios*, individuals with no law degree or authorization to practice law who charge immigrants to fill out their applications for immigration benefits. Hiring *notarios* can cause immigrants who might otherwise obtain legal status to file applications incorrectly, to be found ineligible for relief, and to be potentially fast-tracked for deportation. Over the course of more than four years of fieldwork, I never once saw youths or their family members ask attorneys to provide credentials or otherwise demonstrate their competence to represent them. This reflects the power asymmetry between legal brokers and their young clients: unaccompanied minors seldom feel empowered to make specific demands and requests of their attorneys. Youths are instead relegated to a passive role in the preparation of their own cases for humanitarian relief. Even Danny, the savvy fifteen-year-old from Honduras we met in the last chapter who came to the United States knowing that he had the right to seek asylum, fell victim to fraud. The first attorney Danny hired turned out to be a *notario*. Danny lost hundreds of dollars before he realized his mistake and found a legitimate immigration attorney who took on and won his asylum case.

There are three types of legal representation that immigrants can obtain: pro-bono, low-bono, and full-price services in private practice (Table 6). Pro-bono legal representation is completely free. These services are provided either by attorneys on staff at nonprofit legal aid organizations, funded by a combination of public and private funds, or by volunteer attorneys who work in private practice and take on cases under the supervision of a managing attorney at the nonprofit. These private practitioners usually have limited experience practicing immigration law, and they take on the cases of unaccompanied minors to learn about new aspects of the law or for personal (or firm-level) humanitarian motivations. During interviews, managing attorneys at nonprofits lamented the challenges of coordinating and providing training to these volunteers so they could successfully represent new and unfamiliar cases. They noted that this could be a waste of resources because some pro-bono volunteer attorneys tired of and abandoned the cases assigned to them, which were taking increasing amounts of time to be resolved, especially during the Trump administration.

Low-bono legal representation is carried out by nonprofits or individual attorneys motivated by humanitarian and social justice concerns

Table 6   Types of legal service providers

	Who offers services?	Cost
Pro-bono representation	Nonprofit organizations that employ full-time legal staff and/or supervise attorney volunteers	Entirely free or free except for some fees paid directly to the government
Low-bono representation	Nonprofit organizations that employ full-time legal staff and/or supervise attorney volunteers Individual attorneys motivated by humanitarian considerations rather than profit	Fees paid to government and legal service provider (affordable relative to private practice)
Full-price services	Individual attorneys in private practice motivated by profit	Extremely costly for unaccompanied minors

rather than profit. These legal brokers charge small fees to their clients, much less than what attorneys in private practice would charge. Nonetheless, covering even those lower fees could still be challenging for immigrant families and, even more so, for unaccompanied minors who could not count on any financial support from their US-based relatives. To give one example of the price of low-bono legal services, in 2015, an asylum application for an unaccompanied minor cost $700, plus a $250 fee each time the attorney attended court with, or on behalf of, the youth. Youths unable to access pro-bono or low-bono legal representation had no other option but to hire attorneys in private practice, who could charge between $2,500 to $4,000 to prepare an application or even just one component of an application. For example, they might prepare just the asylum office component of an asylum claim, but not the appeal in court if the case was denied. They might prepare only the USCIS component or the California State court component of SIJS cases. The fees charged by private attorneys were prohibitive for most Central American unaccompanied minors and their families.

In the absence of funding for universal legal representation for all immigrants in removal proceedings in the United States, nonprofit legal aid organizations must find ways to distribute the scarce resources at their disposal to represent unaccompanied minors. The organizations where I did my research in Los Angeles did so by selecting their clients through two different organizational models: the *quasi-universal representation model* and the *triage model*. Both approaches used eligibility screenings, but the outcomes of these screenings—the decision about whether to represent the individual immigrant youth—varied quite starkly based on what model was used.

Eligibility screenings are brief interviews in which legal brokers ask potential clients questions to determine their likelihood of acquiring legal status under various categories in US immigration law. To assess whether each client had a "strong" or "weak" claim to humanitarian forms of relief like asylum or SIJS, legal brokers evaluated what I have called humanitarian capital. Legal brokers identified and attributed value to instances of suffering in each immigrant's account by drawing on their professional knowledge to mine formal legal definitions and anticipating the subjective element characteristic of discretionary humanitarian adjudication.

The quasi-universal representation model meant that organizations selected clients using a low eligibility bar. In other words, cases needed to be eligible for relief but not necessarily "strong" (i.e., deemed likely to win). For asylum, this essentially meant *not* having what is called a "frivolous case." If youths claimed that they feared returning to their home country, this was considered sufficient reason to legitimately apply. For SIJS, any eligible experience of abuse, abandonment, or neglect was considered enough to apply. Low-bono legal service providers adopted this model, taking on all clients who could afford to pay their reduced fees and who met the low eligibility bar. Of course, in addition to their social justice mission, which centered on the idea that all immigrants have the right to legal representation, these organizations also had an incentive to take on more cases because the small fees charged to clients helped subsidize their operations. Both these goals could be accomplished by interpreting legal definitions expansively and representing more clients. Youths were usually connected with low-bono legal service providers by other non-profits and family, and other members of their immigrant communities who had used these services in the past to apply for immigration benefits.

Pro-bono legal service providers adopted either the quasi-universal representation model or the triage model. Organizations that adopted the former model took on clients on a first-come, first-served basis, whom they were connected with by certain ORR shelters and other non-profits. In these cases, youths' access to an attorney hinged somewhat on luck, for instance, on the shelter where they stayed. This, in turn, usually depended merely on the availability of beds in a certain shelter at any given moment.[17] Similarly, some funding sources limited pro-bono service providers to serving only clients that resided in a certain area. For example, the city of Los Angeles's "LA Justice Fund" allowed organizations to represent only immigrants who lived in certain zip codes in the sprawling city, making access to legal representation contingent on where unaccompanied minors' sponsors lived. Immigrants from many other parts of Southern California also attend court in Los Angeles. For them, securing legal aid could be more challenging due to these organizational constraints, as well as due to the need to travel longer distances to access services and attend court.

Despite these limitations, low-bono and pro-bono organizations implementing the quasi-universal representation model were able to represent unaccompanied minors with an array of diverse experiences who could apply for relief if they met the low eligibility bar, as determined in initial screenings. Lawyers working in these organizations were thus enabled, and more likely to, engage in creative lawyering by filing cases that did not necessarily closely correspond to preexisting case law. This approach, for one, allowed legal brokers to manage risk and protect their clients who feared for their lives in their home countries by, at the very least, trying to buy them some time during which they could safely live in the United States while their cases were pending. This could also be a means to obtain temporary legal status for their clients. During the Obama administration, Central American families and unaccompanied minors who did not win their asylum or SIJS cases could still qualify for a form of prosecutorial discretion, which allowed them to stay in the United States with a two-year work permit if the immigration judge found their cases to have merit on humanitarian or other grounds.[18] Filing "weaker" cases thus had the benefit of facilitating access to, at least temporary, deportation relief for certain clients.

Second, this approach allowed legal brokers to file asylum cases that challenged narrow interpretations of US asylum law in hopes of creating new expansive precedents that recognized previously discounted experiences of escape from violence. Legal brokers could also file different types of SIJS cases with the goal of increasing the scope of considerations of the child's best interests. Thus, legal aid organizations that implemented the quasi-universal representation model imposed lesser constraints on their staff and enabled legal brokers to try to expand access to protection for unaccompanied minors and asylum seekers in the United States. By representing those who feared returning to their home countries because they escaped from violence but who did not experience the "right" types of suffering according to established case law, these legal brokers recognized Central American youths to be de facto refugees and enabled them to exercise their right to seek asylum.

Conversely, the triage model involved managing limited resources by identifying and selecting those clients who were perceived to have the "strongest" cases for asylum and SIJS. Organizations could be incentivized to adopt this approach because, if they achieved high grant rates for their clients, this would reflect positively on the organization, potentially making it easier to secure funding for their future operations. The implementation of the triage model resembled the practice of medical practitioners who manage their patients by "assessing severity" and "deciding what suffering needs to be taken care of first."[19]

In the triage model, eligibility screenings were high-stakes encounters during which youths needed to disclose as much information as possible in a short amount of time to convince legal brokers to take on their cases. During interviews usually lasting no more than ten minutes, legal brokers determined if the youth was eligible for relief and decided whether to take the case. There were two main complications in the triage approach to client selection: (1) the process of selecting only the "strongest" cases incentivized legal brokers to apply existing legal definitions narrowly; (2) due to the short amount of time available to interview youths, legal brokers effectively decided which cases to represent based on an insufficient amount of information about potential clients' experiences. To illustrate the limitations of the triage approach, I present two cases: Salvadoran siblings Jonathan and Darwin; and Guatemalan unaccompanied minor Estefania.

Jonathan and Darwin migrated from El Salvador at ages seventeen and sixteen to join their mother, an undocumented immigrant who had been living in Los Angeles for over ten years. Having arrived in the United States as an unaccompanied minor, Jonathan turned eighteen on the day he was released from ORR custody to his mother. The siblings were interviewed to determine their eligibility for relief just two months after they had arrived in Los Angeles. The paralegal interviewed the eldest sibling first and the youngest second. Both boys told us the same story about why they left: they were living with their grandmother who became too elderly and ill to take care of them. When their aunt took them in, they changed neighborhoods, which exposed them to threats and forcible recruitment from gangs. Their mother tried to protect them by sending money from the United States to move them from the dangerous public school to an expensive private school but, even so, they continued to receive threats. The gangs approached the brothers to recruit them on two occasions, threatening that there would be repercussions if, on the third attempt, they did not join.

As Darwin recounted, attempting to state the unspeakable, "They warned us, they said that we knew what was going to happen to us if we refused a third time. We saw cases that didn't end well, so we decided to come here." This account clearly suggests that the siblings received some kind of threat, but, as is often the case, they were both initially reticent to describe this explicitly as a death threat. It should come as no surprise that it is frightening for youths to relive moments such as these while they describe the interactions that caused them to flee, fearing for their lives. After hearing this story from each sibling in turn, the paralegal asked them follow-up questions.

Jonathan, the eighteen-year-old, was asked:

PARALEGAL: Did they [gang members] ever hit you?

JONATHAN: No, but once they came to our house, they were outside, yelling at us. I was too afraid to go out.

PARALEGAL: What was your relationship with your grandmother like?

JONATHAN: She was like our second mom. We told her everything, but she died.

PARALEGAL: I'm sorry.

JONATHAN: Thank you. She was like our mom. My dad never helped us.

PARALEGAL: Did you ever work?

JONATHAN: Sometimes, in a bakery, just to pay for our books. . . .

PARALEGAL: So, you never met your dad?

JONATHAN: We know who he is, but he never helped us, we never had a relationship.

PARALEGAL: Did anyone else hurt you?

JONATHAN: No.

PARALEGAL: Are you scared to go back to your country?

JONATHAN: Yes, that's part of why I don't want to go back.

PARALEGAL: It's difficult now to get asylum based on gangs, you're going to need police reports about what happened, or news reports, or you're going to need to talk about other people that you know, someone in your family who went through similar things.

Darwin, the seventeen-year-old, was asked:

PARALEGAL: When the gangs threatened you, did they have weapons?

DARWIN: Yeah.

PARALEGAL: Where is your dad?

DARWIN: No idea.

PARALEGAL: You never met him?

DARWIN: I have met him, but he never helped us. Ever since I can remember, it's just been my mom who supports us. He even had a letter prepared to say that he wasn't going to take responsibility for us.

PARALEGAL: You could have an asylum case, but right now cases based on gangs are really hard because a lot of people come for the same reason, and it needs to be due to something particular.

DARWIN: Yes, but like I was telling you, our grandmother who took care
[INTERRUPTING] of us, she died.

PARALEGAL: That could qualify you for SIJS. You have one year to apply before you turn eighteen.

The first set of questions the paralegal asked (Did they ever hit you? When the gangs threatened you, did they have weapons?) served to determine the degree or number of instances of victimization that the two brothers suffered at the hands of the gangs. The paralegal thus assessed the siblings' humanitarian capital and decided whether it was "enough" to meet the bar of persecution. As noted in chapter 1, the legal criterion of persecution was purposefully created to be narrow and grant protection only to limited numbers of cases by excluding victims of the "nefarious political routine."[20] The paralegal engaged in legal translation as she explained the narrowness of the persecution criteria to the brothers by saying, "A lot of people come for the same reason, and it needs to be due to something particular." She thus told the brothers that their story needed to be unique, different from those of others who fled the region. As victims of gang violence, the boys could be considered victims of the nefarious routine. What's more, as we will see in the next chapter, US case law considers experiences of forcible gang recruitment to be ineligible for asylum.

The paralegal used her knowledge of US asylum case law to determine that the brothers did not have a strong asylum case. She let them know that their odds of success were low, "It's difficult now to get asylum based on gangs." However, as the paralegal explained the narrowness of the law itself, the brothers perceived her to be discounting their experiences of flight. Darwin pushed back by telling her that they *were* hurt for a unique reason: their grandmother passed away and could not care for them anymore. Of course, the paralegal was merely translating the law, and it is US asylum case law that discounts Darwin and Jonathan's experiences of victimization at the hands of the gangs. There is nothing inherently problematic with simply assessing that the siblings' case for asylum was likely weak. What was problematic was the fact that this assessment was also a reason for the organization *not* to represent their case. When organizations reproduce narrow existing interpretations of the law to decide whether to represent cases, they limit access to free legal representation. They thus inevitably further curtail the chances of obtaining asylum for de facto refugee youths who demonstrate the "wrong" type of suffering.

The paralegal also determined that the organization would not take the siblings' cases after asking these questions to determine eligibility for SIJS: "How was your relationship with your grandmother?" and "Did anyone else hurt you?" to screen for potential abuse; "Did you have to work?" to screen for potential child labor, legally considered neglect; "Did you know your father?" to screen for potential abandonment. Both siblings acknowledged that their father abandoned them, even signing paperwork that formalized his refusal to provide for them. Abandonment is one of the legal criteria that qualify youths for SIJS. However, because eligibility for SIJS is also based on age cut-offs (eighteen years old for those applying for SIJS based on abandonment by one parent), the paralegal determined that only seventeen-year-old Darwin was eligible.

The two siblings were just one year apart and had lived through virtually identical experiences. Yet the hard line of age-based eligibility excluded eighteen-year-old Jonathan, leaving him only the option of applying for asylum with a weak case. If Jonathan, who aged out while he was detained, had enjoyed access to an attorney in ORR, he might have been able to apply for SIJS. Instead, unaccompanied minors can usually secure legal representation only when they are released. Jonathan was detained for fifty-two days in the ORR shelter, and this exacerbated his liminality and undermined his ability to remain in the United States for the long term. During my fieldwork, I often saw cases of vulnerable and seemingly eligible youth who were excluded from relief in arbitrary ways due to matters of timing that penalized them for things they had no control over, such as their length of stay in ORR, bureaucratic scheduling problems in the courts and the asylum office, or the exact date of their birthday or arrival in the United States.

Importantly, while Darwin *was* eligible for SIJS, the organization decided not to represent his case either. This was, in part, due to pragmatic "client management" strategies.[21] Some organizations chose not to represent SIJS applicants over sixteen because looming deadlines might require them to put other cases on hold to file applications for youths like Darwin before they aged out. Yet immigration attorneys working in organizations that used the quasi-universal representation model routinely successfully managed such competing deadlines in the total workload of cases they represented. This type of client selection strategy made it more difficult for older unaccompanied minors to obtain free legal representation. If organizations overwhelmingly represent the cases of younger children—who generally fit more passive narratives—and fail to represent older teenagers—whose lived experiences may challenge existing cultural and legal conceptions of childhood—this will have broader implications in keeping the scope of humanitarian legal categories narrow, so they protect only those with the most humanitarian capital. Nonprofits thus reify ideals that consider younger children more deserving of compassion and protection because they are more innocent and distant from adulthood.

If Darwin and Jonathan's eligibility had been assessed using the approach of the semi-universal representation model, this preliminary interview would have dictated a very different outcome. The attorney assigned to the case would have prioritized filing Darwin's time-sensitive SIJS application immediately before he aged out. She would then have moved on to applying for asylum for Jonathan, and possibly also for Darwin,[22] both of whom would have been deemed eligible because they feared returning to their home country. Indeed, the information and supporting documents that the paralegal mentioned would be necessary to build a stronger asylum case by consolidating Jonathan's humanitarian capital—including "police reports about what happened, or news reports, . . . other people you know who went through similar things"—are not meant to be insurmountable barriers to access legal representation. Rather, these are things that legal brokers routinely compile, over time, as they prepare asylum applications.

The two boys and their mother were visibly confused by the paralegal's determination that day. The boys did not understand why the paralegal had said that their lived experiences of escape from violence were unlikely to satisfy the legal requisites for asylum. Their mother was upset. She asked several times that the paralegal explain why Jonathan could not apply for SIJS like his brother. She did not understand why the two boys, so close in age and experience, would be treated differently under the law. Situations such as these, with siblings who lived through virtually identical experiences falling in or out of eligibility for relief in arbitrary ways, reflect the capriciousness of humanitarian protections for children in US immigration law that are based on the hard-line eligibility of age cut-offs. These dynamics are likely to produce even more mixed-status immigrant families in the United States, as younger unaccompanied minors are better positioned to obtain legal status than their older siblings. The family left the legal clinic that day without legal representation and with only discouraging information. They would have to find legal representation elsewhere as soon as possible, which could prove challenging, since they could not afford to pay for a private attorney.

Another key limitation of the triage model as a means to select clients was the limited amount of time available for youths to disclose information that could potentially be relevant. Not all youths were as apt to quickly share information as Jonathan and Darwin, who made the paralegal's job relatively easy by recounting their story in a clear, detailed, and linear fashion. In the triage model approach, the lived experiences of suffering that youths disclosed in the narrow temporal window of a five- or ten-minute interview were the ones that could potentially "buy" them access to legal representation if they were considered to yield enough humanitarian capital.

Yet, as I will describe in the next chapter on case preparation, a significant amount of time was usually necessary for legal brokers to build rapport with youths and obtain information from them. This meant meeting with youths on multiple occasions, gaining their trust, explaining legal criteria repeatedly, and working with their family members to obtain information relevant to the case. New and valuable information that shifted a case significantly from being deemed "weak" to being considered "strong" often only emerged after several meetings. This is because youths need time to understand the complex legal requisites of applications and what information is relevant to disclose. Youths also have more trouble than adults providing the information necessary to prepare a successful asylum case. They generally have less access to information, especially about events that occurred during the early years of their childhood. Youths also have more difficulty remembering and verbalizing their experiences of suffering because of the strong effects of trauma on young and developing minds.[23]

The case of sixteen-year-old Estefania from Guatemala reflects the negative consequences of having limited time available for the disclosure of information in client selection using the triage model. After listening to a legal orientation presentation, Estefania sat down for her eligibility screening interview. She told the paralegal that she thought she qualified for asylum and SIJS.

PARALEGAL: Why do you say SIJS?
ESTEFANIA: Because my mom died; you said that's abandonment.
PARALEGAL: What about asylum?
ESTEFANIA: When she died, the gangs threatened us.

PARALEGAL: How did she die?

ESTEFANIA: She had a tumor at first, then it became cancer.

PARALEGAL: How old were you?

ESTEFANIA: I was fourteen.

PARALEGAL: What about your dad

ESTEFANIA: He's been here [in the United States] since I was born.

PARALEGAL: Who did you live with when your mother died?

ESTEFANIA: My older brother.

PARALEGAL: Who provided for you?

ESTEFANIA: My dad sent money; my brother worked too.

PARALEGAL: How was your relationship with your mother? Did she ever hurt you?

ESTEFANIA: Maybe, just when I behaved really badly.

PARALEGAL: How did she hit you?

ESTEFANIA: With her hand.

PARALEGAL: Okay, I think you qualify for the *visa juvenil* [SIJS] since your mom died and you're under eighteen. Would it be difficult for you to pay for an attorney?

Estefania, nods, yes.

PARALEGAL: Are you afraid to go back?

ESTEFANIA: Yes.

As I observed the above interaction, I checked off Estefania's eligibility in my mind, as it had become second nature for me after years shadowing legal brokers. I thought: death of mother qualifies her for SIJS; threats to her family and fear of return qualifies her for asylum. The paralegal also determined that Estefania was eligible for SIJS. However, for asylum, in order to qualify, the paralegal said that Estefania would need to have a conversation with her older brother to ascertain more details, including why they were being threatened and what exactly had happened in Guatemala. Estefania had told us that she fled Guatemala with her eighteen-year-old brother after he was threatened by gang members. Like Darwin and Jonathan, Estefania and her brother were left without the support of a caretaker after their mother's death, which, as we saw in chapter 2, can make youths more vulnerable to gang violence.

Estefania and her brother had been separated at the US-Mexico border: Estefania (a minor) was admitted, while her older brother, who was over eighteen, was immediately deported. They had not spoken since shortly after his return to Guatemala. Estefania was no longer sure where he lived. She thought that he had likely gone into hiding because his life was in danger. Estefania had limited knowledge about the threats they received because her older brother was the one who had the direct interactions with the gangs. It was not at all uncommon for loving caretakers and older family members to shield younger children from such painful or frightening information.

The paralegal's concerns about needing details to build a strong asylum case were, of course, warranted. I had often observed how, to obtain the detailed facts necessary to determine asylum eligibility and for case preparation, legal brokers in organizations using the quasi-universal representation model requested information from family members both in the United States and in Central America. Obtaining information from family members in the home country was challenging, and it required time and patience, but it was often possible thanks to technology. For example, one afternoon, an attorney, a young asylum seeker, and I spent almost one hour trying to reach the boy's father in El Salvador who was waiting for our call. After we made about ten calls over speaker phone, all of which were cut off after a few minutes and resulted in nearly inaudible short conversations, we were able to reconstruct a one-paragraph account of the threats the family had received after the boy left, which the attorney submitted as part of the asylum application. Obviously, tracking down Estefania's brother during a ten-minute interview to determine whether she met the asylum eligibility bar necessary for this organization to accept her case would not have been feasible. By selecting clients in this way, however, these organizations were assessing whether youths were eligible and likely to win their cases based on insufficient information and a very partial picture of what youths had experienced in their home countries. The fact that Estefania was likely eligible for asylum was dismissed by this organization because she did not immediately have and disclose the necessary amount of information.

What surprised me that day was that Estefania, who was also eligible for SIJS, was so promptly dismissed as a potential client, first by the paralegal, and then by the supervising attorney. This assessment was made because the suffering that she disclosed in the context of the brief meeting was determined not to yield sufficient humanitarian capital to "buy" her access to free legal representation. I asked the supervising attorney why they would not represent Estefania. The attorney explained that they only chose to represent youths eligible for SIJS if neither parent was in the United States, which gave them more time to prepare applications (i.e., until youths turned twenty-one), for the "client management" considerations mentioned above, or "if it's something very compelling, like, not just abandonment by death but, for instance, if there was abuse."

Legal brokers who implemented the triage model spoke little about eligibility and, instead, used terms like "compelling case" and "sensitive case." When I asked legal brokers what they meant by this, I was particularly struck by one of the answers I received. An attorney and a legal assistant, talking simultaneously, volunteered a list of examples to explain: "if there is self-harm," "sexual violence," "LGBTQ cases," "health problems." Then the attorney said to the legal assistant, "Remember that kid without the hand?" After nodding to the attorney, the legal assistant looked at me, and offered an even more "compelling" example, "We once had a kid missing both arms and legs." Both the attorney and the legal assistant agreed in ranking this last case highest in the constructed hierarchy of suffering that legal brokers use to compare the cases they have worked on in the past, which serves as a basis to evaluate humanitarian capital.

With limited time to obtain information about lived experiences of suffering and victimization from the youth and many potential cases to choose from, Estefania was dismissed with an immediacy that I found both surprising and alarming. The suffering of the child missing body parts was embodied through a stark physical expression and was thus easier to read and translate into humanitarian capital. Conversely, the limited information that Estefania possessed about the threats that she and her older brother received was not taken as an indicator of the need to do more "fact finding," as attorneys working in organizations using the quasi-universal representation model would have done. Instead, it was quickly determined to be insufficient to meet the higher bar of suffering that securing access to legal representation through the triage model requires. After a limited amount of time gathering information, the organization dismissed Estefania's asylum case. Her SIJS case was also dismissed because it was based on "just abandonment" and was not sufficiently "compelling." This is notable, as my interviews with attorneys working in all types of organizations confirmed that it is possible to win SIJS cases based exclusively on abandonment by death under California law.

That day, Estefania told her story, but her suffering did not yield "enough" humanitarian capital. She left with only a list of private attorneys that she could not afford. Notably, the youth's financial need was not considered during triage-model eligibility screenings beyond asking, "Can you afford an attorney?" Even after immigrants admitted that they could not, this did not affect the decision about whether to take the case. When organizations use the triage model, youths' lived experiences of suffering become important even before their humanitarian petitions for legal status are assessed by the asylum office, by USCIS, or in immigration court. This had the effect of commodifying youths' suffering, which became a currency of sorts that could "buy" them access to the scarce and coveted good of free legal representation.

THE IMPLICATIONS OF SCARCE RESOURCES FOR LAWYERING STRATEGIES AND YOUTHS' ACCESS TO PROTECTION

The organizational models that legal aid nonprofits use to select clients crucially structure constraints on the innovative legal strategies that attorneys can carry out. In the triage model, legal brokers can represent only a handful of cases that exhibit exceptionally high levels of the "right" types of suffering. They are thus constrained to reproduce narrow humanitarian categories of admission in the immigration system, exacerbating a process in which compassion is treated as a scarce resource to be sparingly distributed to few. This approach produces an additional, significant barrier that youths must overcome—by quickly disclosing stories with enough humanitarian capital to "buy" them access to legal representation—before even dealing with their actual applications for legal status. Attorneys who implemented the triage model were not unaware of its problematic effects. As one of them put it, "I worry that selecting clients like this doesn't allow us to serve the children most in need."

Conversely, the quasi-universal representation model is a more inclusive means to select clients because it uses a lower eligibility bar and does not reproduce narrowly interpreted legal categories a priori as a criterion to select cases. This approach acknowledges that, especially with young asylum seekers, it takes time to acquire a full picture of youths' past experiences. Information that shifts a case from being considered "weak" to "strong" often only emerges after several meetings. This model enables legal brokers to represent a more diverse array of cases that do not necessarily correspond to existing case law. They can thus carry out an advocacy role, potentially expanding legal categories to recognize more immigrants' lived experiences of escape from violence. Yet, while this model seeks to approximate universal representation, these organizations still have limited funds and can hence represent a finite number of clients. Who ends up getting access to these services on a first-come, first-served basis largely depends on factors outside of youths' control.

No matter what client selection approach is used, when only limited funding is available for organizations to represent small numbers of clients, this creates a context in which free legal aid becomes a scarce resource that immigrants must effectively compete for. The less funding is available, the more this dynamic becomes exacerbated, as the supply of free and affordable legal services shrinks. Even in relatively service-provider-rich Los Angeles, demand for legal services has always exceeded the supply. When nonprofit organizations can only represent limited numbers of clients, due process is undermined because not all immigrants are able to obtain legal representation and apply for relief that they may ultimately qualify for.

The next chapter follows youths who successfully made it to the next juncture of the bureaucratic maze when attorneys take on their cases and help them apply for asylum and SIJS. The examples I discuss there are drawn from my fieldwork in organizations using the quasi-universal representation model, where legal brokers represented youths with a broad array of lived experiences. This allowed me to distinguish problems related to organizational practices from those related to humanitarian categories of admission. I explain the myriad, often arbitrary ways that youths fall in or out of eligibility for protection, highlighting the mismatches between the lived experiences of de facto refugee youth and the narrow formal refugee definition.

5 Lawyering with Unaccompanied Minors

HELPING YOUTHS APPLY FOR ASYLUM
AND PROTECTIONS FOR ABANDONED,
ABUSED, OR NEGLECTED CHILDREN

"Asylum law does not make common sense." Reflecting on years of experience representing Central American unaccompanied minors, one attorney explained, "I had more than one case where the thing that actually pushed them out the door wasn't the thing that made their asylum case winnable." She paused and parsed her words. She was wary that the legal framing of asylum narratives is often misconstrued as problematic lawyering. Like all attorneys practicing during the Trump years, she was also somewhat defensive. I could understand why. After all, the president himself had demonized asylum lawyering as a "big fat con job."[1] Then, she resumed, saying:

> I'm starting to feel a little nervous saying that to an outsider because I think it plays into the narrative this administration is trying to push, that asylum claims are somehow fraudulent. That people are asking for asylum on a basis that is different from what actually brought them here. But to me, instead, it exposes the illogic of asylum law. That a person can be legitimately terrified, and a child can have every right to claim a safe place to live from a commonsense perspective but not from a legal perspective.

The commonsense understanding of asylum as a form of protection for people who fear returning to their homes is a far cry from how asylum

law works in practice. This chapter lays bare the tension between the formal refugee definition and the lived experiences of de facto refugee youth.
US asylum law does not adequately recognize how exposure to violence is
patterned along the key dimension of age in El Salvador, Guatemala, and
Honduras. The *type* and *amount* of suffering youths experienced in their
home countries and the timing of their escape play out in the asylum process in ways that they could never have anticipated. Legal brokers assess
and assign value to youths' experiences of suffering to transform them into
humanitarian capital. This symbolic resource is legible to the adjudicators
in the immigration bureaucracy who grant tangible benefits: deportation
relief, legal status, a path to citizenship.

What counts and what doesn't in this exercise of translation of human
suffering is by no means intuitive or logical for migrant youths, nor for
any nonexperts for that matter. To qualify for asylum, youths' accounts
must satisfy US asylum case law that recognizes only experiences like
child abuse, which reify notions of childhood as a state characterized by
lack of agency and dependency on adults. Conversely, US asylum case law
is biased against those targeted by gangs. This stance is at odds with the
position of the UNHCR, which instead recognizes forced recruitment by
any violent group to be a form of persecution.[2] Victimization and forced
recruitment by gangs are key reasons why youths flee Central America
today. Yet those who faced these realities usually have slim odds of winning their asylum cases if their experiences cannot be reframed to fit existing, infantilizing case law. These interpretations of deserving refugeehood
in the US asylum system often clash with youths' subjective understandings of the reasons for their escape. Unaccompanied minors' legal socialization continues during their asylum applications as they work with legal
brokers to reinterpret their experiences. Not all youths are equally receptive to the lessons their attorneys try to teach them. Those who learn to tell
their stories of escape, not as they understand them, but in the language
of the law, fare better during their interviews at the asylum office and in
immigration court.

This chapter is structured as follows. First, as existing literature has
focused on adults, I explain how and why lawyering with asylum-seeking
youths differs. Second, I discuss US asylum case law and the legal arguments that attorneys commonly use to prepare the cases of Central

American unaccompanied minors. Third, I trace asylum case preparation from start to finish, examining how youths and legal brokers co-construct narratives and prepare for interviews with asylum officers and immigration judges. Fourth, I examine the SIJS application process, which, unlike asylum, considers the *best interests of the child*. Legal brokers may advise youths who escaped from violence for the "wrong" reasons to apply for SIJS instead, thus using this form of relief to compensate for the limitations of asylum law. To prepare SIJS cases, legal brokers reinterpret youths' home country experiences using California child welfare laws to determine whether these would constitute parental abandonment, abuse, or neglect if they had occurred in the United States. Finally, I discuss how legal brokers adjusted their Obama-era legal strategies to manage increased exclusion and indeterminacy during the Trump administration.

In this chapter, I argue that youths who escape from violence fail to obtain refugee recognition not only when their asylum cases are denied but also when they gain legal status through other forms of relief or when they win asylum for reasons that clash starkly with youths' own understandings of why they fled. Of course, the most important thing for the individual youth is to obtain substantive relief and legal status through any path possible. However, when adjudicators apply the law to exclude de facto refugee experiences that do not conform to infantilizing expectations and narrow formal eligibility criteria in individual cases, this serves to uphold the restrictive nature of the asylum system, one in which compassion is treated as a resource in scarce supply. In this way, the ostensibly protective asylum institution falls short of its promise and remains ill equipped to protect youths who escape life-threatening violence.

I discuss how legal brokers work in the context of these constraints, finding means to manage risk and maneuver in the system to obtain favorable outcomes for their clients. Legal brokers can, and sometimes do, try creative arguments and strategies to expand eligibility categories. Yet this is no easy feat. The risks of doing so are high and fall directly upon their young clients for whom deportation could be a death sentence. It is generally a safer bet to work within the confines of the system and prepare youths' claims by strategically selecting, reframing, and interpreting their lived experiences of suffering to satisfy existing narrow legal categories. Under Trump, the legal and political context became far more volatile, and legal brokers had to find new ways to manage the heightened risks their clients faced. Yet, as we will see, this unexpectedly created incentives to try creative lawyering strategies aimed at expanding existing legal categories.

WHAT'S SO SPECIAL ABOUT REFUGEE YOUTH?

Existing scholarship has almost exclusively examined the profession of legal brokers and other humanitarian actors who work with adult immigrants and asylum seekers to mediate their access to legal status and aid.[3] When I started my fieldwork, I observed legal brokers work with adults and youths.[4] Stark differences quickly came to light. Compared to adults, youths have more difficulty remembering and discussing traumatic experiences, they are less likely to volunteer information, and they have more trouble contextualizing their experiences in the social and political dynamics of the home country. Legal brokers use youth-specific interviewing strategies to overcome these challenges.

As noted in chapter 4, young asylum seekers generally have less access to information than adults, especially about events that occurred during their early childhood. To obtain the detailed accounts necessary for asylum cases, legal brokers requested information from family members in the United States and the home country, particularly adults but also other youths, like older siblings. Managing these conversations between recently reunited family members was a delicate process. Youths did not always feel close enough to caretakers from whom they had long been separated to discuss sensitive issues with them. Caretakers sometimes also shied away from conveying raw and personal accounts in front of their children, and they might ask legal brokers to interview them separately. For instance, it could be deeply distressing for a mother to describe the sexual violence she had endured at the hands of her child's father. Yet when the victimizer pushed out one generation after the other in cases of domestic violence, these events were relevant to the youth's case. When adults' stories entered their asylum declarations, youths had to become familiar with these because they might be asked about them during their interviews at the asylum office. In legal clinics, youths thus discovered painful stories that their protective caretakers had sheltered them from. These caretakers had behaved exactly as parents are expected to according to Western conceptions of "priceless childhood" that assume adults to be responsible for safeguarding the innocence of children.[5] Ironically, during their asylum applications, youths were simultaneously infantilized, and depicted as lacking agency, and adultified as they were made aware of painful family histories that only adults had previously been privy to.

Even when youths did have access to information about events that occurred in their home countries, they generally had more difficulty than adults discussing their experiences. Youths had sometimes normalized the violence that shaped their lives, which might not necessarily seem worth disclosing from their perspectives. What's more, asylum seekers experience posttraumatic stress disorder (PTSD), which makes remembering past experiences and sharing stories difficult.[6] Research on developmental psychology has found that PTSD has stronger impacts on youths than it does on adults. This is because children and youths retain and process information differently due to neurological characteristics of the brain, which is not fully developed until late adolescence, in the early twenties.[7] Yet the legal age of majority is eighteen in the US asylum process, a mismatch with the biological age of maturity.

Having ample time and meeting with youths on multiple occasions was the best way to gather the information necessary for their asylum cases. With time, legal brokers could build rapport with youths so they would trust them enough to tell them their stories. Several meetings were also usually necessary to ensure that youths understood complex and evolving eligibility criteria for asylum and SIJS. While the eligibility screenings described in the last chapter could take as little as five minutes, interviews to prepare written declarations for applications took multiple, hours-long meetings. However, in all legal aid organizations, legal brokers worked within severe time and resource constraints. Each attorney could be responsible for between forty and seventy cases at a time, sometimes more. Legal brokers also worked against deadlines imposed by the age-based eligibility criteria of policies and by administrative scheduling priorities in court and at the asylum office.[8]

Toward the end of my fieldwork, I attended a course for lawyers where a psychiatrist who specialized in working with children and youths discussed strategies for interviewing them in ways that would not cause discomfort or be retraumatizing. One of the key recommendations was to use open-ended questions, like those that researchers use in semi-structured interviews. Yet the recommendation to ask questions like, "Tell me about your relationship with your parents," starkly contrasts with how legal brokers interviewed youths. Instead, legal brokers asked questions based on potential scenarios or examples of relevant things that could have happened in the home country. Their young clients could then "select" from these scenarios, which seemed to help move interviews forward more quickly. Legal brokers drew these scenarios both from legal definitions and their past experiences working with other clients. My field notes are full of examples of these types of questions, for instance, about child abuse: "In addition to using the belt, did they hit you with other things? Did they throw things at you or talk to you using strong, hurtful words? Did they hit you in your back, your legs, your arms? Did they throw their shoes at you? Did they hit you three, four, or five days a week? Did they ever leave marks?"

These questions elicited details that served to build humanitarian capital and satisfy eligibility for asylum based on child abuse. These details were also important for SIJS purposes since California law has specific definitions about what type of corporal punishment parents can inflict on their children. Nonetheless, this type of questioning made interviews inherently pathologizing and victimizing. While child abuse certainly was a migration driver, many youths had grown up in loving homes in Central America. In my role as a volunteer in legal clinics, I was trained to ask these types of questions as I interviewed youths to help prepare their asylum cases. I noticed how youths pushed back. When I interviewed fifteen-year-old Geovanny from Honduras, he frowned and grew visibly offended when I asked him whether his grandmother had been abusive. When I asked again, this time about his grandfather, he responded firmly, "No. I called my grandmother, *mama* and my grandfather, *papa*. They were like our parents." While we asked these questions to ascertain information that could help unaccompanied minors obtain legal status, I was troubled by the subtext to these interactions. That day, I wondered if I had implied to Geovanny that being loved by someone other than your parents was somehow a less legitimate way of growing up.

During the course, the psychiatrist suggested other important strategies that legal brokers did use often in their practice, including reading body language to anticipate when the young person was getting overwhelmed by the interview, offering chances to take breaks, and empowering youths to ask for those breaks when they needed them. The psychiatrist also suggested some small and easy-to-use strategies, such as providing something tactile for youths to fidget with during the interview, like a slinky, and having drawing materials and toys at hand for them to play with. The legal brokers in attendance were especially excited to hear these tips. They animatedly participated in the discussion by volunteering examples of other props they had used, like stuffed animals, stress-relief toys, even soap bubbles. While I had seen these props in some legal aid offices, I seldom saw legal brokers who worked under strict time constraints actually incentivize the use of toys, gadgets, or art. Indeed, I only saw toys being used on one occasion by an eleven-year-old while his older sibling was being interviewed.

As I listened to the psychiatrist's course, I wondered whether it is possible for lawyering to evolve to be truly sensitive to the substantive needs of children and youths, beyond cosmetic remedies like the toys sitting in the offices of legal clinics where staff work mostly with older teenagers. Perhaps, in the context of all the constraints that currently exist on the work of legal brokers who mediate humanitarian claims for legal status, this is an unattainable goal. Even the psychiatrist giving the talk admitted that, to a certain extent, legal brokers just had to recognize that their work inevitably had "side effects." This is to say that the interviews conducted to prepare humanitarian petitions for legal status are inherently retraumatizing. The psychiatrist noted that the best thing that legal brokers could do was to explain to youths that, if they endured these preparatory interviews, their asylum or SIJS adjudication interviews, the visits to court, and all the rest required, this could reap real rewards: legal status and a secure life in the United States.

The legal brokers alongside whom I worked in legal clinics clearly cared about the well-being of their young clients, whom everyone referred to affectionately as "the kids." They demonstrated an almost parental attitude of care and protectiveness that went beyond a strictly professional attorney-client relationship. They tried to mitigate the negative "side effects" of their work by empathizing with their clients and acknowledging the high emotional cost of applying for humanitarian relief. When possible, lawyers also altered their legal strategies to mitigate the negative "side effects" of undergoing a process that they recognized to be retraumatizing for their clients. For example, one attorney, who was representing an unaccompanied girl who had been raped, was waiting to hear back from the asylum office about the result of the application. The attorney strategized in advance that, if the case were denied, she would help her client apply for SIJS instead of appealing in immigration court. At the asylum office, the girl had been interviewed one-on-one by a female asylum officer. Appealing the asylum case in immigration court would instead require the girl to give testimony about being raped in a trial setting and to be cross-examined. Without question, this would be a traumatizing experience. By strategizing to apply for SIJS instead, which would not require the girl to discuss the sexual violence she had endured, as a plan B if the asylum office denied her case, the attorney chose the strategy that sheltered her client from a hostile bureaucratic space. This not only maximized the youth's chances of obtaining legal status but also considered her emotional well-being.

PROTECTIONS FOR UNACCOMPANIED MINORS IN THE US ASYLUM PROCESS

The US government has, to some extent, acknowledged that refugee youths are different from adults by introducing protections for unaccompanied minors in the US asylum process. As we saw in chapter 3, these include exempting unaccompanied minors from credible fear screenings at the border, as well as from the filing deadline; adults have one year from their date of arrival to submit their asylum claims. What's more, unlike their adult counterparts who are apprehended at the border and who can apply only in immigration court, unaccompanied minors can first apply at the USCIS asylum office (Figure 7).

The importance of this protection is reflected in the discrepancies between asylum grant rates for Central Americans in immigration court—between 17 and 28 percent—and for unaccompanied minors at the asylum office—between 28 and 70 percent.[9] These discrepancies can, in part, be

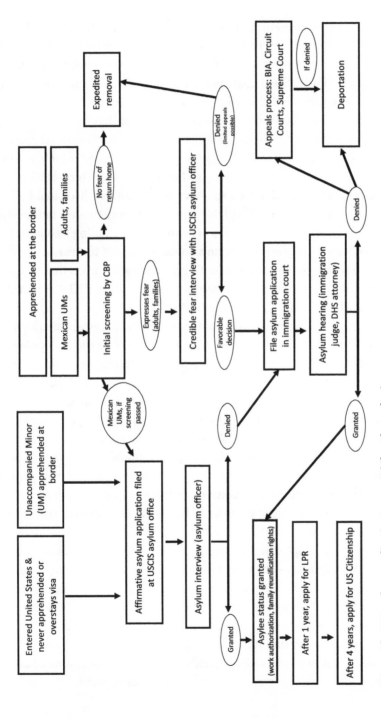

Fig. 7. The US asylum application process. (Chart by author)

explained by the different nature of the proceedings. The trial setting of hearings in immigration court requires more supporting evidence and involves heightened scrutiny of the case during cross examination. Conversely, the asylum office decides cases during one-on-one interviews that, at least as a matter of official policy, are not meant to be adversarial.[10]

However, these discrepancies also reflect the fact that, unlike immigration judges, asylum officers are trained to implement agency-level protective guidelines for working with asylum-seeking children,[11] which include "child-friendly" interview practices and child-specific interpretations of refugee law. Asylum officers learn about the strategies discussed by the psychiatrist above, like reading body language to anticipate whether the interview is causing the young person distress. This training also prompts asylum officers to implement accommodations relative to the age and developmental capacity of youths, adopting strategies for protecting asylum-seeking children similar to those recommended by the UNHCR and the UN Committee on the Rights of the Child.[12]

Although the US asylum system does not explicitly enshrine the best interest of the child, these guidelines have important implications when it comes to satisfying the refugee definition for unaccompanied minor asylum seekers. For asylum seekers of all ages, the amount of harm suffered in the home country must be determined to be "enough" to meet the eligibility bar of persecution; they must also show the right type of suffering. The latter must fit under one of the five protected grounds in the refugee convention: political opinion, religion, race, national origin, or membership in a particular social group.[13] When dealing with unaccompanied minors, these guidelines and trainings prompt asylum officers, first, to take into account that the *amount* of harm youths suffered can be less than the bar used for adults and still be considered persecution. Second, the guidelines prompt officers to consider that children's testimonies need not spell out eligibility—the right *type* of suffering, or why the persecution took place—as clearly as those of adults to qualify. These "child-friendly" guidelines are not always implemented consistently in practice, as we saw in the case of Hector's dehumanizing asylum interview in chapter 3, but they are meant to be binding for asylum officers.[14] Conversely, no binding guidelines exist in immigration court, where the asylum claims of unaccompanied minors are essentially treated like those of adults.[15]

THE RIGHT TYPE OF SUFFERING: US ASYLUM CASE LAW
THAT APPLIES TO UNACCOMPANIED MINORS

It was not usually readily apparent or easy for youths to explain *why* they had been persecuted in their home countries. When attorneys asked youths why they fled, this prompted answers that were intuitive to youths but incompatible with successful case law, such as "They wanted me to join" (forced gang recruitment). To look for evidence of motive, attorneys asked youths to remember conversations that had taken place with their persecutors. One attorney reflected on the challenges this posed, "The most important fact to a person who was in great danger is the danger they lived through. . . . They have a lot of trouble understanding why you keep wanting to shift the conversation to what was their [persecutor's] motivation for wanting to hurt them. That's just not something that makes a lot of intuitive or logical sense."

Access to protection thus hinged on asylum-seeking youths' ability to remember and recount their conversations with the people who victimized them. These were conversations that induced fear, with enduring traumatic effects. Having to ask youths these questions made the interviews necessary to prepare asylum declarations inherently unpleasant and re-traumatizing. Expecting youths to remember such details about traumatic events also goes against research on the effects of trauma on memory. The research shows that children who have experienced repeated traumatic events from an early age tend to have poorer autobiographic memories. Further, individuals typically develop the ability to tell memory narratives that center not just on the "who" and "what" of a story but also on causality—the "why" of a story—only in later adolescence.[16]

This requisite in asylum proceedings also seemed to paradoxically condition access to protection on whether persecutors in the home country ever verbalized their motives for hurting their victims. As one attorney bitterly put it, "Gang members will have to be like, 'Oh, you're anti-violence, and I attack you because you're anti-violence.' . . . It's like saying that the persecutor knew about [asylum law], and [this is why he] did this." If these conversations did not occur or youths could not recall them, as was often the case, the reason *why* the persecution took place had to be deduced through the critical and creative work of interpretation on the part of legal brokers.

The vast majority of Central American unaccompanied minors escape forms of violence that do not neatly fit the ideal-type of refugee captured by the post–World War II Refugee Convention: adult, male, and targeted by oppressive regimes. Most apply for asylum based on membership in a particular social group (PSG). Because of its ambiguity and malleability, the PSG category has allowed for some expansion of the refugee definition historically, for instance by recognizing persecution based on LGBTQ+ sexuality as an eligible experience.[17] At the same time, however, this very same ambiguity can pose risks for individual asylum seekers applying for relief because the PSGs considered eligible for asylum at any given time can change as US asylum case law evolves. While the definition of "social group" has also been contested, the generally agreed-upon standard is that the social group must be visible and recognizable enough in society that individuals could be persecuted because they are members of that group.[18]

In preparing asylum cases, attorneys typically presented as many PSGs and arguments as they could think of to explain why persecution took place. This was a means to maximize chances of success, in hopes that the asylum officer would pick at least one argument and grant the case. Unlike immigration court, the asylum office—where attorneys working with unaccompanied minors had all, or most, of their experience representing cases—does not provide written decisions detailing *why* particular cases are granted or denied.[19] In the absence of written decisions, attorneys did not know for certain on what grounds—based on what *type* of suffering—each client's case had won or lost at the asylum office. This reflects the indeterminacy inherent in the asylum process. In addition to expertise, legal brokerage with asylum-seeking youths involved a good amount of guesswork to anticipate whether a case was likely to win and to interpret why a past case was granted.

Nevertheless, during the first four years of my research (2015–2018), the consensus among attorneys was that, for unaccompanied minors, asylum cases based on two PSGs were "easy" to win at the asylum office: family membership and child abuse. The family membership PSG meant that youths could be granted asylum if their family members in the home country had been victimized, and this, in turn, had put them at risk. The child abuse PSG stems from precedent-setting case law that recognized domestic violence as a valid basis for asylum in 2014 (Matter of A-R-C-G-), which was an important victory in the decades-long battle to correct the gender bias of the post–World War II refugee definition. Advocates applied this case law to expand asylum eligibility to victims of child abuse by arguing that, just as women are persecuted because of their subordinate position in society and inability to leave abusive domestic relationships, children are dependent on abusive caretakers and unable to leave these relationships.

Experiences that fit the child abuse and family membership PSGs were considered the "best" types of suffering, the ones valued most when it came to consolidating humanitarian capital. Conversely, experiences of gang violence and forced recruitment were considered the "worst" types of suffering, for two reasons. First, cases based on these experiences risked associating youths with the very same criminal actors they fled. This was dangerous in a US context that criminalizes Central Americans, conflating them with MS-13 gang members. Criminalization became official policy at the asylum office under Trump. All Central American teenagers were flagged as security threats and had to undergo new invasive background checks, which delayed case outcomes for months.[20] Any mention of gangs raised a red flag and could be interpreted as a security risk in this context, despite the fact that, from a legal standpoint, even some minor gang involvement does not disqualify youths from asylum eligibility.[21]

Second, unfavorable case law on gang violence has long been a constant in the US asylum process.[22] Legal brokers were critical of the "floodgates" argument behind this case law: the idea that gang violence is too commonplace to be recognized, as it would mean too many people would qualify for asylum. Legal brokers could, and sometimes would, file applications based on forcible gang recruitment and victimization. However, their clients had much better chances of winning if their cases could instead emphasize the child abuse or family membership PSGs, even if the main reason or the exacerbating event that led the minor to flee was related to gang violence. In other words, the least risky legal strategy, most likely to result in a case grant for the individual client, was also the one that reified child-specific interpretations of asylum law, keeping its overall protective scope narrow. Asylum lawyers worked under the constraints of a system where conservative legal strategies and playing by the rules of the game reaped the highest rewards.

Asylum case outcomes can play out in particularly cruel ways in a context that rewards certain types of suffering rather than the need to escape from life-threatening violence. For example, in the cases of certain siblings: the (usually older) youth who was directly targeted by gang members was more at risk of being denied asylum than his (usually younger) sibling who had not been targeted directly. This was because the younger sibling could claim a family PSG, which was considered a valid type of suffering, while the older sibling could only claim gang recruitment, which was not recognized by case law. These outcomes underscore the mismatch that exists between de facto and de jure refugeehood. As we saw in chapter 2, siblings may indeed be targeted, and flee in turn, from eldest to youngest. Thus, of course, it makes sense to use the family PSG to *extend* protections to younger siblings in victimized families who are either at immediate risk or likely to be at risk soon after. Conversely, using these legal criteria to disqualify older youths from relief reflects how legal formalism can be weaponized to transform an ostensibly protective institution like asylum into an exclusionary tool of immigration control. While asylum-seeking adults must show that they are singled out as targets, for unaccompanied minors, childlike dependency and passive victimization yield more humanitarian capital.

Unaccompanied minors' attorneys sometimes used PSGs other than family or child abuse, as well as arguments based on other protected grounds in the refugee definition: religion, political opinion, or race. For example, legal brokers probed youths with questions about their sexuality. However, LGBTQ+ youths might be understandably reticent to be forced to come out before they were ready and to do so in the menacing space of the asylum process. Legal brokers could also argue cases based on religion, for instance, if youths who were being recruited by gangs had gone to church often or were part of very religious families. The legal argument would then emphasize that youths did not want to join because their religious beliefs viewed gang activity as immoral or sinful. While attorneys noted that religion cases could be successful, they agreed that, when they tried to present youths' resistance to gang recruitment as a political opinion—as an anti-gang activist—this was generally not an effective way to win the case.

Legal brokers had to teach youths enough about the law so they could participate in co-constructing asylum narratives that satisfied the formal criteria for refugee status, showing the right amount and type of suffering. The many interviews and conversations that took place between attorneys and their clients to prepare an asylum application comprised a crash course of sorts, the most intensive exercise of legal socialization that youths would undergo yet. Youths often referred to their asylum interviews as something they had to study for, like an exam. The stakes of the exam were, of course, extremely high. To "pass," youths had to learn to tell their stories of escape, not as they intuitively understood them, but in the language of the law.

The next sections present the cases of three de facto refugee boys who escaped from violence: Francisco, who was denied asylum in immigration court; Edgar, who was granted at the asylum office; and Diego, who experienced the wrong type of suffering and was advised to apply for SIJS instead. These cases highlight the contradictory, emotionally costly, and labor-intensive process of humanitarian legalization, in which intangible emotions and past experiences of suffering are transformed into humanitarian capital so that they may be legible to the adjudicators who decide whether to grant migrant youths protection—deportation relief, legal status—or exclude them.

FRANCISCO IS DENIED ASYLUM: HOW EMANCIPATORY LEGAL ARGUMENTS CAN BACKFIRE

Francisco was an indigenous youth from a remote rural village whose family survived on subsistence agriculture. Francisco fled after a Ladino man—a member of the majority racial group—threatened to kill him if he did not give up the family plot of land that he cultivated. Francisco's case was denied at the asylum office. Like other young asylum seekers, when Francisco fled his country at age seventeen, he knew little about the broader political context in his village and the particular role that his family had played in the struggles over the use of communal land. Francisco had since learned more from his mother, but it had been difficult to communicate with her from Los Angeles. There was no phone service in their village, and the nearest town was hours away.

Given these challenges, it had been impossible for Francisco's attorney to obtain a written declaration from his mother to support the case. Based on the limited additional information Francisco could obtain, his attorney strategized that his asylum appeal in immigration court would focus on the grounds of race and political opinion. Francisco's case centers emancipatory legal arguments and a rights-based discourse that starkly contrast with the victimizing and infantilizing frames used in the asylum claims of most unaccompanied minors. Yet using sophisticated legal arguments to explain why persecution took place can backfire when youths are unable to understand and internalize these discourses enough to articulate them during their interviews.

The challenging aspect of preparing asylum cases based on race was that indigenous Central American unaccompanied minors did not generally arrive in the United States having mastered the terminology of indigenous rights or a historical critique of colonialism, which the legal arguments for these types of cases centered on. Many indigenous youths I met during my fieldwork did not speak the native language of their indigenous group. Their parents had decided not to teach them the language in hopes that speaking Spanish would protect them from discrimination. This sheltering by parents contributed to why youths did not strongly identify as indigenous. Since youths had not reflected on how being indigenous had shaped their experiences in their home countries, they commonly rationalized that they had been harmed, bullied, harassed, and denied services in school or hospitals because they were "poor" and not due to their indigenous backgrounds. This field note excerpt of a meeting between Francisco and two legal brokers shows some of these challenges:

> The attorney asked, "Who are the Ladinos?"
>
> Francisco explained: "People who are different from us; they have more experience; they know more. Since we come from the mountains, we know less; we are ignorant."
>
> The attorney corrected him: "When you say who they are, think about this. Are they the descendants of the Spanish? They are not part of an indigenous group like you are."
>
> Reflecting out loud, Francisco said, "They have a different culture."
>
> The legal assistant intervened to ask, "Are they Catholic?"
>
> Francisco: "I don't know, I don't think so."
>
> The attorney noted, "Most people there are Ladinos right? Not indigenous." [Francisco nodded yes.] "You can say Ladinos speak Spanish and identify with the majority population."

The legal assistant, a Latina woman, touched her arm to highlight her medium skin tone so as to provide context, asking, "Ladinos, they are mestizos, right? They are like me?"

Francisco, whose skin color was a darker hue, looked confused. He paused to think, then said, "My family says that Ladinos don't have indigenous blood."

The attorney replied, "OK, that is good; you can say that they don't have indigenous blood, and they don't identify as indigenous."

Next, the attorney suggested that Francisco rephrase his earlier statement "we are ignorant," and the legal assistant asked, "What do you mean by that?"

Francisco explained, "Because we live in the mountains, and we don't know the culture of our country. That is what they tell us, and it sticks in your head."

The attorney explained, "It's better if you say that this is what [Ladino] people think, because otherwise it will seem like you think that this is true. You don't think so, right? I want to present to the court that you have a political opinion, that you think your people should have their own government, autonomy.

Legal assistant: "Do you know what autonomy is?"

Francisco: "Not really, I don't know much. Is it having your own laws?"

Legal assistant: "Exactly."

Attorney: "It's more or less like what you have already, but Ladinos are stealing your land. You want your people to have their own land, right?"

Francisco exclaimed, convinced, "Yes!"

Attorney: "At the interview, I want you to be like an activist for indigenous rights."

Francisco: "Like an activist? I don't really understand."

Legal assistant: "You are like a voice representing your community."

Attorney: "Like your uncle, he is an activist."

The legal brokers attempted to reconstruct the dynamics of the sending context with Francisco so that he would be able to articulate his experience of persecution based on the legal grounds of race and political opinion. Yet Francisco found it challenging to describe who Ladinos are, and why they occupy a privileged position in Guatemalan society. He was puzzled by the legal assistant's reference to skin color and the attorney's remarks on the history of Spanish colonialism. Instead, he repeated the demeaning language that the dominant group uses to describe his indigenous group because it was "stuck in his head." The attorney suggested that he instead use more emancipatory language that does not reflect his internalization of symbolic violence but rather an awareness of racial hierarchies and his political opinion in opposition to the Ladino's dominance in society, which allows them to steal indigenous lands with impunity.

The problem is that the legal brokers used a conceptual vocabulary (i.e., indigenous rights activism, colonialism, autonomy, etc.) that Francisco completely lacked. For a youth with limited formal schooling, who had been sheltered from dangerous land rights activism despite being part of a politically involved family, this was to be expected. Francisco met in person with his attorney on two occasions for multiple hours just to practice for his interview in court, in addition to all the meetings they had previously to prepare his I-589 asylum application and declaration. Despite all this preparation, the meetings that Francisco had in the legal clinic were not sufficient for him to gain an understanding of such complex issues.

When Francisco's case was heard in immigration court, the Department of Homeland Security (DHS) trial attorney made several counterarguments to claim that he was ineligible for asylum and should be deported. First, the trial attorney argued that "discrimination" (based on being indigenous) does not amount to persecution. In other words, Francisco had not suffered *enough*: his humanitarian capital did not rise to the level of persecution but, rather, should be considered "just discrimination." This argumentation was striking, considering that Francisco was threatened by an armed man on multiple occasions, and one of his relatives had been killed after refusing to give up his land. All of this had been meticulously enumerated and documented in his application to build his humanitarian capital. Second, the trial attorney made two sets of arguments to claim that Francisco did not have the right *type* of suffering: he did not articulate a political opinion; and race could not have motivated the persecution because the persecutor was a member of the same racial group. Since Francisco did not internalize an indigenous rights language, and he had difficulty articulating his claim in terms of race or political opinion in court, he was especially vulnerable to the trial attorney's attacks.

During a long conversation after the hearing, Francisco's attorney vented passionately, criticizing the trial attorney's arguments. She complained that the US government lacked an understanding of racial hierarchies in Central America. A Ladino man threatened Francisco and his family but, because this person had indigenous relatives, the trial attorney said they belonged to the same racial group. Yet, unlike in the United States, where race is constructed in terms of the "one-drop rule," in Latin America, those who intermarry are considered mestizos and can blend into the dominant group. The attorney's legal argument was based on the fact that this position of dominance allowed this man to persecute and threaten Francisco and his family and steal their land with impunity. Irrespective of the violence youths faced, the following two factors combine to make cases like this vulnerable to denial: US government officials' lack of understanding about the social, political, and historical context in sending countries; and youths' difficulties internalizing and verbalizing the emancipatory racial and political discourses that their attorneys try to teach them. The stakes of not learning to speak the language of the law are high: the fear and suffering of this de facto refugee youth were discounted. In the tug of war over refugee recognition, the exclusionary prerogatives of the state prevailed, and the trial attorney convinced the immigration judge to deny protection to Francisco.

EDGAR: PREPARING A STRONG ASYLUM CASE WITH THE RIGHT AMOUNT AND TYPE OF SUFFERING

Edgar fled from El Salvador at age seventeen. It took five, hours-long, in-person meetings and several phone calls for his attorney to prepare his case. I wrote forty single-spaced pages of field notes just on these meetings, reflecting the enormous amount of work that goes into asylum case preparation. As the attorney and I met with Edgar over time, I observed that he became better acquainted with us. He smiled more often and began to relax. He seemed less anxious, and he was willing to tell us more about what had happened in El Salvador. This change in demeanor underscored the importance of rapport building with asylum-seeking youth.

Yet, from the start, Edgar was especially articulate compared to other youths I met during my fieldwork. The son of a police officer, Edgar was studying in a private school in El Salvador, and he had never had to work. He was of a higher socioeconomic status than other unaccompanied minors. Already during our first meeting, despite the fact that he was visibly nervous and speaking quickly, Edgar was able to tell us his story in a linear fashion. He explained the reason why he fled without being prompted: MS-13 targeted him and threatened to kill him because his father was a police officer. The gang members had said that this was why they were targeting Edgar. This allowed his attorney to argue that the persecution took place on account of the family PSG, as well as on a more specific PSG: family members of police officers.

During a later meeting, when the attorney had developed a better understanding of Edgar's circumstances, she probed whether she could also frame the case in terms of political opinion, according to the legal strategy of presenting as many eligibility grounds and arguments as possible to maximize chances of success. Of course, emancipatory arguments based on political opinion were directly at odds with the infantilizing arguments more commonly used in unaccompanied minors' cases. Reconciling both types of framing in a single case was inherently contradictory.

ATTORNEY: Did you ever talk to anyone besides your parents about the threats you received from the gangs? Did you ever mention that you didn't agree with the gangs and their illicit activities? Did you ever mention that you agree with the police?

EDGAR: Like to who? No, I didn't really talk about these things.

ATTORNEY: I'm asking because sometimes if you believe something strongly, that it's against your ideals, and you are very vocal about it and active in the community, you can be a target for that reason.

EDGAR: I never did that. If I had, they would have killed me for sure. They kill those people.

ATTORNEY: OK, the reason why I'm asking is to see whether we can also include an argument about political opinion in your case. So, you never had any of those conversations?

EDGAR: No, the truth is I never did.

Edgar had told us in a previous meeting that he thought his father was doing important police work to stop gang violence, while voicing his concerns about the state of his country. The attorney asked Edgar if he had ever been vocal about these views, which would have given her material to frame his case on the grounds of political opinion. Edgar explained that, while he felt comfortable expressing his views about the police from the safety of the Los Angeles legal clinic office, this was not the case in El Salvador. There, he tried to attract the least amount of attention possible because he felt that otherwise he would certainly have been killed. This, of course, was a concern shared by other youths targeted by gangs in Central America, which creates challenges for framing their asylum cases under the political opinion grounds.

Each time we met with Edgar, the attorney asked new follow-up questions, which served the purpose of clarifying the narrative, avoiding inconsistencies, and obtaining more details. Asylum officers and immigration judges consider asylum claims credible when they are detailed and consistent.[23] Details allow legal brokers to build humanitarian capital, lending concreteness to intangible emotions like fear, and showing how these had tangible effects on the lives of youths. For example, fear could lead to changes in behavior, like dropping out of school and hiding out at home, or to symptoms of distress, like insomnia or loss of appetite. Interviews to construct the testimonies of asylum seekers usually involved enumerating relevant past events—when someone was threatened, when they interacted with their victimizer—that were then described painstakingly in written declarations. In this way, legal brokers made emotions and past experiences legible to asylum officers who determine on discretionary grounds whether the youth suffered "enough" to meet the eligibility bar of persecution. Edgar had been threatened on multiple occasions, and it was important to portray the escalating nature of the threats made against him:

> The attorney spent a long time figuring out what happened between two different incidents with the gangs that Edgar told us about.
> She asked Edgar, "How scared did you feel? How many times did you see the gang members [outside your house]?
> Edgar thought about it, then suggested, "Maybe three times."
> The attorney wrote down the number of times in the declaration.
> Later during the meeting, the attorney asked, "Why did you take the threat more seriously the second time? Did it feel more severe? More real?"
> Edgar replied, "Because this time, they pointed a gun to my chest."
> The attorney asked, "Did the gun touch you?"
> Edgar pointed to his chest, "Yes, it touched me here."

The attorney transformed Edgar's suffering into humanitarian capital by quantifying his fear, asking how many times he saw gang members outside his house, why the second threat he received was worse ("more severe," "more real") than the first. After these questions, Edgar told us that a gang member pointed a gun to his chest, something that would make anyone afraid, providing an image that would be clearly visible to the asylum officer reading his declaration. All these details served to present Edgar's fear as real and "objectively" plausible. According to USCIS, asylum claims based on "general ambiguous fears" are insufficient. Instead, "an applicant must have a genuine fear of persecution and that fear must be objectively reasonable."[24]

Because all humanitarian claimants are viewed with suspicion, the testimony of suffering by itself, detailed as it may be, yields less humanitarian capital than testimony that is backed by documentary proof. This includes both documents that asylum seekers bring with them from the home country, such as police reports, and those that can be produced in the United States, like a psychiatrist's report documenting trauma and PTSD. Neither document was easy to come by. The psychiatrists that provide these services were in limited supply and obtaining these documents could be costly for youths, both financially and in terms of the investment of time and emotional energy necessary. Edgar did not undergo psychological evaluation, but he did have a police report describing the threats he received in El Salvador. This was likely possible since his father was a police officer. Most Central American asylum seekers could not provide this type of proof.[25] Oftentimes, they simply fled with too much urgency to think about obtaining proof before they left. Other asylum seekers recounted that they had been too scared to approach the police or, even if they had, police officers refused to write up reports, either because they feared the gangs themselves or because they were corrupt and colluding with the gangs.

Indeed, as attorneys stress in their legal arguments, Central Americans flee their home countries precisely because they are unable to count on the state to ensure their safety and safeguard their human rights. Yet, ironically, the documents produced by the very governments that fail to protect their citizens yield more humanitarian capital than the testimonies of asylum seekers. In this way, asylum seekers are made more dependent on sending states, contradicting the purported aim of asylum law. On the whole, however, attorneys agreed that documents were more crucial to win asylum cases in immigration court, where a higher burden of proof is required. Conversely, asylum officers can do independent research into country conditions and individual circumstances to grant cases. Since they have the chance to apply at the asylum office first, unaccompanied minors are somewhat more insulated than adults from reliance on documentary proof.

In preparing youths' asylum narratives, it also was important to make sure that they did not mention things that could be misconstrued by the asylum officer and work against their claims. During one meeting, Edgar mentioned that he saw on the news that things were getting worse in El Salvador, "The police are losing control; there have been reports of grenades being thrown into police buildings." The attorney asked, "When you say, 'getting worse,' do you mean in your neighborhood, your city, or the country?" Edgar replied, "Everywhere, the whole country is dangerous." The attorney cautioned Edgar, "We don't want to say that everything, everywhere is dangerous in El Salvador. We want to make the case that *you* were in danger because of your relationship with your father, which is the truth." The attorney thus taught Edgar that it was key for him to convey the uniqueness of his circumstances to avoid being seen as one among many in a bulk of similar applications. Indeed, Edgar's case both fit inside existing case law (family PSG) and was distinctive enough to separate him from others (son of a police officer).

This conversation reflects the contradictions of the asylum law in action. On the one hand, the attorney cautioned Edgar to be careful in saying that everywhere in El Salvador was dangerous so as to better highlight the specific dangers he personally faced in the town he hailed from. On the other hand, however, one of the standard questions that asylum seekers are asked at the end of their interviews is whether they could safely relocate elsewhere in their country of origin. Of course, the answer to this last question must be *no* to establish the applicant's fear of return. Noting that all of El Salvador is dangerous is therefore helpful to answer that question. In sum, the home country must be dangerous enough, in all places, so that return and relocation to safety would not be possible, producing the need for international protection. Yet danger must not be perceived as too routine or pervasive throughout the entire country so as to discount the unique nature of a case or raise concerns of "opening the floodgates" to asylum arrivals.

When preparing youths to answer questions about relocation in their home countries, legal brokers especially emphasized dependency on adult caretakers. Because unaccompanied minors occupy a liminal state between childhood and adulthood, legal brokers constructed asylum narratives that distanced their young clients from the traits of maturity and independence and instead emphasized childlike traits. The latter were better suited to satisfy US asylum case law and asylum officers' assumptions about how refugee children deserving of protection should behave. As an older teenager, Edgar inched dangerously close to adulthood. This is how he reacted when the attorney asked if any adults in El Salvador could care for him if he were to return:

ATTORNEY: Do you have any other family in El Salvador?

EDGAR: My grandmother.

ATTORNEY: Does she live close to where your parents live?

EDGAR: Yeah, just down the street.

ATTORNEY: Could you support yourself if you went back to El Salvador? Could you work to live on your own elsewhere?

EDGAR: No, well, I want to be prepared before I start working. I want to study because I want to get a good job, I don't want to break my back to make super little money.

ATTORNEY: Well, we don't want to mention that, because the point is that you can't *survive* if you go back. Not that you don't want to do a particular job.

Edgar did not have family he could live with in El Salvador other than in the town he fled. The attorney asked him if he could live elsewhere on his own, to see whether his answer would satisfy the adjudicator's expectations for childlike behavior: that children cannot work and independently provide for themselves. Edgar, however, did not understand the goal of the question. He said that he would not want to have to support himself because he wanted to go to college first. The irony of this interaction is telling. On the one hand, unaccompanied minors are held to middle-class standards in the United States—get an education, go to college—and are expected to achieve them, even when the odds are stacked against them (see chapter 6). Yet, at the same time, if they come to the United States with middle-class aspirations and express them at the wrong moment, like during an asylum interview, this can dangerously position youths away from the refugee-victim frame.

Of course, Edgar would be in danger if he were deported to El Salvador, but he also had aspirations for the future and ambition. These two things are not mutually exclusive. De facto refugee youths seek not only safety from harm when they migrate but also a home where they can continue their transitions to adulthood and pursue a full social existence. Yet, these two points become incompatible in the asylum narrative where there is no space for complexity ("the point is that you can't *survive*"). Child-victims must be portrayed as one-dimensionally helpless, defined solely based on the persecution they suffered. Similarly, asylum-seeking youths from poor families had to be careful not to mention their desire to work in the United States, or they risked being associated with the economic migrant frame. Thus, both coming-of-age pathways—through higher education and work—that demonstrated youths' aspirations and future goals could backfire in the asylum process. The asylum application required youths to undergo a rite of reverse passage, discursively regressing to childhood in their narratives rather than highlighting elements that conveyed their desire or actions aimed at moving forward in their transitions to adulthood.

A few days before his interview at the asylum office, the attorney gave Edgar some tips that underscored the performative aspect of the asylum interview. It was important that Edgar look the part, to express with his body the same things he would convey with his words. His clothing had to reflect his respect for the asylum officer and signal him not as a deviant teenager but as a "good" kid. On the day of our meeting, Edgar looked far too fashionable in jeans, a DKNY T-shirt, a baseball cap that read L.A., and a metal chain necklace. The attorney told him that this was not an appropriate outfit for the asylum interview. She singled out the necklace as something to definitely not wear because it might suggest gang jewelry. They discussed what clothing he should choose, something formal, but not too adult-like, so as to not make Edgar, who was tall and big, look older.

The attorney also advised, "If you feel emotion, that's OK, don't try to repress it. If you feel like crying, that's OK. In fact, that's good, it shows that your fear is real. [In El Salvador] did you cry?" Edgar replied, "Yes, I cried often, sometimes I still cry when I think about it." Edgar was far more willing to admit his vulnerability than other male teenaged asylum seekers. Boys often denied that they had cried while experiencing harm in their home countries. They tried to repress their emotions because behaviors like crying clashed with their understandings of masculinity. Yet "acting like men" would not serve boys well during their asylum interviews. Since legal brokers were aware of the potentially harmful consequences of performing masculinity in that space, they tried to normalize and validate the show of emotion.

When it was time for his interview, Edgar asked me to accompany him as his interpreter. That morning, I arrived at the asylum office at 6:45 a.m. The waiting room was almost empty but Edgar and his aunt Luisa—his ORR sponsor—were already there, visibly anxious. I asked Edgar how he was doing. Luisa answered for him, "He is nervous, we didn't sleep well." Edgar had taken his attorney's advice and was smartly dressed, wearing plain black Nike sneakers and a nice button-down shirt with thin white and blue stripes. The attorney arrived slightly late, which she was apologetic about. She was also smartly dressed but had deep black circles under her eyes, poorly hidden by her makeup. I had seen this look on her often. On other occasions, she had confided that she felt tired and burned out by the job.

While we were waiting to be summoned by the asylum officer, the attorney buried herself in legal briefs to catch up on work that never ceased to pile up. I made small talk with Luisa to pass the time. Edgar, who was usually talkative and funny, sat taciturn and fidgeting apprehensively with his phone. Our boredom and worry were interspersed with texts and phone calls from Edgar's family members. "Your uncle says good luck," Luisa told Edgar, reading him the text message from her husband on her phone. "Tell him I say thank you and that I love him," Edgar replied before going back to staring at his own phone. Edgar's father and grandmother then called from El Salvador. When she hung up, Luisa told me, "Back home, they are worried." After four hours in the freezing air-conditioned waiting room, we were finally called in for the interview. These long wait times were not at all uncommon. With so much at stake, making asylum seekers wait for hours before they are called in for their interviews is a cruel manifestation of the power asymmetry between the asylum seeker and the state.

Due to the confidentiality of interviews at the asylum office, I could not take notes during Edgar's interview (see methods appendix). However, I later wrote some general reflexive notes informed by this experience and others I had working as a volunteer interpreter. Each of my glimpses into the asylum office made apparent the legal violence of the asylum interview interaction. Despite "child-friendly" interviewing accommodations and the fact that individual asylum officers may very well be dedicated to the humanitarian mandate in their job description, the asylum office remains an intimidating bureaucratic space. It is not at all straightforward to assume that youths will perform well in that space, even with extensive preparation.

With such long interviews, the level of burnout of all parties involved is notable: for the asylum seeker, who is giving an emotional testimony about traumatic past experiences; for the asylum officer, who has to keep track of a story that she read for the first time right before the interview; and for the interpreter, who must deliver a precise and accurate translation of the youth's account. Toward the end of Edgar's four-hour interview, I was exhausted and having trouble translating. Research shows that the quality of interpreters' work decreases over time due to physiological stress and the high level of concentration required, compounding the potential for errors.[26] Yet an accurate translation of the asylum narrative is key to avoid producing inconsistencies that can lead to case denials and to convey the complex legal and discursive strategies that asylum seekers and their attorneys carefully co-constructed.

The importance of the legal socialization that youths undergo by interacting with their attorneys was especially apparent in Edgar's case. He understood what details he needed to disclose and how to tell his story in the language of the law. He performed well during his interview, speaking clearly, waiting for the translation, and volunteering information by bringing up things that were in his declaration but not tied to the narrow question that the officer had asked. Edgar performed well even though he was anxious and glassy-eyed, and at a certain point, even breathing with difficulty. A smart young man, Edgar demonstrated his transformation, in just a few months, from someone who "doesn't even know what asylum is"—in the words of the CBP officer he interacted with at the border—into someone with a sophisticated understanding of asylum law. Edgar was an educated and articulate older teenager, and he was more knowledgeable about the political situation in El Salvador than other youths. He had excellent legal representation.

Not all cases were prepared as thoroughly as Edgar's. Legal aid organizations are under-resourced, and much of the case preparation work was often done not by lawyers but by legal assistants or volunteers. What's more, not all asylum seekers were accompanied by their attorney on the day of the interview. Youths with private or low-bono attorneys may be charged additional fees for this service. If attorneys are present at the asylum office, they can make sure that interviews are not adversarial. Attorneys can also deliver closing statements in which they reiterate the main arguments of the case and the criteria in child-friendly asylum office training to hold the officer accountable for implementing these criteria when making their decisions. Attorneys argue, first, that the applicant experienced the right *amount* of suffering in the home country, enough to rise to the level of persecution. They note that the severity of the suffering does not have to be same for children and adults. In other words, children can qualify for asylum with less humanitarian capital. Second, attorneys argue that their clients experienced the right *type* of suffering: the reason for the persecution satisfies at least one of the protected grounds in the refugee definition. They note that children can be granted asylum even if there are inconsistencies or the testimony does not spell out why the persecution took place as explicitly as the officer might expect from an adult.

After we finished Edgar's interview that day, Luisa asked the attorney how she thought it went. Cautiously, the attorney said, "I think [Edgar] did a good job. You said everything that you needed to say. You did the best you could, and I did everything I could." We went our separate ways, hoping Edgar's case would be granted but unsure and anxious. Months later, we heard the happy news that Edgar was granted asylum, obtaining recognition as a de jure refugee to match his lived experiences of escape from violence.

DIEGO: REFRAMING HOME COUNTRY EXPERIENCES AS ABANDONMENT, ABUSE, AND NEGLECT FOR SIJS

Diego was sixteen when he migrated from Honduras, where he lived with his mother and younger siblings. He had witnessed a gang member shoot and kill his best friend during a birthday party. The gang member

threatened to kill Diego too if he did not leave the country. Diego immediately went into hiding at a relative's house while his family quickly put
together enough money to pay for his trip with a coyote. After hearing his
story of escape from violence, I was surprised when the attorney advised
Diego to apply for SIJS. When I asked her why, she explained, "If he had
a really strong asylum case, then he could apply for that, but he just witnessed the death."

The attorney's rationale was that there was nothing to show that the
gang member could find Diego to carry out the threat. The attorney explained that, if he had gone to Diego's house to look for him, the case
would have been stronger. Since Diego left, it would be difficult to argue
that he was at risk because we did not know what would have happened
if he had stayed. This example highlights yet another catch-22 situation
asylum seekers face: the timing of their escape. The longer youths stay in
their home country, the more proof they might have that their persecutors
tried to carry out their threats. But who would stay put after receiving a
death threat in a country with so much violence and impunity if they had
the means to flee? Also, staying in the home country for too long, and
being lucky enough to survive without suffering substantial harm, could,
conversely, be construed as proof that the danger was not real. While
Diego's flight after witnessing a murder and receiving a death threat can
hardly be considered preventative, his attorney still determined that he
did not have enough humanitarian capital to build a "strong" asylum case.
Youths' migration decisions—how they and their family members assessed
the level of risk and the cost of staying in the home country— play out in
paradoxical ways in the US asylum process.

Of course, Diego's claim to asylum was also "weak" because it was based
on the wrong type of suffering: gang violence. Instead of bringing these
cases to the asylum office, legal brokers often strategized to apply for
SIJS instead if the youth was eligible. This legal strategy was confusing
to youths, as one attorney acknowledged: "It's hard for some clients to
understand why we're applying for SIJS, saying that their father, who they
don't really know or care about, abandoned them. They are like, 'Why are
we making this about my dad? If I go back, the gangs will kill me.'"

Unlike asylum, SIJS enshrines the principle of the best interests of
the child. The first step in the SIJS application takes place in state-level

family, probate, or dependency courts, where attorneys request a written approval called a SIJS order.[27] In these orders, judges place youths in the care of a legal guardian in the United States and determine that returning to the country of origin is not in the child's best interests because he or she was abandoned, abused, or neglected by one or both parents. Unlike immigration bureaucrats, judges in state courts are well-versed in making determinations about the best interests of the child. During the second step of the SIJS application, bureaucrats at USCIS examine these cases— on paper only, without in-person interviews—to complete the approval process so youths can become lawful permanent residents.

The SIJS application process is complex because it involves bureaucracies in both the child welfare and immigration realms (Figure 8), and it presents unique challenges. Most importantly, starting in 2016, the number of SIJS applications surpassed statutory limitations on how many of these cases can be granted per year. As the backlog grew, it took over four years on average for the SIJS cases of applicants from El Salvador, Guatemala, and Honduras to be resolved, leaving youths in lengthy legal limbo.[28] Complications could also arise when there was conflict between youths and the family members in the United States serving as their guardians, or difficulties locating parents in the home country who had to be served paperwork and notified of the proceedings. Nonetheless, attorneys still widely perceived SIJS to be far "easier" to win than asylum. It was easier to fit youths' home country experiences in state laws defining abandonment, abuse, and neglect than in the narrow refugee category.

Diego was applying for one-parent SIJS since he had reunited with his father, who had been living in Southern California since Diego was seven years old. For the purposes of his application, which would be based on neglect, his mother in Honduras would be framed as the "culprit" parent, despite the fact that Diego had no ill words to say about her. To establish neglect, the caretaker does not need to have had an intent to harm the child. One attorney explained, "If the kid were here in the US, and they were doing what they did in their home country, would the Department of Child and Family Services intervene? If the answer is yes, we usually use that as an argument for neglect." Lawyers argued neglect based on state-level (in this case, California) education, labor, and penal codes, looking for home country experiences that violate provisions in these laws, for

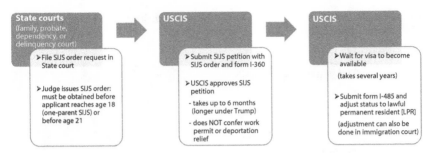

Fig. 8. The SIJS application process. (Chart by author)

example, about the minimum age of mandatory schooling or limitations on how many hours minors can work in different occupations. The contradictions of these evaluations were not lost on legal brokers. One attorney expressed discomfort in what she saw as the necessary evil of interpreting youth's lives with, "somewhat of a Western-centric view. . . . But [this is] for the sake of advocating for them."

Attorneys took youths' lived experiences in the home country and strategically transformed them through the definitions of California law, reading childhood *there* through the lens of childhood *here*, as a time to be protected and sheltered, to play and study. The attorney's line of questioning in Diego's case thus centered not on the events that led to his escape from violence but on his working conditions, which could serve to establish neglect.

ATTORNEY: How many hours did you work? How many days? [in construction]

DIEGO: Like 8, 9. Every day.

ATTORNEY: Did you ever get hurt?

DIEGO: Once.

ATTORNEY: How?

DIEGO: I fell and scraped my knee.

ATTORNEY: Was it bad?

DIEGO: No, just a little scrape.

ATTORNEY: Anything else?

After some conversation about the work Diego did in Honduras, he disclosed that he operated dangerous heavy machinery to make cement.

ATTORNEY: Did you ever get hurt while you were working in the fields? [in agriculture]

DIEGO: No.

ATTORNEY: Did you use pesticides?

DIEGO: Yes.

ATTORNEY: Did you use gloves? A mask?

DIEGO: No. My hands got all white.

ATTORNEY: Did it hurt?

DIEGO: Yes, it burned.

ATTORNEY: How did you feel about having to work?

DIEGO: Good, I liked it.

ATTORNEY: Did your mom tell you that you had to work?

DIEGO: No, but I felt that I should work.

ATTORNEY: What did you use the money for? Did you provide for your family?

Diego said he did not make much money. He paid for his clothes and, sometimes for food. A few times, he gave his mother the money he made.

The conditions that constitute neglect based on California legal definitions may very well be normalized by youths, since it is common in Central America for children in poor families to work (see chapter 1). When Diego was not responsive to the question about whether he ever got hurt while working, the attorney used her repertoire of experience and knowledge of California labor protections for underage children to provide potential scenarios and screen for incidents that would constitute neglect: using pesticides, working without protective gloves, operating heavy machinery, and working long hours.

When the attorney moved beyond gathering details about objective labor conditions to ask Diego how he subjectively understood his circumstances in Honduras, she ran into his resistance to a narrative that reinterpreted his experience in an infantilizing US-centric lens. Diego told her that he liked to work and did not feel his mother was coercing him. From Diego's perspective, in Honduras, he was a young man and not a child, so it was quite normal that he worked full time. Entering the workforce is a rite of passage to adulthood, particularly for boys. Many of my male study participants relished the independence afforded to them by work and enjoyed their jobs, despite the fact that they were often employed in strenuous and even exploitative conditions. Yet it did not matter for SIJS, like it does for asylum, that youths internalize and be able to verbalize these new understandings of their past experiences. Youths were often not required to provide oral testimony to family or dependency court, and a written declaration was enough. Even when youths were required to testify, the scrutiny of SIJS cases is lower than for asylum claims.

That SIJS case preparation was less intensive than the "crash-course" of asylum preparation was apparent in how youths spoke about their applications. They often misnamed *"la visa juvenil"* (the youth visa, as attorneys refer to SIJS in Spanish), with other forms of relief, like the similarly sounding *"visa U"* (Spanish for U-Visa for crime victims). Likewise, I was troubled to find that some unaccompanied minors who had applied for SIJS did not seem to be aware of the important limitations that this path to citizenship would have for their family reunification rights. Whomever legal brokers present as the "culprit" parent, youths who become permanent residents (and eventually, US citizens) through SIJS permanently forfeit the right to reunify both of their parents and their siblings. In Diego's case, he would never be able to bring his "negligent" mother to the United States or regularize the status of his undocumented father, who became his primary caretaker.

During my fieldwork, I observed how attorneys explained to SIJS applicants this limitation to their future family reunification rights. Yet, even when attorneys were diligent in explaining their legal strategies to their clients, youths often remained confused and did not fully understand these. Some of the youths I met through interviews who had applied for SIJS aspired to reunify parents they had left behind and legally bring them to the United States. This knowledge gap shows that legal brokers were not always able to teach their young clients about the law. These dynamics contributed to making the legalization process disempowering for unaccompanied minors, who often did not fully understand their rights.

When I finished my fieldwork, Diego's SIJS case was still pending, but his attorney was confident that it would be approved based on his working conditions in Honduras. According to the attorneys I interviewed, compared to SIJS cases based on abuse or abandonment, cases based only on neglect, like Diego's, were the ones most likely to encounter resistance at

the state-court level. Judges could consider youths' circumstances to reflect "just poverty" instead of going against the best interests of the child.
In response, attorneys would argue that the judge's role was not to decide
whether certain living conditions might be commonplace in the home
country, but, rather, merely to assess whether these experiences met California legal definitions of neglect.

California state-court judges generally understood their role in these
terms and were willing to grant SIJS orders. Attorneys representing
unaccompanied minors had worked over the years to educate judges
in Southern California about SIJS, as this became a form of relief that
they increasingly pursued. This meant that the legal context for SIJS applicants was more favorable and focused on protection in Los Angeles.
By contrast, judges in other jurisdictions apply child welfare definitions
more restrictively and lack the familiarity and willingness to grant SIJS
orders.[29] When that occurs, a branch of the state that is formally mandated to protect the best interests of the child can instead play a role in
upholding immigration control and exclusion.

THE TUG OF WAR BETWEEN EXCLUSION
AND PROTECTION: LEGAL STRATEGIES
UNDER OBAMA AND TRUMP

The struggles that unaccompanied minors, and indeed all asylum seekers, face were by no means novel to the Trump era. Thus far, this chapter
has highlighted challenges common to the Obama and Trump contexts.
I now turn to discussing what changed. The Obama administration combined exclusion and protection in its policies toward unaccompanied
minors. Under Trump, exclusion was the sole focus of dozens of reforms,
which were introduced at a rapid-fire pace, making an already indeterminate legal context increasingly volatile. Challenging exclusionary policies required massive amounts of work from organizations involved in
impact litigation. Many of these legal battles were ultimately successful
in safeguarding existing protections. However, while litigation was pending, the work of direct representation attorneys became more challenging.
They had to continuously refashion their legal strategies to diversify and

mitigate the heightened risk of case denial and deportation their young clients faced.

First, the hard line of age-based eligibility became an even bigger obstacle under Trump. While some applicants previously had until age twenty-one to apply for SIJS, the Trump administration restricted eligibility for all SIJS cases to under age eighteen. Advocates eventually blocked this change through two class action lawsuits, restoring the original age-based deadlines for SIJS.[30] The Trump administration also tried to deny unaccompanied minors their right to apply for asylum at the asylum office by stripping them of their protected status when they turned eighteen. Under Obama, the asylum office had heard the cases of those who had been designated as unaccompanied minors at the border even after they turned eighteen or reunited with their parents.[31] To protect their clients' access to the asylum office, attorneys now had to file their asylum cases before their eighteenth birthdays, racing against yet another deadline. While attorneys submitted asylum and SIJS applications ever more quickly, the government, on its part, was taking far longer to decide cases.

Second, interpretations of asylum eligibility shrank progressively from only two "right" types of suffering to seemingly none at all. A former asylum officer thus described working at the Los Angeles asylum office between 2014 and 2018:

> [In 2014], some creative PSGs worked, for example, young teenage boys who went to this particular school, but that's not recognizing any major case law. And that has not since worked. We also used to have cases where the PSG was lacking parental protection: kids who resided in a household without their parents, and therefore were targeted because [gangs] treat them like orphans. Then we no longer recognized it. Forced gang girlfriends worked for a while but it doesn't anymore. So really, the last two years [2016–2018], the two [PSGs] that worked were family or child abuse. . . . It's not clear yet whether [child abuse] is going to work anymore because of new case law.

This account of the shifting interpretations of eligibility reflects the uncertainty inherent in the asylum process. Notably, the protective scope of asylum law had already narrowed under the Obama administration. Until 2014—the year that arrivals of unaccompanied minors increased—the asylum office accepted a number of "creative" PSGs that more closely corresponded to an array of different lived experiences of escape from violence, such as "teenage boys who went to this particular school," or "forced gang girlfriends." This is notable since, unlike immigration court, the asylum office does not, in principle, have the ability to create new case law to grant "original" cases.[32] It is instead reliant on case law established by the courts. That these "creative" cases worked at the asylum office reflects the protective discretion that officers could use. The asylum office had also accepted a PSG defined as "lacking parental protection." Attorneys would argue that children were victims of violence, both in and outside the home, because their parents could not protect them. This PSG framing fits the narratives of some of the stories presented in chapter 2 quite closely: children whose parents migrated to the United States and whose relatives in the home country could not care for them were more vulnerable to forced gang recruitment and abuse in the home. After 2014, the narrower experience of child abuse replaced the broader idea of children and youths being vulnerable due to the lack of parental protection. Under Obama, asylum eligibility for unaccompanied minors was consolidated under the two relatively narrowly defined criteria of family membership and child abuse.

Yet the scope of asylum protections was far more severely undermined by the Trump administration. Attorney General Jeff Sessions issued a series of decisions to quickly overturn decades of litigation that had expanded access to protection for asylum-seeking women and children, disqualifying the PSGs of domestic violence (Matter of A-B-, 2018) and family (Matter of L-E-A, 2019). These decisions also disqualified victims of "private actors," like family members or gang members. As we saw in chapter 2, virtually all Central American youths are harmed by so-called "private" rather than state actors. However, these acts of interpersonal violence are rooted in broader unequal power structures and enabled by the state's unwillingness to protect the human rights of its citizens in El Salvador, Guatemala, and Honduras. Attorneys viewed the Sessions decisions as unjust and illegitimate or, as one of them put it, "definitely trying to close the door on asylum." In response, they continued to help their clients apply for asylum using the family and child abuse arguments that would have won based on the Obama-era status quo. They also tried out new arguments and PSGs, deliberately filing cases that sought to expand the refugee category.

Third, a series of policies that were largely invisible to the public un-dermined the use of protective discretion both in immigration court and at the asylum office. Immigration judges lost their ability to manage the cases on their dockets. They could no longer grant applicants more time to apply for relief or exempt those with pending applications from attending court, which placed some youths at greater risk of deportation.[33] Judges were also stripped of the power to use prosecutorial discretion to grant temporary permits to youths who lost their asylum cases but were still deemed to merit deportation relief.[34] To comply with new pressures from supervisors, asylum officers began to interview unaccompanied minors like adults, evaluating their credibility and holding their testimonies to the same standards.[35] Child-friendly interview practices were thus under-mined, and it became even more important for youths to show the right amount and type of suffering to win their cases. In response, legal brokers changed how they prepared unaccompanied minors' asylum cases. They became more cautious about obtaining details, which had previously been crucial to establish eligibility and credibility. They feared that cases would now more easily be denied if youths made mistakes reporting specifics, such as the date a certain event took place or how many people were present. An absurd balancing act ensued as legal brokers found themselves having to prepare cases both detailed and vague enough to pass muster at an asylum office increasingly focused on exclusion.

Fourth, the Trump administration introduced a host of procedural changes that made SIJS cases more difficult to win. USCIS ceased to defer to state court expertise in determining the best interests of the child. Instead, additional details and proof about home country events were requested to evaluate the court's SIJS orders, using what attorneys characterized as "bogus arguments." One attorney complained about this happening to her client, "USCIS wants evidence that the judge considered . . . whether or not the child could live with other relatives in the home country before it issued the finding that it's against her best interests to return to her home country." The attorney noted that USCIS was inappro-priately applying the relocation and fear of return assessment typical of asylum to the best interests determination central to SIJS. Legal brokers believed that the Trump administration was instrumentally using proce-dural hurdles like these to grant SIJS at lower rates. Attorneys responded by contesting negative decisions at USCIS and submitting additional memos, emails, and paperwork or even by returning to court to request more detailed SIJS orders from judges.

As the likelihood of success of each individual application became more uncertain, and case resolution times for both SIJS and asylum became more drawn out, legal brokers diversified risk by changing how they strategized the best path toward legalization for their unaccompanied minor clients. During the Obama administration, the most common strategy was to advise youths to apply for their "strongest" relief first, the one estimated to be most likely to yield a positive outcome. If the youth's cases for both asylum and SIJS were deemed equally strong, legal brokers prioritized the application that was most time sensitive, usually SIJS, which was already subject to age-based deadlines. The second application would then be a plan B if the first was denied. Each application for relief is complex and time consuming, and this strategy allowed legal clinics to save scarce resources. It also eased the burden on youths and their caretakers who had to take time off school and work to attend meetings and who sometimes paid additional fees for each application. By 2019, the Trump administration's policies had had enough of a negative impact that legal brokers changed their strategy and began to immediately and simultaneously apply for both asylum and SIJS when their clients were eligible. By not putting all their eggs in one basket, so to speak, attorneys found a way to diversify the heightened risk of case denial that their clients now faced.

These new risk diversification strategies had some undesired effects. At the organizational level, more legal hours went into the preparation of each client's deportation defense. Organizations were not able to represent as many clients unless they could obtain more funding. Managing risk in these ways taxed attorneys who were already overworked. The dark circles under the eyes of Edgar's attorney became an all-too-common sight during the Trump years. The vicarious trauma and exhaustion of a job that was already difficult under "normal" circumstances were further exacerbated. Attorney burnout, in turn, had negative consequences for youths. High staff turnover meant that youths were often assigned different attorneys as their cases progressed. Each time, youths had to tell their stories to a new stranger, which exacerbated the retraumatizing nature of the asylum process.

Not only was keeping up with all these changes grueling for legal brokers, who had to constantly update applications, but each change also prompted new conversations with clients. I listened to many phone calls where attorneys informed youths about how obscure and highly technical policies *could* have an impact on their case. Explaining these issues in simple terms was near impossible for legal brokers, who were still themselves trying to predict how each particular change might play out in practice. As policies changed continuously, this further undermined youths' ability to understand their rights under US immigration law. Legal brokers played a delicate balancing act when discussing the law with youths during the uncertain Trump years. On the one hand, they managed youth's expectations, giving far more cautious assessments than they had under Obama about whether and when their cases might be granted. On the other hand, legal brokers also tried not to express cynicism. They did not want to undermine their young clients' trust in the legal process and hopes for finding safety and stable futures in the United States.

THE PARADOXES OF RECOGNITION: WHO COUNTS AS A DE JURE REFUGEE?

The migration decisions that unaccompanied minors and their families made while facing violence in their home countries later play out in unexpected ways during their asylum applications. Youths had to flee at the right time, escaping early enough to survive, yet staying long enough to experience a sufficient *amount* of suffering to meet the bar of persecution and the right *types* of suffering to satisfy US asylum case law. During high-stakes asylum interviews, youths had to describe their experiences of escape, not as they understood them, but in the language of the law. Legal brokers play an indispensable role in the legal socialization of youths, teaching them about asylum and SIJS and thus enabling them to claim rights vis-à-vis the state.

In mediating the asylum process, legal brokers can, and sometimes do, prepare applications based on narratives that challenge narrow US asylum case law. Yet this comes with significant risks. Their clients are more likely to obtain relief if their cases can be reframed to satisfy existing case law. Thus, the legal strategy most beneficial for the individual youth's chances of obtaining refugee status is also the one that keeps the scope of asylum protections narrow. During the Obama years, after 2014, when asylum eligibility became relatively stable and consolidated under the two criteria of child abuse and family membership, legal brokers had strong incentives to stick to these types of cases to maximize chances of success for their clients.

During the Trump era, even narrow infantilizing asylum case law was attacked. As legal brokers continued to file cases using the arguments of the Obama years, what had been conservative legal strategies became strategies of resistance to protect the status quo of asylum eligibility for children against the new wave of exclusion. As asylum applications based on all types of arguments became far more risky endeavors, this also created incentives for creative lawyering strategies. Legal brokers experimented with new PSGs and legal arguments. Some of these arguments were shared through mailing lists, so attorneys at different organizations were working together. Direct representation attorneys employed these strategies mindfully to get their clients into the asylum system in hopes that, before their cases were heard, there would be positive developments in case law and through impact litigation. Hence, during the Trump years, the direct representation of individual youths worked in synch with broader advocacy goals of expanding access to protection for more immigrants. Of course, exclusionary policy changes and new legal strategies meant more risks for individual clients, which legal brokers tried to mitigate through creative, yet time-consuming and resource-intensive means.

What remained constant during both administrations was that the US asylum system did not adequately recognize how age and stage in the life cycle shape exposure to violence, causing youth migration from Central America today. As long as this continues to be true, in the best-case scenario, there are two possible outcomes for youths who escape from violence but have not experienced the right *types* of suffering. Some, like Diego, may obtain relief through pathways like SIJS. Others may be granted asylum for a reason other than what precipitated their flight, as they subjectively understand it. This has important implications because, as we saw in the cases of Edgar and Francisco, not all youths are equally receptive to the "crash-course" of asylum preparation. Learning to tell their stories in the language of the law is especially challenging for youths with limited formal education, for those sheltered by protective caretakers from frightening family histories, and for younger applicants who, for developmental reasons, do not have the same capacity as those who have reached the age of biological maturity to tell causal narratives, explaining not just *how* but *why* they fled.

To be sure, in both of those circumstances, individual youths still obtain essential substantive protections: deportation relief and legal status. Yet only true *recognition* of their experiences of escape in the US asylum process would open the door to others like them. This is crucial because not all youths who escape from life-threatening violence but present the "wrong" *types* of suffering had experiences that qualified them for SIJS or that could be reframed as winning asylum cases. Legal brokers used only the facts that youths recounted to them and their legal—and sometimes also quite sociological—interpretation of these past events to construct cases. As long as narrow criteria are used in the US asylum process to decide who is a de jure refugee, the worst-case scenario will be that de facto refugee youths who have very real vulnerabilities are excluded from protection and risk deportation back to life-threatening danger.

6 Coming of Age under the Gaze of the State

Linda had turned eighteen a few weeks before we met at a park in Los Angeles. A legal clinic staff member told me that she was a "very sweet kid" and suggested that I interview her. Petite as she was, and without any makeup on, Linda looked younger than her age. The atmosphere was relaxed as we sat under the LA sun together. Linda told me all about her life in Los Angeles and Honduras, treating me with the familiarity of a confidant. Her demeanor changed, and she took on a serious air when she started talking about her high school. She was afraid of getting in trouble. She was avoiding the kids whom she saw as "*malas compañias*" (the wrong crowd). Those kids got bad grades and smoked marijuana, things she could not afford to do as an immigrant in legal limbo. She explained, "You have to be really careful. You have to follow the laws. There are lots of things that one can't do. . . . Immigration is seeing the things that I'm doing. They have my case number, they have all my information, they know everything I'm doing."

As they adapt to life in the United States while their immigration cases are pending, Central American unaccompanied minors experience heightened state scrutiny. They come to feel, as Linda put it, that their every move is being watched. This chapter explores the everyday lives of unaccompanied minors as they come of age under the gaze of the state. The increasingly lengthy application process for asylum and Special Immigrant Juvenile Status (SIJS)—usually taking over two and over four years, respectively, under Trump—spills over to affect other facets of youths' lives as they navigate school, work, and family reunification after long periods of separation. What happens in those realms, in turn, can influence the outcomes of their applications for immigration relief. The United States is a temporary safe haven from the violence youths fled in El Salvador, Guatemala, and Honduras. Yet, these de facto refugee youths still face many challenges to continue their life course transitions and find stable futures in their new homes.

The independent migration of past cohorts of mostly male teenagers has been conceptualized as a "rite of passage" through which children transition to adulthood by finding adventure, emancipation from adult control, and employment in the receiving country.[1] Conversely, I have argued that unaccompanied minors undergo an infantilizing and victimizing rite of reverse passage as they navigate asylum and SIJS applications in the United States: their petitions require them to discursively regress to childhood in their narratives, rather than move forward to adulthood. In this chapter, I argue that the legal process has spillover effects, shaping the decisions that youths are able to make vis-à-vis their life-course transitions, like getting a job, going to college, or getting married.

Under the pervasive gaze of the state, unaccompanied minors' coming-of-age does not necessarily occur in a straight line from childhood to adulthood as the classic idea of rites of passage implies. The legal and social dimensions of youths' dual liminality interact. Whether their applications for immigration relief are granted or denied, and how long these are pending, affects when and how youths can take steps toward adulthood. Many remain stuck in a protracted in-between state, neither children nor adults, and subject at once to both infantilizing and adultified expectations. Within these constraints, unaccompanied minors make gendered coming-of-age decisions. Girls are more likely than boys of the same age to conform to US expectations for childlike behaviors and to delay life-course transitions by staying in school and living with family member caretakers for longer.

Compared to other groups of immigrant youths studied in prior scholarship, Central American unaccompanied minors experience "cumulative disadvantages."[2] That is, after fleeing violence in their home countries, they encounter unique challenges in US institutions that are ill-equipped or unwilling to support them during their incorporation. As the professional field of legal brokerage with unaccompanied minors expands, some legal aid organizations have hired case managers who help youths navigate challenges outside the legal realm. This has somewhat freed attorneys who work with unaccompanied minors from "wearing multiple hats" so they can focus on their area of expertise.[3] Like attorneys, case managers can be conceptualized as brokerage figures. These brokers facilitate unaccompanied minors' access to the limited state services and public benefits for which they are eligible, as well as to aid from individuals and nonprofits. Case managers thus help guide youths' "bureaucratic incorporation" in different state systems—such as health care and public education— beyond the maze-like US immigration system.[4] This support is especially important because only about 30 percent of unaccompanied minors nationwide receive ORR-funded post-release services; even for youths who qualify, the assistance provided through this program is very limited due to social workers' high caseloads.[5]

Just as attorneys transform youths' past experiences of suffering into humanitarian capital to help them obtain legal status, case managers assess whether youths' current needs and behavior yield sufficient humanitarian capital to obtain aid from private donors that complements limited state support. In making these assessments, case managers anticipate and respond to gendered and racialized societal expectations. Boys and girls differ in terms of how they are perceived in US society, which has implications for their treatment in state systems and their access to aid from other sources. Boys are more readily criminalized and excluded in schools and neighborhoods. Girls are more readily perceived as innocent victims deserving of protection and assistance, unless they engage in behaviors seen as too sexual and woman-like.

Not all legal aid organizations offer case management services. Youths who cannot benefit from these services rely exclusively on their family members for support. Yet the caretakers of unaccompanied minors are usually undocumented immigrants who have long lived in the shadows and thus have little experience navigating state systems. Many lack the resources necessary to help youths because they are working exploitative jobs and must meet demands from other family members in need. Indeed, the migrant networks of Central Americans are resource poor, a disadvantage that stems from the denial of refugee status to past generations, including some of the parents and relatives of unaccompanied minors (see chapter 2).[6] Unaccompanied minors who can rely neither on case managers nor on family are left to navigate challenges on their own, with little state support, despite being a formally recognized vulnerable group.

This chapter is structured as follows. First, I describe how case managers help unaccompanied minors navigate challenges outside the legal realm and play a role in their legal socialization, educating youths about their rights and obligations regarding health care, school, work, and the state and federal laws that affect their everyday lives. Second, I discuss how family members help youths navigate these same challenges, as well as the gendered patterns that emerged in youths' family reunification experiences, as they strive to gain familiarity with caretakers from whom they have long been separated or have never met. Third, I turn to the experiences of youths in long-term foster care who do not have the support of family. Finally, I discuss unaccompanied minors' gendered coming-of-age trajectories through work or higher education in the United States.

CASE MANAGEMENT: HELPING "SWEET" KIDS AND THOSE IN NEED; MANAGING REBELLIOUS TEENS

My observations shadowing case managers as they helped unaccompanied minors navigate challenges outside the legal realm revealed important information about how different institutions beyond the immigration bureaucracy—such as school, work, family, and the health care system—operate to include or exclude this relatively new population of immigrant youths. Interactions between case managers and youths also made apparent the pressures and contradictory expectations that are imposed on unaccompanied minors as they navigate humanitarian paths to legal status and seek belonging in their new homes while under the scrutiny of the state.

As brokers who mediate a context of reception characterized by exclusion and protection, similarly to attorneys, case managers worked both to control and empower their young clients. On the one hand, usually with the benevolent goal of protecting youths, case managers not only educated them about their legal obligations but also transmitted specific messages about how unaccompanied minors should look and behave to gain acceptance and support. They thus inevitably reproduced normative notions about deserving youth citizenship. On the other hand, case managers were also advocates who educated youths about their rights and the benefits they could access as California residents, notwithstanding their legal status.

Even in legal clinics that offered case management services, meeting youths' needs beyond the legal process was seen as secondary in importance to their petitions for immigration relief. As a result, case management services were even more under-staffed and under-resourced than legal services, making it impossible for case managers to provide individualized support to all the young clients of the organization. At the time of my fieldwork, the role of the case manager was still relatively new and slowly becoming professionalized. Staff members working in this role were usually not trained social workers. Case managers were better prepared to assist their clients in some areas of need more than others. For example, the case managers I shadowed were still compiling a list of shelters for homeless youths at the time. They were faced with challenging work, which many were learning while on the job, and they had to find ways to manage the limited resources at their disposal to help their clients.

Case managers were able to have short one-on-one meetings with most youths when they went to the legal clinic to meet with their attorneys. During these meetings, they provided youths with basic information about their rights and entitlements, mainly their eligibility for free health insurance. They thus played an essential role as brokers to health care, teaching unaccompanied minors about their right to health insurance in California until age nineteen under Medi-Cal, irrespective of their immigration status.[7] Case managers explained what documents were needed to qualify, helped youths fill out applications, and handed out information about the health care providers nearest to them, all while encouraging youths to use Medi-Cal to take care of their physical and mental health needs.

To provide more individualized support, case managers relied either on youths' attorneys to alert them to needs or on youths themselves to proactively ask for help. I found that case managers enjoyed working with kids they saw as being "on top of things": those who reached out to them, promptly answered their calls, and prioritized working with them over other commitments they might have had at the time. When youths asked for help more often than case managers deemed appropriate, however, they could be perceived as problematic, taking up too much individual attention and diverting it from other cases. Linda was one of these clients. Unlike most youths, Linda had no family anywhere in the United States. She very much relied on her attorney and the case managers at the legal aid organization. Because she was correctly perceived to be in need, staff members were happy and, initially, enthusiastic, to help her. After a while, however, they tired of her questions about Medi-Cal, school, and work. They wished that Linda would be more independent and fend for herself. Indeed, it seemed to me that this was exactly what Linda was doing when I last spoke to her; she was living with a friend and looking for a job to support herself after school. This was all the more difficult because Linda could not legally work since she was an SIJS applicant. Unlike a pending asylum case, a pending SIJS case did not confer a work permit during the time of this research. This would change under Biden in 2022, following a major advocacy victory seeking to attenuate the vulnerabilities of SIJS applicant youth that I describe in this chapter (for more on this, see conclusion).

Over time, Linda also lost her standing as a favorite among staff—a "sweet kid"—because she failed to meet normative gendered behavioral expectations. The "sweet kid" was a client who staff members knew would be a good face for the organization because he or she would elicit the compassion of those wanting to donate resources to help unaccompanied minors. In the aftermath of the Trump administration's separation of Central American families, legal aid organizations in Los Angeles received a veritable outpouring of support from other nonprofits, churches, businesses, and concerned citizens, all of whom wanted to help the small children separated from their parents at the border. Yet, at the time, these legal aid organizations worked almost exclusively with unaccompanied minors who were teenagers and not small children.[8] Therefore, staff had to find ways to manage donors' expectations while ensuring that resources would continue to flow in to support their mostly teenaged clients, for whom limited state support was available. To establish durable partnerships, case managers strategically initiated interactions with donors and volunteers by using the case of a "sweet kid" as the first case they would advocate for. This allowed them to present an image of the unaccompanied child to donors, which, while not exactly corresponding to the children separated from their parents at the border that they saw in the news, was at least not too discordant from it. In this way, case managers secured resources both for that particular client and for future ones.

Linda was one of the clients selected to this end. Not only was she in great need of support because she was alone in the United States, but she was charismatic and pretty. Petite as she was, even at eighteen, Linda looked younger than her age. A group of potential donors had reached out to the organization offering to support unaccompanied minors with in-kind donations, which would be funded through an Amazon wish list account. The case manager asked Linda to go to the Amazon website to create a "wish list" with items that she needed. A few days later, after seeing the list of items that Linda had chosen, the case manager laughed as she incredulously recounted, "You have no idea the things she sent me! Like black stilettos, and five-inch platforms, and super short miniskirts. And all of that is fine by me, but people aren't going to donate that! The idea is that she is an *unaccompanied minor*. I thought she could ask for sanitary pads because then people are going to be like, 'she needs that and can't afford it, poor thing.'"

Wary of the liminal status between childhood and adulthood that unaccompanied minors inhabit, the case manager did not want eighteen-year-old Linda to be perceived as a menacing teenager who dressed in a way that signaled her as a seductive woman. The case manager recommended that Linda present herself as a "poor kid" because she predicted that only that image would elicit compassion and aid from the donors. I do want to emphasize that, by telling Linda to pick a different set of items, the case manager—who was a Latina child of immigrant parents and an outspoken feminist and immigrants' rights advocate—was not doing so in a way that reflected her own beliefs about "appropriate" female behavior. Nor was she making these recommendations uncritically. Rather, the case manager was mindful that, particularly for these types of initial requests, the innocent self-presentation of youths helped to ensure future support to fill gaps and supplement the organization's scarce resources. She strategically advised Linda to perform her innocence and need as a "poor kid" as a pragmatist trying to help as many clients as possible. The case manager and I had discussed the limitations of compassion for unaccompanied minors on more than one occasion. I did not have to point out to her the contradictions of the liminal position these youths inhabit in the United States. She was well-attuned to them herself, as this interaction shows:

> The floor of the office was increasingly covered in donations, bags of clothing for much smaller children than those that the organization served. This made the donations difficult to distribute quickly, and they sat on the floor until enough smaller children or petite teenagers came to the office to collect them. I commented on this, noting, "If this was for teenagers, this stuff would be long gone already."
>
> The case manager replied, "I know but this donor organization only serves children up to age twelve." A colleague suggested, "We could just give the individual items to our clients, I feel like most of that stuff isn't for small kids necessarily, there's towels, backpacks, and other useful things in the bags."
>
> The case manager said, "Yeah, we could do that, I guess. I think they don't want us to give it to the kids [the teenagers]. But how would they find out? Right?"
>
> I chimed in, "It's interesting that this NGO that specializes in things for babies is donating to an organization that largely serves teenagers."
>
> The case manager replied with an ironic tone, "You know, with all the family separation coverage in the media, they wanted to donate stuff for the little brown kids at the border."
>
> I responded, "Teenagers are less sympathetic, right?"
>
> The case manager said, "You know it."

With a limited set of tools at their hands, case managers learned to play the game to secure what resources they could within the constraints that existed. They tried to be strategic in accruing donations like those described above because these could also benefit older clients who did not fit into the clothing but could use other items, such as shampoo, towels, backpacks, and school supplies. What's more, since some unaccompanied minors were parents themselves, they could take advantage of items like diapers and formula. It was to secure valuable resources like these, that case managers used the strategy of presenting the stories of "sweet kids."

However, even if the case manager did not personally agree with the gendered messages about how deserving youths should look and behave, by instrumentally telling Linda how to conform to the "sweet kid" behavior, she inevitably transmitted and reified notions of deservingness based on childlike innocence that characterize the contradictory US context of reception. While Central American boys are readily criminalized in the United States, it was easier for girls to appear innocent, but only if they did not demonstrate a woman-like sexuality. By telling her to change her donations wish-list, the case manager reminded Linda that, as an unaccompanied minor, she was allowed needs but not desires. Unaccompanied minors must embody a one-dimensional identity as poor refugees or abandoned children, one that leaves little room for the aspirations and desires that young people typically express in their transitions to adulthood.

A few months later, another female client named Cristina, who was from El Salvador, failed to meet the behavioral expectations of the "sweet kid." Like Linda, Cristina had recently turned eighteen but looked years younger. A volunteer from a local church had offered to house Cristina because she could no longer stay with her aunt, who had left the country to care for a sick relative in El Salvador. The case managers received a phone call from the volunteer hosting Cristina who wanted to report an "incident" that happened when they were shopping together. Apparently, Cristina had taken pictures of herself in her underwear and sent them to boys. The volunteer said, over the phone, "I'm not at all saying this in an uptight or judgmental way, but we just thought that you should know." After another occasion when Cristina skipped school to hang out with her friends and lied about where she was, the case manager complained that cases like this made the organization look bad and presented an unacceptable strain on the limited resources available to help so many clients in need:

> On the one hand, I get it, she's a teenager. On the other hand, though, she needs to step up and take responsibility because otherwise it's not fair to all the other clients I have. I told her, "You don't have the privilege to do that, you are representing all unaccompanied minors now. You can't lie to me. If you lie again, I won't help you. . . . We found you housing for a month, but if you don't cooperate, do you realize that you will be homeless after that?! It's not my job to find you a place to stay; it's yours."

Helping unaccompanied minors like Cristina who were on their own without any family support in the United States posed particular challenges for case managers, especially when their behavior did not correspond to the ideal child who elicits compassion but rather signaled that of the rebellious teenager, needing to be disciplined. When youths were over eighteen and thus, legally speaking, adults who could have been self-sufficient but did not always have the tools and resources to do so, case managers struggled with how much, and in what ways, to both help and discipline them. They also struggled to decide how "parental" to be in these interactions. Like Linda, Cristina depended on aid to survive because she was an SIJS applicant who did not have a work permit. While Linda was looking for a job, Cristina was still in school, yet struggling to stay focused and advance, due to what case managers suspected was an undiagnosed learning disability. They worried that Cristina would not fare well now that she could no longer rely on her aunt.

I observed case managers genuinely worry about their clients while managing multiple difficult situations, including risk of homelessness, at the same time. Like immigration lawyers, they had a stressful job that included emotional labor and the toll of the sense of responsibility they felt for their young clients, which could lead them to experience burnout. At the same time, however, in serving as brokers in a context of reception characterized by limited compassion, case managers inevitably transmitted normative notions of deserving citizenship. They reinforced youths' understandings that, to be found deserving of support and to claim belonging, they had to embody an ideal-type of innocent child and not behave "like teenagers." Through comments like "you are representing all unaccompanied minors now," the presence of the state's gaze in youths' lives was amplified, bolstering youths' impressions that their actions were constantly being scrutinized. As reflected in the words of Linda that open this chapter—"immigration is seeing everything I'm doing"—unaccompanied minors experienced this scrutiny strongly.

To be sure, youths *are* subjected to intense scrutiny as they navigate removal proceedings. Making just one mistake can have dire consequences, including deportation. Thus, reinforcing behavioral restrictions was a means to protect their clients from immigration enforcement. As mentioned in previous chapters, attorneys also counseled youths about how to look and behave in the spaces where they were particularly visible to the state, like court hearings and asylum interviews. They made youths aware that their behavior, looks, and demeanor could push their cases toward denial or approval based on discretionary criteria. Assisting youths with their needs outside the legal realm, case managers reinforced these messages and transferred their significance to the realm of everyday life.

Case managers transmitted messages that not only had to do with complying with laws but also with racialized societal norms that police minority youths in the United States. For example, youths were told that while marijuana consumption is legal in the State of California, it is illegal under federal law, and this meant that, as immigrants, it was illegal for them. Case managers warned youths not to use drugs and not to hang out with peers who did, because they might find themselves in the wrong place at the wrong time and get into trouble, the very type of situation that Linda told me she fretted about while in school. When youths, especially boys, had tattoos, case managers would tell them that these could signal them as "bad" kids or even be read as an indication of gang affiliation. They advised youths to get tattoos removed and connected them with organizations that would do so for free.

Case managers also had awkward conversations about sex with youths, most often boys, who were nearing age eighteen. They informed them that, under US law, having sex with a minor is considered statutory rape, and this could get them in trouble. One day, a case manager had this conversation with two Salvadoran brothers, ages sixteen and eighteen. The younger brother looked absolutely mortified, blushing, and looking down at his feet. The older brother, whose name was Marcos, laughed loudly and said, "That's not a problem for me, my girlfriend is eighteen." The case manager replied, "OK then, just make sure that you treat her well, so you don't get in trouble." Tellingly, the case manager noted that Marcos should treat his girlfriend with respect, not to have a conversation about consent, but rather to make sure that he avoided "trouble" that could negatively affect his chances of securing immigration relief. The criminalization narratives that affect male unaccompanied minors are apparent in this example, as the case manager warned the young man against committing an illegal act of domestic violence or sexual abuse. While Linda's sexuality was seen as problematic because of her "seductiveness," Marcos's sexuality was framed as potentially violent and problematic in criminal terms. These gendered frames and narratives of threat around sexuality resonate with other historical examples of racialized stereotypes about immigrants and minorities in the United States.[9]

Over the course of my fieldwork, case resolution times for asylum and SIJS became increasingly long, a problem exacerbated by Trump-era policies. This prolonged unaccompanied minors' state of legal limbo, making it all the more important for them to conform to behavioral restrictions because of the "probationary logic of legalization."[10] In other words, youths remained in the state of heightened scrutiny and evaluation that all undocumented immigrants seeking to legalize their status face. The longer the period of legal limbo lasted, the more challenging it was for youths to comply with state-mandated restrictions. This was particularly true for youths with pending SIJS cases, like Linda and Cristina, who were not allowed to work. As a form of immigration relief designed to protect the best interests of the child, SIJS enshrines the Western notion that childhood is a time for school rather than work, and it effectively suspended applicants in the phase of childhood, even after they turned eighteen.

Some attorneys and case managers told youths with pending SIJS cases that they should not work under any circumstances. Yet others, well-aware that youths were in financial need and had to work to support themselves and help their families, were willing to give more nuanced advice like, "I'm going to remind you that you can't work, but, for me, the most important thing is that you don't work with fake papers because that can affect your case." In this way, case managers and attorneys acknowledged that it was inevitable that many of their clients would work. They let youths know that while using fake or "borrowed" papers was illegal—considered immigration fraud and identify theft—and could harm their chances of obtaining legal status, working without authorization was more of an extra-legal gray zone.

Of course, without papers—valid, fake, or "borrowed"—it was more difficult for youths to find jobs that would allow them to adequately support themselves. The prohibition on work created significant challenges for SIJS applicants, including food and housing insecurity, especially for those youths who could not rely on family to support them. Complying with these rules meant postponing life-course transitions, including entry in the labor force and marriage (only unmarried individuals qualify for SIJS), far beyond the legal age of adulthood. In the context of lengthy case resolution times, if an unaccompanied minor applied for SIJS at age sixteen or seventeen, she might not become a permanent resident with the right to legally work until age twenty or twenty-one.

HELPING EXTRAORDINARY ACHIEVERS: EDUCATIONAL ATTAINMENT AND BELONGING

Attorneys were motivated to keep doing their jobs despite the burnout and challenges they faced on a daily basis when they won the case of one of their clients. Similarly, case managers found motivation for their difficult work, which involved hearing innumerable stories of unaccompanied minors' struggles, by celebrating and supporting the accomplishments of clients who were exemplary achievers. This was unsurprising as they came across some truly inspiring stories of youths who had managed to succeed against all odds, despite bringing with them "cumulative disadvantages," such as interrupted schooling and traumatic experiences in the home country and during transit migration, which position unaccompanied minors at a greater disadvantage than other cohorts of immigrant youths.[11]

These disadvantages were further compounded by the challenges youths faced during their incorporation as they navigated a series of state systems not designed to welcome or accommodate them. Case managers and attorneys were often angered by what they perceived to be injustices that youths faced in institutions like school. Extraordinary achievers gave case managers confidence in youth resilience and hope that these obstacles could be overcome. From the perspective of case managers, extraordinary achievers were youths who satisfied middle-class expectations for young people in the United States. They excelled in school, getting good grades in high school, and, in some cases, making plans to attend college. They were the ones who, similarly to 1.5 generation undocumented youths, were able to claim belonging based on meritocratic discourses that reward hard work and educational attainment as an expression of the American Dream.[12]

Juan was one of the extraordinary achievers. He migrated from El Salvador at age sixteen and had applied for asylum and SIJS shortly after arriving in the United States. While Juan had a work permit thanks to his pending asylum case, his personal coming-of-age goal was to focus on school rather than work. Juan had always dreamed of going to college. His family valued higher education: his mother had completed her high school degree and would have liked the chance to keep studying herself; his older sister had gotten her bachelor's degree in El Salvador. Juan's plan was to go to college and work only part-time to help his mother pay for his books and tuition. During his senior year in high school, Juan asked a case manager for help filling out his college admissions applications. Understandably, this paperwork was unfamiliar to Juan who had arrived from El Salvador just two years earlier, where he was used to navigating a completely different educational system. It was his liminal legal status, however, that posed the main challenge. Juan did not understand how to fill out the box on his college application that asked about his immigration status. He asked the case manager, "Can I say that I am a resident?"

This was a complex question. Juan was potentially eligible to become a lawful permanent resident through both asylum and SIJS. Indeed, his SIJS order (the first component of the SIJS application, see chapter 5) had been granted. Yet SIJS and asylum cases were taking longer and becoming increasingly difficult to win in the context of the Trump administration. Well over a year after applying, Juan was still waiting to hear back about the results of both of his applications for relief. Permanent residents and approved refugees qualify for in-state tuition and federal fellowships. However, because of the timing of his college application, Juan was unable to fill out the federal financial aid application to get the support he needed to pay tuition.

As a recently arrived unaccompanied minor, Juan also did not qualify for financial aid for undocumented youths. He had spent less than three years in a California high school, which is the minimum amount of time necessary for undocumented youth to qualify for in-state tuition through the California Dream Act. This legislation was passed to support the Dreamers, a different, bigger, and more visible population of 1.5 generation children who migrate at a young age with their parents and are educated in the United States since primary school. These entitlements were obtained after years of advocacy by immigrant youth activists.[13] Yet they benefit only this specific group. Because of his age at arrival, like most

unaccompanied minors, Juan fell outside of eligibility for state aid for undocumented students.[14] When the time came to apply for college, he was
neither a Dreamer, a resident, nor a refugee. Instead, Juan was classified
as a foreign student. As such, he would have to pay expensive tuition, an
onerous burden for his single mother.

Since Juan fell outside of these categories, the college application process was daunting and confusing, not just for him but also for the high
school counselor and college admissions officers who wanted to help him.
These school officials were not accustomed to working with this new population of immigrant youths. They did not understand how Juan could
have a work permit and yet be neither a resident nor a DACA recipient,
the renewable two-year permit that most Dreamer-generation youths
qualified for. The case manager from the legal clinic inserted herself as a
broker between the school and Juan. To advocate on his behalf, the case
manager decided with Juan to disclose information about his asylum case
to the college admissions officer to educate her about his particular situation of legal limbo. She used his inspirational story, hoping to convert her
into an advocate for Juan and to try to convince the college to waive part
of his tuition. During a phone call with the admissions officer, she noted
that Juan numbered among her favorite clients: "He came to the US two
years ago, he is a stellar student, he has a 3.6 or 3.7 GPA. . . . Honestly, he
is like top two out of hundreds of clients. I just want to make sure that he
can continue his education."

Juan was grateful for the special support he received from the legal
aid organization staff, and the case manager noted that he was "sweet" in
expressing this, which made it all the more rewarding to work on his case.
One day, Juan texted her a thank-you message, "Thank you so much! [cry-
ing smiley face emoticon] I don't know what I would do without you." To
this, the case manager replied, "Juan, don't make me cry. People like you
inspire me, so thank *YOU*. But yes, let's keep in touch about this, and we'll
figure it out together!"

In spite of the case manager's help, when I finished my ethnographic
fieldwork in 2019, Juan had still not been able to enroll in college. One key,
insurmountable obstacle remained: his pending asylum case. Suspended
in this unique type of legal limbo that unaccompanied minors face, Juan's
chosen coming-of-age trajectory through higher education—a key step

toward his transition to adulthood—was stalled. Seeing no way out of this conundrum and unable to afford even a discounted tuition rate, Juan decided to delay his college applications for a year in hopes that his asylum case—the one likely to be resolved earlier—would be approved, so he would qualify for federal aid. I stayed in touch with Juan and interviewed him two years later. He had been able to pursue his dream after all. His asylum application was approved, and he was admitted to a prestigious four-year university, with a full scholarship.

While undoubtedly inspiring, Juan's exceptional story makes all the more apparent the contradictions of the expectations imposed on unaccompanied minors in the United States. These young immigrant newcomers constantly receive messages from state actors (ORR staff, immigration judges, asylum officers) and brokers who mediate their interactions with the state (attorneys, case managers) about models of deserving youth citizenship. These models reflect middle-class values that privilege school and higher education over work and normative measures of successful youth assimilation centered on educational attainment. Yet, while school has been identified as a key institution for the inclusion of 1.5 generation undocumented youths, unaccompanied minors, who arrive as high-school-aged older teenagers, often face exclusion in the education system. While all immigrant and minority students face structural disadvantages in US public schools, the elementary school years of K–12 education are more inclusive. In high school, class and race inequalities are amplified.[15] The state does little to support unaccompanied minors in high schools. Instead, they must succeed against the high odds stacked against them. Unaccompanied minors are left with the mark of middle-class expectations and the idea that they must behave this way to belong and, for some, a sense of inadequacy if they are incapable of meeting the near-impossible goals imposed on them.

Juan overcame a host of barriers that caused others to fall out of the educational pipeline. Unaccompanied minors face added burdens in school due both to their newness and unfamiliarity with the US education system and to their state of legal limbo as humanitarian claimants. They face obstacles already when first enrolling in high school. Sometimes youths—like Cadmael, whom we met in chapter 2—were ineligible to enroll because they arrived in the United States at age seventeen, were detained for months in ORR custody, and had turned eighteen by the time they were released. Those youths had reached the marker of adulthood that legally disqualified them from enrolling in high school. What's more, the Associated Press released a report in 2016 finding that schools nationwide were also keeping recently arrived unaccompanied minors who were still under age eighteen from enrolling in high school because they lacked legal status and documents proving physical presence.[16] These exclusions violated the protections in *Plyler v. Doe*, the Supreme Court decision that guarantees access to K–12 schooling to all children, irrespective of their immigration status.

Juan's mother, Julia, described their initial interactions with staff at their neighborhood high school as negative and discriminatory. Juan was initially placed in the wrong grade. He was then encouraged to leave by one of his teachers because he was not the "right age" for high school. The teacher had assumed Juan was nineteen instead of his actual age of sixteen. Julia told me that this deeply pained Juan, "He would come home and cry, he couldn't sleep or eat. He would tell me, 'Mami, what am I going to do about my studies? Nobody is supporting me.' He would ask questions and get no information. . . . That was until I went to the teacher and I told her, 'That's it! He can either be here or not. But the attitude that you all have here is rude, discriminatory, and you are making my boy sick.'" Julia said that, after she confronted her, the teacher admitted that she had never checked Juan's paperwork and instead just assumed that he did not belong in high school.

Julia felt empowered to advocate on her son's behalf, which was certainly not true for other undocumented parents and relatives of unaccompanied minors. These caretakers usually did not have experience with high schools. If they had other children in Los Angeles, they were almost always considerably younger, born in the United States, and attending more inclusionary elementary schools. Having a mother who was a strong advocate would prove indispensable for Juan's access to, and ultimate integration in, his high school. Julia was well aware that nobody would have helped Juan had she been, as she said, "a careless mother." Julia eventually found an ally in a Salvadoran counselor who helped Juan change grades so he would have time to get enough credits to graduate and choose a lesson plan that he would excel in. As has been found in prior literature on 1.5 generation immigrant youths' K–12 education in the United States, the presence of supportive school counselors and teachers was also key to help unaccompanied minors integrate in their schools, feel welcomed, learn English, understand class materials, and complete their education.[17] Many unaccompanied minors told me that their English-Spanish bilingual teachers and teaching assistants were key figures who had supported them in this sense. In sum, in addition to his smarts, Juan had key resources in the United States, which enabled him to succeed and that other unaccompanied minors often lack: a case manager and mother who advocated on his behalf and an ally among school staff.

Juan also brought the academic skills necessary to succeed in school with him from El Salvador. Before migrating, Juan had nearly finished his *bachiller*, the equivalent of a high school degree. This was not the case for many other unaccompanied minors, whose schooling in El Salvador, Guatemala, and Honduras had been interrupted by violence. Neighborhood commutes to school and even schools themselves could expose youths to dangerous interactions with gang members. These risks often caused youths to drop out of school months, or even years, prior to their migration. Others had dropped out of school at a young age to work and help support their families. For indigenous youths who arrived in the United States speaking no English, and sometimes no Spanish either, catching up was particularly difficult, in the context of limited support. Unaccompanied minors who lacked Juan's academic skills and resources often had little to do in high school except attend English language courses for newcomers, which do not count as credit toward high school completion. Treated in discriminatory ways similar to other Latinx youths in the Los Angeles Unified School District, unaccompanied minors who accumulated little progress toward the high school degree at age eighteen were often pushed out of school by administrators who had an interest in keeping graduation rates high, due to concerns about funding.[18] Other times, youths were pushed out at age eighteen for no apparent reason, even if they were doing well. Sadly, I came across push-outs happening all too often over the course of my fieldwork.

PREVENTING HIGH SCHOOL PUSH-OUTS: RIGHTS EDUCATION WORK WITH UNACCOMPANIED MINORS

In informal conversations and formal interviews with case managers and attorneys, we often discussed how schools were imposing additional barriers on unaccompanied minors' access to education and violating their rights by pushing them out at age eighteen. Under California law, if youths enroll in public high school before eighteen, they have the right to stay to finish their degrees until age twenty-one. Case managers felt particularly strongly about educating youths about their rights in school, and they shared this information with all the clients they met. They thus played a role in the legal socialization of unaccompanied minors. During one meeting, a case manager thus counseled a fifteen-year-old client and her mother:

> "You're still a bit young but I want to tell you this because I want you to know what your rights are. You have the right to stay in high school until you turn twenty-one. Sometimes schools tell students that they have to leave when they turn eighteen. In fact, it happened to one of our clients just this morning. This is against the law. I want you to know that you do have rights here in the United States. There are certain basic rights that you have, and it doesn't matter that you don't have papers." Sounding slightly surprised to hear this, the client's mother replied, "Oh, good, thank you."

Sometimes, we were able to see the positive impact of this rights-education work. When his high school principal threatened to kick out eighteen-year-old Antonio from El Salvador, he demonstrated his knowledge of his rights and defended himself. The principal wanted to kick Antonio out as a punishment after a school official had mistakenly reported him, instead of another boy with a similar-sounding last name, for a minor violation of school rules about parking. Tellingly, this would have been an extraordinarily punitive response to a minor act of noncompliance even if Antonio truly had been responsible. Many unaccompanied minors, in particular boys, were criminalized in such ways by staff and administrators in the high schools they attended in Los Angeles. That day, Antonio called the case manager to report what had happened. He recounted how the principal responded when he mentioned his right to stay in school: "He said to me, 'Your attorneys might have their rules, but we have our own rules at school. You are over eighteen, so we are giving you the privilege to stay in school. If you mess up, we will kick you out. We have done it before to a kid who was just two weeks shy of graduating.'"

After this phone call, the case manager was angered by the principal's treatment of Antonio, and she was brooding for the remainder of the afternoon. She expressed her frustration, noting that schools were supposed to be helping her clients but instead they were making it impossible for them to get an education. She told Antonio's attorney what had happened. The attorney was impressed that Antonio had claimed his rights and exclaimed, "Good for him!" To cheer her up, I added, "This really speaks to the rights-education work that you are doing here." With these encouraging words, we managed to bring the smile back to the case manager's face. The next day, she went to school with Antonio and intervened with the principal to defend him. Antonio had changed several households, living with different family members in the United States, and he did not have another supportive adult figure who would advocate on his behalf. The case manager's support would have a lasting impact: when I spoke to Antonio two years later, he proudly reported that he had completed his high school degree.

When unaccompanied minors learned about their rights from brokers in nonprofit organizations, they could feel more empowered to defend themselves or ask for help. When youths lacked this support, they were more vulnerable to being pushed out of school and otherwise denied resources. For example, Yesenia, whom we met in chapter 3, was just a couple of classes shy of graduating at age eighteen when her high school counselor told her to switch to an adult school. Yesenia had done well in high school, and she wanted to go to college to study medicine. Her parents supported her goals. Neither Yesenia nor her mother thought to protest because they were unaware of their rights in the public education system. Yesenia's case had been prepared by a low-bono organization with high caseloads that did not offer case management services. Yesenia struggled with the transition to adult school and lamented that she would have more quickly and easily finished her degree had she stayed in high school.

For these young immigrants who arrive in the United States during a liminal stage in the life cycle, between childhood and adulthood, and on the verge of aging out of eligibility for limited sources of state support (age nineteen for Medi-Cal; age eighteen for enrollment in high school), promptly accessing government resources and services is crucial. The case managers working in the legal clinics that prepare immigration cases can provide unaccompanied minors and their families with indispensable information to be able to do so. Just like legal brokers worked as intermediaries between youths and the immigration bureaucracy, case managers worked as intermediaries who helped youths navigate other state systems that support different dimensions of their incorporation in the United States beyond obtaining legal status.

YOUTHS' EXPERIENCES OF FAMILY REUNIFICATION: NAVIGATING LOVE AND CONFLICT

In addition to their brokerage vis-à-vis state institutions and private donors, another challenging task that case managers took on was to mediate conflict between youths and their families. One case manager who did not have a background in social work commented on feeling unprepared for this, "We're not trained for this! At least if we were family therapists, it would still be hard, but we would have more tools and skills to work with." With limited training, case managers did their best to manage these situations, usually by taking the side of the youth. They particularly struggled with those family member sponsors whom they perceived to be "unreasonable" because they did not help them support youths. Another case manager remarked on her frustrations with the stepmother of a nineteen-year-old from El Salvador, venting to me characteristically, "I found a place for the kid to do therapy near their house, and now [the step-mother] says she doesn't want to take him there because it's too close to her house. She doesn't want to be seen there because of the stigma associated with getting mental health services in *those types* of places."

This young man had asked the case manager for help getting therapy after he came out as gay to his attorney, unbeknownst to his stepmother. Even though this nineteen-year-old was, legally speaking, an adult, his stepmother made the case manager's work more challenging, as she positioned herself as an unwanted and uncooperative intermediary rather than allowing them to interact directly. The case manager eventually conceded to the "unreasonable" stepmother and spent more time finding a place where he could do therapy farther away from their house. Case managers preferred to interact with youths directly, partly because this usually made their jobs easier, but also because they were trying to help youths take ownership over their lives and make decisions independently from their caretakers. These types of empowering strategies and adult-like expectations, of course, directly contradicted other messages that case managers directed at youths, which instead incentivized them to be as childlike as possible, once again reflecting the mixed expectations that unaccompanied minors face in the contradictory context of reception.

Case managers characterized sponsors as "bad" when they believed that they were not caring for youths well enough. Cristina's aunt was characterized as a "bad" caretaker, even before she left her alone to return to El Salvador. The aunt had been very involved in her niece's case, but she was also perceived as unduly harsh and controlling. She once reprimanded Cristina several times in front of the case manager, saying, "She doesn't listen in school, she doesn't do what she is told." The case manager intervened to tell the aunt to take it easy on Cristina and to let them speak alone so Cristina would feel comfortable expressing herself. It is telling that the case manager went from defending Cristina to being similarly frustrated by her behavior after her aunt left. Without her aunt present during the meeting that day, Cristina went from silent to very talkative, telling us all about her life, and reporting in a matter-of-fact way on all of the rules she had been taught since she arrived in the United States: "The [ORR] social worker explained the rules of this country. That I need to go to court and respect my elders. That I should listen to my attorney. . . . My aunt also explained the rules to me. She said I shouldn't dress, like sexy, that I shouldn't be a flirt, that I shouldn't wear makeup, that I should only wear long skirts. Now, I have to sleep with a long nightgown."

That Cristina rebelled against all these rules and expectations once her aunt left is unsurprising. According to case managers, their clients followed one of two patterns when reacting to exacting rules and control from their caretakers: "They either all-out rebel or overcompensate and follow rules even more than what sponsors expect because they know sponsors owe them nothing. So, they behave like this because they're grateful that sponsors are taking them in." My research suggested that compliance was much more common than rebellion. The feelings of gratitude that the case manager mentioned were particularly common when youths lived with supportive nonparent sponsors. However, sometimes youths felt guilty to receive this support, or they felt out of place in their new homes.

In some cases, youths' family members were the ones who asked attorneys and case managers to help them mediate conflict with youths and provide what could be characterized as a parenting-support function of sorts. Parents and relatives struggled to discipline recently arrived teenagers and to navigate new living arrangements that disrupted established family dynamics. As we saw in chapter 3, family members who served as youths' ORR-designated sponsors—and who had signed a formal agreement with the state to be responsible for them—were concerned about youths getting in trouble. They feared that this could not only put the youth in danger but also affect the broader household, which usually had one or more undocumented members. While case managers might intervene in these circumstances by telling youths to listen to their caretakers, they usually made it clear that "they are our clients, so we are going to meet with them alone, to understand their point of view." They thus positioned themselves as youths' allies in these delicate family reunification dynamics.

Not all unaccompanied minors could rely on case managers to mediate the conflict that could arise during family reunification. These youths had to navigate these challenges on their own. The outcome of these struggles was important since family is a key institution that mediates immigrant incorporation. Once released from ORR custody, unaccompanied minors entered two types of families, each of which presented different dynamics. Some reunified with one or both of their parents, most often their mothers, from whom they had usually been separated for ten or more years. Others reunified with other family members, whom youths had typically never met or barely knew. These relatives were aunts, uncles, cousins, and older siblings who sometimes had children of their own to care for, both in the United States and in their home countries. Youths living in both types of families recounted having positive and negative experiences in their new homes but, overall, youths reunifying with nonparent sponsors reported more conflict than youths reunifying with parents.

Family reunification experiences were also gendered: boys were more likely than girls to report conflict with their families in the United States. After experiencing conflict or lack of support, youths sometimes left the homes of their sponsors. This was more common when youths lived with nonparent caretakers. Out of the forty-five youths I interviewed, thirteen had left their sponsors' homes, ten of whom were boys (Table 7). This

Table 7   Coming of age and family experiences in the United States by gender

Experiences in the United States	Male (n = 25)	Female (n = 20)
Unaccompanied minor is a parent (has US citizen child)	2	3
Falling out with nonparent sponsor—youth leaves home	10	0
Falling out with parent sponsor—youth leaves home	0	3
Reports conflict with family	12	4
Reports support in family	16	18
Working	11	2
Studying (high school)	8	16
Both working and studying	6	0
Neither working nor studying	0	2

SOURCE: Formal interviews (n = 45).

pattern can be understood in terms of traditional gender norms that tie females more closely to the family than males.[19]

Boys expressed two somewhat contradictory motivations for leaving their family-member sponsors' homes. Sometimes, they resented the control their relatives wanted to exercise over their lives, reflecting their desire to feel like adults and be independent. Other times, however, their motivations reflected a childlike desire for dependency. They had expected the adults in their lives to financially provide for them once they arrived in the United States. When their relatives were unable to do so, this made youths feel abandoned. These contradictory feelings, which some boys felt concurrently, reflect how youths experience the liminal position they inhabit in the United States, suspended between childhood and adulthood.

After experiencing a falling-out with their caretakers, five of the boys whom I interviewed had moved into a youth shelter that housed immigrant minors in Los Angeles. They were all indigenous and hailed from Guatemala, where they lived with both parents, and they had left due to a combination of violence and poverty. As the first of their nuclear families to migrate to the United States, they had reunified with a family member who had initially agreed to support them. However, after their release from ORR, these family members had told the youths that they would need to work to support themselves. These youths never showed up for their hearings in immigration court. Some feared they would be deported if they showed up without an attorney, and they did not have money to pay for one. For others, their sponsors had either never received or had never given them the notice with the time and date of their hearings. When they entered the care of the youth shelter, a space they found through their peer networks, these youths started going to school again and were connected to legal aid organizations that, when possible, reopened their cases to help them apply for relief.

Felipe was one of them. He had come to the United States with hopes of going to school. He moved in with an uncle he barely knew. Felipe was disappointed to discover that, despite what his uncle had told ORR, he could in fact not support him because he was already providing for his own children in Guatemala. Felipe and his uncle shared a one-bedroom apartment in Los Angeles with four other immigrants, taking turns to sleep and shower. Paying rent, expenses, and the $7,000 debt he owed for his journey was difficult for Felipe since the only work he was able to find was as a day laborer, sporadically picking up jobs outside of Home Depot. Employers did not want to hire this diminutive fifteen-year-old who seemed "too small to work" in physically taxing manual labor. Young and undocumented, Felipe worked only about two or three times a week, making nine dollars an hour on average. He eventually left the apartment he shared with his uncle. He moved around the state, working various exploitative jobs and facing housing insecurity, until he found the youth shelter. There, he was able to access resources to support his education and pursue his immigration case. When I met him at age twenty-one, Felipe was sharing an apartment with other immigrants and was about to graduate from high school. He had learned English and had his work permit, which allowed him to find a better-paying and more stable job in a Beverly Hills restaurant.

Finding affordable housing in an expensive city like Los Angeles was a common challenge for unaccompanied minors who could not rely on family. Case managers often intervened to prevent or address homelessness. Yet finding a shelter for homeless youths over age eighteen—who did not qualify for minors' shelters like the one that had taken in Felipe—was especially complex. The most important challenge in getting a bed in a long-term shelter was that it was a requirement for youths to either be working or actively searching for work. This disqualified SIJS applicants, who could not legally work while their cases were pending. In this way, a humanitarian provision meant to protect children instead exacerbated

unaccompanied minors' vulnerabilities, increasing their risk of homelessness and undermining their ability to meet their basic needs.

Only three of the girls I interviewed left the homes of their sponsors
after a falling out. One of them was Lilian who was pregnant when she
migrated from El Salvador to the United States at age seventeen. She reunified with her mother, from whom she had been separated for fourteen
years. Lilian had great hopes for her relationship with her mother, who
had promised to support her. However, once she arrived in Los Angeles,
Lilian felt excluded when she discovered that her mother had made a
new life for herself, with a partner and stepdaughter. Lilian felt that her
mother preferred to spend time with her new family rather than with her.
The night before her asylum interview, Lilian had a fight with her mother,
who kicked her out. Lilian was distressed and spent a few days sleeping
on a friend's couch, missing her asylum interview. Her attorney had to file
a formal request for the interview to be rescheduled, explaining what had
happened. If Lilian had not been represented, she likely would have been
ordered deported after missing her interview at the asylum office.

When I interviewed her, Lilian was living with her child and older
brother. She had since tried to make amends with her mother, who helped
her sometimes, watching her baby while she worked. Yet the way Lilian
spoke of her relationship with her mother conveyed a raw pain. She felt
that they would never really overcome their estrangement. Lilian said that
she wanted to win her asylum case so that she would not be separated
from her own daughter, who was born in the United States. Lilian did not
want her daughter to grow up without her mother like she had, paying
a steep personal price for the US immigration policies that keep Central
American families apart. Months later, I received the happy news that Lilian had indeed won her asylum case. She could look forward to the safe
future alongside her daughter that she needed and desired.

Notably, while many youths described feelings of abandonment,
betrayal, and estrangement, like those expressed by Lilian and Felipe,
youths who had a falling out and left the homes of family members on
bad terms were a minority. When asked the question "Who helped you
most since you arrived in the United States?" many youths mentioned
their parents and other relatives. Most families stuck together, overcoming conflict, and providing important support. Youths who reunified with
their parents after years apart described emotional first encounters at

the airport where they were flown in and dropped off by ORR staff. After an initial "honeymoon phase,"[20] families went through a transition period characterized by conflict or a lack of closeness. Youths and parents tried to overcome these challenges over time, a process they characterized as *"retomar la confianza"* (taking back the trust). For parents, this sometimes meant taking control of "rebellious teenagers." This was how Marcela described her son Jesus, whom we met in chapter 3. When I interviewed this mother-son pair together, Marcela looked at Jesus both reproachingly and tenderly, while she vented to me, as mothers often did:

> It was hard because he was spoiled, and he misbehaved. He went out with his friends and didn't come home. I worried that something might have happened to him. . . . He screamed at me. He told me that I wasn't his mom, just to make me suffer. He told me all about the hardships that he went through [in Honduras] because of me. He doesn't know how much I suffered here too. But now, he behaves. I have been scolding him, "Don't do this, don't do that." It's really hard for a single mom having a son that's already grown up, instead of having him since he is little.

During the interview, Jesus shared his perspective as well. I asked him why he had feelings of resentment toward this mother. With a soft tone that conveyed the reconciliation that had taken place since those turbulent early times, he explained, "I wasn't used to being with her. I was used to doing my own thing, by myself. In Honduras, we're more independent, more self-reliant. The government doesn't help you there for anything. You just have to fight however you can." Jesus thus linked the protection he received from his mother with the protection he received from the US government as a de jure refugee. He aptly characterized this protection as intrinsically paired with a measure of control and an expectation for his childlike dependency by contrasting it to his independence—albeit a perilous one—and the lack of state protection in Honduras.

For families, "taking back the trust" also meant spending time together and doing fun activities. Jesus and Marcela went on excursions to the beach and local parks. Jesus behaved not only like a "rebellious teenager" with his mother but also in a childlike way. Mother and son slept in the same bed in their small studio apartment, and Jesus liked it when Marcela stroked his hair to help him fall asleep. This loving ritual was a means for the two of them to catch up for lost time and become closer. Marcela had not gotten the chance to mother Jesus affectionately since she left Honduras when he was just a toddler. To "take back the trust," youths and their parents also spent time talking, not just about their daily lives, but also about the difficulties they had each endured during their time apart. These conversations were painful but brought many closer together. For example, a mother who migrated to flee an abusive relationship with her children's father told me that having a conversation about this with her children, who had joined her in the United States and were now old enough to know, had finally helped them understand why she left them behind. She believed that these conversations had helped her children become less resentful of her and overcome their feelings of abandonment.

Most parents and relatives provided love and emotional support to the newly arrived youths in their care. Some provided material support so youths could attend school full time. Mobilizing their migrant networks, other family members helped youths find jobs, recommending them to their employers in restaurants, construction work, factories, shops, and fast-food chains. Parents and relatives, who had usually lived in the United States for ten to fifteen years, also served as brokers vis-à-vis receiving country institutions, enrolling youths in school, taking them to seek health care, helping them find attorneys, covering their legal expenses, and accompanying them to appointments in legal clinics, immigration court, and the asylum office. Yet their undocumented status hampered family members' ability to serve as brokers vis-à-vis the state because living in the shadows meant many had limited knowledge of state systems. During the Trump years, undocumented adults also avoided this role as spaces previously assumed to be safe acquired a frightening new quality as sites of potential apprehension and deportation. Family is a crucial social institution that mediates immigrant incorporation. Youths who lived in supportive homes had resources that better positioned them to overcome the challenges they faced as they adapted to their new lives.

TRULY UNACCOMPANIED MINORS
IN THE CONTINUED CARE OF THE STATE

Unaccompanied minors are especially reliant on their families because, despite the fact that they are a formally recognized vulnerable group, they benefit from limited state support. Notably, even when youths win their asylum cases, they do not qualify for integration support services like those that the state provides to individuals admitted from refugee camps through the resettlement process.[21] The only exceptions to this rule were unaccompanied minors placed in long-term foster-care arrangements, like Fernando, whom we met in chapter 3. By definition, youths are placed in foster care if they cannot rely on family. They instead benefit from state support—access to free legal representation and housing—at least until age eighteen. In addition, these youths could qualify for a program called Unaccompanied Refugee Minors (URM) that allowed them to continue living with their foster families until age twenty-one. Youths qualified for URM if, before age eighteen, they either won their asylum cases or had an approved SIJS order.

The stated goal of the URM program is to ease the transition to adulthood and foster the independence of unaccompanied minors who are completely on their own by providing them with support beyond the usual eligibility cut-off age of eighteen. The URM program provides support to help youths continue their education, as well as to help them find jobs. However, SIJS applicants could not legally work and hence could not benefit from the latter services.[22] The prohibition on work for SIJS applicants imposed by the immigration bureaucracy was not only at odds with youths' goals of independence but also with the mission of the URM program: to promote the integration of refugees in US society by fostering economic self-sufficiency. This discrepancy again reflects the contradictory mandates of the different state agencies that unaccompanied minors navigate in the bureaucratic maze that awaits them in the United States.

Fernando qualified for URM because his SIJS order had been approved. Work-oriented youths like him faced a difficult decision upon turning eighteen: they could choose to stay in foster care with the URM program and not work, or they could opt out of URM to live on their own. If they chose to leave, this meant losing access to housing and assistance. Yet it also meant gaining independence and, effectively, the ability to work in the informal economy, like other undocumented immigrants. Youths who found themselves in Fernando's situation were made to choose between two starkly different situations: a precarious independence as young adults in legal limbo, with no support from state or family, or a prolonged and imposed childhood, accompanied by contradictory state support. Fernando wanted to work and had a very different view than his foster mother about what an appropriate coming-of-age looked like:

> She would tell me that if I didn't study, I would be a nobody here. You know what I think? You don't have to study to get ahead in life. With a job in a kitchen, in construction, wherever, the important thing is that you like the job, and you use your intelligence well. You can't just spend all your money. But, if you work and you save, and you help your family in your country, and you help yourself, I think that means you are making something of your life.

Fernando chose to leave foster care at age eighteen to "get ahead in life" on his own terms. He first worked in construction, but this work was too sporadic for him to support himself and send money home. Without a work permit, finding a better job took Fernando a whole year. An older immigrant whom Fernando befriended eventually helped him find housing and a new job in a restaurant working full-time as a chef's assistant. Fernando was nineteen and just starting his new job when I interviewed him. He felt that this work opportunity reflected his positive trajectory. He was motivated to learn new skills in the restaurant and excited to make more money, which would allow him to send more remittances to his mother in Guatemala. Fernando said that she had worked her whole life to provide for him, shouldering a significant burden as a single parent. It was now his turn, as a young adult, to work and provide for her. Fernando had felt stuck while he was in state custody for three years, oppressed by both the legal prohibition on work and the normative expectations to study that his foster mother transmitted to him. Despite his precarious legal and social condition, Fernando felt that his life was finally moving forward since he left foster care.

GENDERED COMING-OF-AGE TRAJECTORIES THROUGH SCHOOL OR WORK

When they arrive in the United States, Central American unaccompanied minors find a place of refuge that provides some respite, at least in the short term, from the life-threatening danger they fled. Yet, since they find themselves in legal limbo with limited state support, unaccompanied minors continue to face many hurdles to pursue a full social existence in their new homes. Based on their pre-migration goals and aspirations, some youths were work-oriented like Fernando, and others school-oriented like Juan. Still others changed their minds once they arrived in the United States, their plans shifting from school to work or vice-versa due to outside pressures, newfound individual aspirations, or a combination of the two. Sadly, what all youths had in common was that they faced challenges in pursuing either of their desired coming-of-age trajectories. Their goals and aspirations were often at odds with the path that they were expected or allowed to pursue as young immigrants in the United States. Youths who wanted to work faced compulsory education laws, which in California apply until age eighteen, as well as normative pressures to study and obstacles obtaining work permits. Youths who aspired to study, on the other hand, encountered countless obstacles in school and often lacked the resources and support they needed to succeed.

Faced with competing pressures and expectations in the contradictory context of reception, the coming-of-age pathways that Central American unaccompanied minors chose to pursue in the United States were gendered (Table 7). Boys were more likely to privilege work over school sooner. They often sought out work with the goal of becoming independent from adult caretakers, both in the United States and in their home countries. Conversely, girls were more likely to conform to US middle-class expectations and prioritize school over work for longer, as well as to reside with family for longer, even after entering the workforce. Yet, for the reasons described above, completing high school could be a serious challenge even for youths who wanted to prioritize their education. Heading to college—the quintessential rite of passage for young people in the United States who increasingly delay other life-course transitions, like work or starting a family—was simply unattainable for the vast majority of unaccompanied minors.

The few who did make it to college all had an approved asylum case, like Juan. When I last spoke to Juan, he had recently moved out of his mother's home to live on campus in student dorms. Juan was happy and satisfied. He was enthusiastic about his classes and filled with optimism for the future. Yet he also conveyed the burden that he felt due to his delayed coming-of-age and transition to university, which was postponed until he won his asylum case.

JUAN: I want to continue to better myself and soak up all the knowledge I can. After my BA, I hope to go to law school. Well, either that or grad school. I still need a bit of time to decide, even though I know I'm running out of time. I want to share my experience and propose solutions to migration issues since I experienced them firsthand.

CHIARA: What do you mean when you say you are running out of time?

JUAN: Sometimes I feel that way because I feel like I don't have a lot of experience yet with all this [college]. So, it makes me think that I'm running out of time. Of course, I do know that I still have time, and that's why I haven't completely decided on a career yet. But, yeah, I feel old. I'm almost twenty-one. Even so, I think it will be a beautiful experience here at [name of University], it's already been better than I expected.

Juan simultaneously felt that he was lacking in experience and "old." Not only was he starting college later than most of his US-born classmates, but he also felt that his transition to adulthood had been considerably delayed by his migration to the United States. In El Salvador, he had been just months shy of graduating from his *bachiller* and enrolling in college, when he was forced to drop everything and flee. A de facto refugee, Juan was nonetheless more than the persecution he suffered. He was an ambitious young man with the goals of the best and brightest, the very immigrants the United States purports to want to attract. Juan essentially felt as if he had been robbed of the years it took him to get back on track in the United States and complete high school, starting largely from scratch. He felt that he lost the years when his asylum application was pending, during which he was unable to go to college and worked at a fast-food chain instead. Despite all his capability and ambition, it was only when he was recognized as a de jure refugee, and hence granted legal status, that Juan was able to pursue his dreams and aspirations.

Other similarly academically gifted unaccompanied minors with college-going aspirations had been thwarted due to their denied or unresolved asylum cases. Elena, an unaccompanied minor from Honduras who fled her country, like Juan, at age sixteen, also had dreams of going to college. Elena excelled in high school, academically and socially: she had a high GPA, participated in several extracurriculars, and had a leadership role in student organizations. She even was prom queen during her senior year, the prototypically American coming-of-age experience of the movies. Elena applied, and got into, two University of California campuses, where she would have been the first in her family to attend college. Yet, she was in legal limbo just like Juan when the time came to apply for federal aid. Tuition was too expensive even with the partial scholarship that she won. While her family and high school counselor had been supportive, they lacked the tools to help her. Elena got discouraged and ended up renouncing her spot. She did not feel like she could move out of her mother's home and away from Los Angeles, pay for tuition and support herself independently, and still have time to enjoy spending with family whom she had missed so much during so many years of separation.

Instead, Elena took a job at a meatpacking plant, where she was still working nearly two years later when I spoke to her again. In the meantime, her asylum case had been approved, but she had since abandoned her dreams of college. At the meatpacking plant, Elena had a stable—if unpleasant and dangerous—job with a relatively good salary and benefits. She had quickly advanced to a supervisory role. Elena still lived with her family; she helped pay household expenses and enjoyed the company of her siblings and mother. She had enough disposable income to enjoy the free time that she spent with her boyfriend. In sum, as a de jure refugee, Elena was happy and living a secure life, even if not entirely serene. Unlike her, her mother was still undocumented, as were two of her siblings, de facto refugees who had escaped from Honduras before her. Elena's siblings had hired someone they thought was an immigration attorney but was likely a *notario*. This person took their money and disappeared without ever filing their asylum applications.

Legal status mattered both for access to higher education and work. Stable legal status was indispensable for most unaccompanied minors who wished to pursue higher education because of the timing of their arrival and late entry in high school. For work, having a work permit was already very beneficial. Like adults, asylum-seeking youths are also granted work permits 180 days after applying for asylum while their cases are pending.[23] With work permits, youths could obtain better paying and more stable jobs. They had opportunities for job mobility, promotions, and raises. In terms of job prospects, asylum seekers were faring better than SIJS applicants. For example, Antonio—the youth who stood up for his rights and finished high school—was still waiting for his SIJS case to be resolved so he could get his green card at age twenty, over three years after he applied. His SIJS order had been approved by the courts, but he was one of many youths stuck in the SIJS backlog, and hence, he could not legally work (see chapter 5).

Antonio did not aspire to go to college and needed to work to support himself because he could not rely on his family. When we last spoke, he was working in a factory that was willing to hire him without papers, where he was paid less than minimum wage. He had started out working nights at the factory while still in high school after his cousin recommended him two years earlier. Antonio said that the job was tedious and the hours extremely long, but working was indispensable for his independence and so he could help support his brother who had long been unemployed due to an injury. While his life-course transitions inched forward even in his liminal state—he was in the workforce, supporting himself and his family—Antonio reflected that life felt precarious as he waited to hear back from USCIS on the final result of his SIJS case:

> Waiting makes me anxious. It's like, I feel nervous just thinking, what will they decide? Am I going to get my residence or not? You know, it still feels like a bit of a mystery. I want to know if it's yes or no. After everything I've been through here, I feel like I deserve it, but I think that, ultimately, it might just be a matter of luck. [My lawyer] gives me reason to feel positive, she thinks that 100 percent I will get it because she always tells me, "When you get your residence, you can do this, and go there," but I don't know, I just don't know if I'll have it someday.

Work permits positioned unaccompanied minors more favorably than Antonio in the workforce. Yet merely having a work permit could not fully appease the anxiety and fears about the future that he expressed. The emotional stability of approved asylees and permanent residents was palpable in the way they spoke. They didn't have to worry about renewing work permits and potentially falling out of employable status due to bureaucratic delays. Most importantly, they could imagine a long-term future in the United States. They could dream about and take steps toward continuing their transitions to adulthood.

THE DUAL LIMINALITY OF UNACCOMPANIED MINORS COMING OF AGE IN THE UNITED STATES

This chapter has shown how the legal process spills over to affect unaccompanied minors' lives and transitions to adulthood as they adapt to their new homes. In the face of limited state support, legal clinic staff and family members help ease some of the "cumulative disadvantages" that unaccompanied minors face compared to other cohorts of immigrant children.[24] Unaccompanied minors inhabit a dual liminal state: simultaneously in legal limbo and in limbo between childhood and adulthood. Aware of the liminal status their clients occupy in a context characterized by limited compassion, case managers strategically counseled youths to behave in ways that signaled childlike innocence so they would be seen as deserving of aid and support. In these ways, case managers helped individual youths demonstrate humanitarian capital to elicit the compassion of donors and accrue resources to complement state support, which could benefit them and other clients of the legal clinic. However, case managers thus inevitably also reproduced normative expectations that infantilize youths and negatively sanction behaviors perceived as deviant or too adult-like. To protect youths from immigration enforcement and punitive policing, case managers educated them about their legal obligations and the behaviors expected of them. Yet these warnings also served to make youths acutely aware of the gaze of the state in their everyday lives.

While intermediation of the contradictory context of reception—characterized by exclusion and protection—has these adverse effects, case managers also carry out important work as brokers. They help youths overcome challenges in state systems, like school and subsidized health care, which their undocumented family members have limited knowledge about. For unaccompanied minors unable to receive these extra-legal support services, since many organizations do not provide them, family is the primary source of support as they incorporate in the United States. Recently reunited families had to overcome the lack of familiarity, resentment, and conflict that resulted from prolonged periods of separation imposed on them by US immigration policy, which keeps immigrant families apart and inflicts legal violence on them. In some cases, this was impossible. Youths were left to fend for themselves in an especially precarious situation, either in youth shelters, strict foster care facilities, or at risk of homelessness. In most cases, however, families stuck together and provided emotional and material support to youths, helping them finish school or find work. While unaccompanied minors demonstrated resilience, and some found ways to pursue their desired coming-of-age goals despite the high odds stacked against them, it was only with legal status that these youths could pursue a full social existence and find lasting refuge in their new homes.

7 Beyond Precarious Protections

LESSONS FOR HUMANE IMMIGRATION REFORM

This book has documented the experiences and perspectives of Central American unaccompanied minors and their immigration attorneys as they pursue applications for refugee status in the US asylum process. I examined how *exclusionary* immigration control laws and legal violence interact with asylum and other policies that have a humanitarian intent: to *protect* vulnerable immigrants by granting them exemptions from enforcement or incremental access to legal status. As a formally recognized vulnerable group, unaccompanied minors benefit from protections in US law that position them comparatively more favorably than adults. These protective policies provide some openings for legal brokers to help youths seek inclusion and claim rights vis-à-vis the receiving state. Yet existing protections are a precarious fix in light of a broader immigration system focused on dehumanizing enforcement practices and an asylum institution that was created with the experiences of adults in mind.

I have argued that the commonsense understanding of asylum as a form of protection for those who fear returning to their homes is a far cry from how asylum law works in practice when applied to the claims of children and youths. Central American unaccompanied minors who escape life-threatening violence are de facto refugees. Yet narrowly interpreted

US asylum law often fails to recognize their experiences, ignoring how age shapes exposure to violence and migration decision-making. Without the help of legal brokers, youths cannot successfully navigate a formalistic asylum system that "does not make common sense." This reality leaves too many vulnerable young people at risk of deportation back to danger in their home countries.

In this final chapter, I synthesize the twofold contributions of this study to scholarly research on (1) the effects of the law on immigrants' lives and (2) lawyering at the intersection of citizenship and humanitarianism. This case study also provides lessons for US immigration reform, and I end the chapter with concrete suggestions for policy change.

THE EFFECTS OF THE LAW ON MIGRANTS' LIVES: RETHINKING THEORIES OF YOUTH MIGRATION

Today's migration of Central American unaccompanied minors requires a rethinking of theories of independent youth migration as a rite of passage to adulthood. These past theories ignored the role of the state and the effects of the law in shaping youth migration and settlement. Unlike past cohorts of teenagers who migrated alone to seek adventure, employment, and emancipation from adult control, migration is not a linear process of transition to adulthood for unaccompanied minors.[1] Three characteristics distinguish them from their "adventurous" peers. First, these youths migrate from countries where they face life-threatening violence. Second, high-stakes asylum applications dominate their settlement process, determining whether they will be allowed to stay for the long term, with legal status, in the country that provided them temporary refuge from harm. Third, unlike male-dominated past flows, about one-third of unaccompanied minors arriving in the United States today are female.

El Salvador, Guatemala, and Honduras are dangerous places in which to grow up, where suffering is distributed unequally among the most disadvantaged members of society. Structural and interpersonal forms of violence are co-constitutive and patterned in age- and gender-specific ways. Youths who migrate alone are members of Central American transnational families divided by borders who cannot legally reunite because of restrictive US immigration policies. These youths have, most commonly, been raised by single mothers or nonparent relatives. Their caretakers sometimes receive remittances from parents in the United States, but they may neglect to care for youths or become too elderly or ill to do so. Both boys and girls are vulnerable to violence at the hands of caretakers in state contexts where laws protecting victims of domestic violence are seldom enforced. When youths reach adolescence, those who lack supportive caretakers and poor and indigenous youths are especially exposed to victimization at the hands of gangs that commit crimes with impunity, unchecked by local justice systems. The risks related to gang violence are also gendered: boys are more at risk of forced recruitment, while girls are at risk of sexual violence.

These conditions threaten youths' lives and make it impossible for them to envision a future in their home countries. Many experienced their blocked coming of age with acute distress, like Brayan, who spent over a year hiding in Honduras, fearing that his brother in the United States would not be able to help him flee (chapter 2). He coped with self-harm behaviors that left permanent marks on his body in the form of small white scars. Youths like Brayan migrate from Central America to find refuge from harm. Yet, like their "adventurous" peers, through migration, they also seek to pursue the aspirations and desires that are part of becoming an adult. Many migrate to join parents from whom they have long been separated to recover a relationship before it is too late. Some pursue aspirations to work, be independent, and help their families. Others seek to continue their studies so they can pursue careers their working-class parents could never have dreamed of.

In the receiving country, unaccompanied minors inhabit a dual liminal position. As teenagers, they occupy a liminal stage in the life cycle, between childhood and adulthood, and they inch dangerously close to the legal threshold that marks the end of protective minor status at age eighteen. As noncitizens, they are in precarious legal limbo between protected refugee or special juvenile status versus perilous "illegality" and the related high risk of deportation. These two dimensions of liminality interact: to be seen as deserving of compassion, considerations of the child's best interests, refugee recognition, and legal status, youths must be perceived as passive child-victims rather than agentic teenagers or adults. During their applications for humanitarian immigration relief, unaccompanied minors' rites of passage to adulthood are *reversed* discursively, as they are made to associate themselves with infantilizing and victimizing legal frames.

The legal process also spills over to affect the everyday lives of unaccompanied minors. By interacting with legal brokers and state bureaucrats, youths absorb normative messages about how they should behave to seek acceptance and avoid being criminalized as deviant Latinx teenagers, "bad" immigrants, or "bogus" refugees. Youths thus become acutely aware of the pervasive gaze of the state. They react by changing their self-presentation and behaviors beyond their petitions in the immigration bureaucracy. For some unaccompanied minors, particularly boys, the need to be perceived as children, in and beyond the legal process, clashes with their self-understandings. They view themselves as independent young adults, who sometimes worked in their home countries prior to migration to support family, who lived independently in contexts of violence, and who made risky journeys to reach the United States. Even for others, more dependent on family or more focused on school in the home country, arriving in the United States means encountering expectations for protracted childlike behaviors that can make them feel "stuck" in their childhood. Within these infantilizing constraints, unaccompanied minors make gendered coming-of-age decisions. Girls are more likely than boys of the same age to conform to expectations and delay life-course transitions by staying in school and living with family member caretakers for longer.

During the Trump administration, decisions on unaccompanied minors' petitions for asylum and Special Immigrant Juvenile Status (SIJS) were delayed significantly, in many cases, taking over two and over four years, respectively. Prolonged legal limbo yields heightened liminality in life-course transitions. Youths waiting for an answer on their cases live with the specter of potential deportation looming large over their lives. They face added challenges to pursue their desired coming-of-age goals. For SIJS applicants, during the time of this research, these challenges included legal prohibitions on work and marriage while their cases were pending.[2] Without work permits, youths who want to become adults by entering the workforce face obstacles finding work, like Fernando, or are stuck in exploitative jobs, like Antonio (chapter 6); as a result, they are at risk of food insecurity and homelessness.

Prolonged legal limbo can mean giving up on dreams of higher education, the culturally acceptable, middle-class goal for "assimilable" young immigrants. Youths like Elena are often ineligible for the fellowships they need to afford college while their asylum applications are pending; as result, they become reoriented toward work out of necessity (chapter 6). De facto refugee youths whose asylum applications are denied, like Hector (chapters 2 and 3), become acutely aware of their position in the disenfranchised group of those seen as unworthy of protection. Even when they are eligible for asylum appeals or other forms of relief like SIJS, these youths can become distrusting of the legal process and pessimistic about the outcomes of their petitions. They may set aside coming-of-age goals, as they lose hope for safe and stable futures in the United States.

Unaccompanied minors are a cohort of immigrant youths who interact intensively with the immigration bureaucracy and come of age under the gaze of the state. I have shown that it is productive to examine their incorporation experiences through the lens of *legal socialization*. Borrowed from research in criminology, this term refers to the acquisition and internalization of ideas about the law and relationships of authority. This particular socialization process occurs throughout the life course but is especially important during childhood and adolescence. While past migration scholarship has focused on the *acculturation* process—how immigrant children learn English and become culturally similar to their "mainstream" US-born counterparts—going forward, scholars should pay more attention to processes of *legal socialization*.

This lens foregrounds an analysis of the effects of the law on the lives of immigrant children and youths during their settlement in the receiving country. It can therefore be helpful to scholars studying the experiences of various groups of immigrant children and children of immigrants in today's era of heightened enforcement. For example, even the estimated six million US-citizen children who are growing up in mixed-status families are not sheltered from immigration enforcement. Many interact directly or indirectly with the state since their family members are targeted for deportation. Understanding the impacts of exclusionary and protective immigration laws at this formative stage in the life cycle has key implications for how future generations in increasingly diverse societies will perceive their relationship with the state and claim rights and belonging.

TRANSFERABLE CONCEPTS FOR THE STUDY
OF LAWYERING AND THE LAW IN ACTION

Legal brokers play an indispensable role in enabling immigrants to access the rights and protections that the laws on the books promise. Indeed, unaccompanied minors are especially vulnerable to rights violations and legal violence before they obtain legal representation, including when they are processed by Customs and Border Protection (CBP) at the US-Mexico border and during detention in Office of Refugee Resettlement (ORR) facilities. By shadowing legal brokers as they worked with unaccompanied minors released from federal custody and represented them in asylum and SIJS proceedings, I addressed two research questions:

1. How do legal brokers navigate the indeterminate humanitarian legalization process—where cases are assessed one-by-one on a discretionary basis—to obtain favorable outcomes for their clients?

2. Under what conditions is the goal of obtaining legal status for the individual immigrant compatible, or at odds with, broader advocacy goals of expanding narrow humanitarian eligibility categories so that more immigrants can potentially qualify for relief?

To explain how legal brokers help individual unaccompanied minors gain membership rights (refugee or special juvenile status, a path to citizenship) on humanitarian grounds, I advanced the concept of *humanitarian capital*. This is a form of symbolic capital that legal brokers activate as they interview their clients by using their skills and expertise to detect and assign value to lived experiences and narratives of suffering. By assessing humanitarian capital, legal brokers anticipate whether cases are likely to satisfy both formal eligibility criteria and the discretionary elements that inform asylum officers' and immigration judges' decisions about whether to grant cases. By illustrating these mechanisms, this framework highlights how legal brokers strategically maneuver within the constraints of the humanitarian system to manage risk and help their clients obtain legal status. At the same time, by revealing exactly how value is assigned to different experiences in this exercise of translation of human suffering, the humanitarian capital framework also starkly reveals the limitations of legal brokerage and the paradoxes of the humanitarian law in action.

In a US asylum process that rewards the "right" *amount* and *types* of suffering, as opposed to the need to escape life-threatening violence, lawyers and their young clients face multiple, sometimes insurmountable, catch-22 situations. Youths had to flee their home countries at the right time, staying long enough to experience sufficient harm to build humanitarian capital. Of course, the terrible truth is that staying too long could mean succumbing to forced gang recruitment or death. Further, not just any type of suffering yields humanitarian capital: US asylum case law discounts the experiences of youths directly targeted by gangs while rewarding experiences that highlight passive dependency on adults, such as child abuse or harm that results from family ties.

Describing the future harm that youths would face if denied asylum yields another catch-22: countries of origin must be dangerous enough everywhere to make it impossible to safely return. Yet home country risks cannot seem too commonplace because this raises alarm about opening the door to too many similarly situated people. While humanitarian capital can be used to obtain key membership rights, if deployed at the individual level, it can paradoxically backfire at the group level when legal status on humanitarian grounds is treated as a scarce resource to be distributed to few. Of course, as I have already noted, the resource constraints in question are self-imposed and largely imagined, since US immigration law does not establish limits on how many asylum cases may be granted per year. Indeed, there are historical precedents for granting asylum much more broadly, for instance, to Cubans arriving at the US-Mexico border.[3]

When compassion is in scarce supply, I have shown that the humanitarian legalization process has significant emotional costs for young asylum seekers and SIJS applicants. To elicit the information needed to build a "strong" case, legal brokers address their clients through pathologizing questions that make case preparation interviews in legal clinics inherently unpleasant and anxiety provoking. Legal brokers teach their young clients to describe their experiences not as they subjectively understand them but in the language of the law, using narratives more fitting to obtain protection as refugees and abandoned, abused, or neglected children. To build humanitarian capital in a system of state selection that rewards victimhood and infantilizing frames for unaccompanied minors, legal brokers inevitably reproduce the disempowering and retraumatizing nature of humanitarian proceedings. Future interdisciplinary research by social scientists, psychologists, and physicians should further examine the costs of applying for humanitarian relief, asking whether these have long-term consequences for the development of children and the well-being of applicants of all ages. Such findings can inform a broader conversation about whether it is acceptable at all to impose such a process on vulnerable and traumatized individuals seeking protection.

The humanitarian capital concept can be leveraged for future case studies worldwide to explain legal brokerage or bureaucrats' status determination practices vis-à-vis various forms of legal status based on compassion, for example, asylum for applicants of all ages, protections for crime victims, or deportation relief for sick immigrants or for the parents of ill children.[4] The concept is also transferable beyond the realm of immigration and citizenship, for instance, to study how nonprofit organizations make use of the narratives of the individuals they serve to raise funds for their operations and humanitarian projects.

As regards the second research question on the relationship between direct client representation and broader immigration advocacy goals, I identified how client selection models (chapter 4) and the legal and political context (chapter 5) shape constraints on lawyering practices. These factors play a role in incentivizing either conservative legal strategies that reproduce existing categories or creative legal strategies that seek to expand eligibility for relief. Some legal aid organizations choose to represent only clients with the "strongest" cases (perceived as most likely to win), based on the belief that it is better to use scarce resources on those who actually have chances of success instead of wasting them on cases likely to be denied. However, this strategy rests on a faulty assumption: with young asylum seekers in particular, information that shifts the case from being considered "weak" to "strong" usually cannot be gleaned during brief eligibility screenings and only emerges after several meetings. This type of client selection model at the organizational level constrains creative lawyering strategies and incentivizes legal brokers to reproduce existing humanitarian categories since these are used a priori to select clients.

Conversely, other legal-aid organizations approximate universal representation by representing all clients who are eligible (broadly interpreted) for relief who are referred to them or who can hire them for small fees. For asylum, this means that, if youths claim that they fear returning to their home country, this is considered a sufficient reason to legitimately apply. This more inclusive approach to client selection imposes less constraints on creative lawyering strategies. When legal brokers can represent an array of cases that do not necessarily correspond to existing case law, they will be more likely to file applications based on arguments that can potentially expand asylum eligibility. Further, this approach to client selection enables de facto refugees to access the legal aid they need to exercise their right to seek asylum.

By comparing how legal brokers worked with unaccompanied minors during the Obama and Trump administrations, I identified how the legal and political context shapes constraints on lawyering. It is generally true that preparing applications based on narratives that challenge existing asylum case law always comes with risks for individual clients, who are more likely to obtain relief if their cases can be reframed to satisfy existing criteria. Yet the risk calculus that lawyers made on behalf of their clients changed during the Obama and Trump years. Under Obama, particularly after 2015, asylum eligibility pertaining to children became relatively stable and consolidated under the two criteria of child abuse and family membership. In that context, legal brokers had especially strong incentives to stick to existing arguments and conservative legal strategies to maximize chances of success for their clients.

The Trump administration introduced dozens of exclusionary policy changes that undermined access to asylum and SIJS protections. With Matter of A-B- and Matter of L-E-A-, the administration tried to do away even with narrow existing asylum case law. Challenging these policies required immense efforts from organizations involved in impact litigation. Many of these lawsuits were ultimately successful in safeguarding existing protections. While litigation was pending, however, direct representation attorneys had to find new means to mitigate heightened risks of case denial and deportation for their young clients. They reacted by continuing to file cases using the child abuse and family arguments of the Obama years. In doing so, what had been the conservative legal strategies became strategies of resistance to protect the status quo of asylum eligibility against the new wave of exclusion. The volatility of the legal context also created incentives for more creative lawyering strategies. As asylum applications based on all types of arguments became far more risky endeavors, direct representation attorneys experimented with new PSGs and legal arguments that did not correspond to existing case law. The Trump era thus unexpectedly yielded a situation where the direct representation of individual youths was closely in synch with broader advocacy goals of expanding access to protection for more immigrants.

Whether these creative legal strategies, in turn, will actually help expand asylum eligibility remains to be seen. Many of these cases are still pending at the time of this writing, delayed by a combination of the growing backlogs in immigration court and at the asylum office and the effects of COVID-19. The latter led to USCIS and immigration court closures, so that the cases of unaccompanied minors and other immigrants in removal proceedings were largely placed on hold for nearly a year. Upon entering office, the Biden administration ordered the Justice Department to resolve the heightened indeterminacy in the asylum system caused by Trump-era policies. In June 2021, Attorney General Merrick Garland vacated Matter of A-B- and Matter of L-E-A-, thus returning asylum eligibility to the Obama-era status quo.[5] When I last interviewed immigration attorneys in early 2021, they had predicted that this change would take place. They were also cautiously optimistic that new case law would allow for incremental expansion of the refugee definition so that more youths would qualify. They identified the new political context as a favorable time to lobby for improved access to SIJS as well.

DISPELLING THE MYTHS OF THE EXOGENOUS MIGRATION "CRISIS" AND THE "BOGUS" REFUGEE

I hope this book will help dispel two myths that hamper goals of humane immigration reform in the United States. The first is the myth of the "crisis": the idea that unaccompanied minors and asylum seekers arriving at the US-Mexico border represent a new problem, one that is externally produced by violent sending countries. In fact, decades of US foreign and immigration policy have led us to where we are today. The nefarious effects of US intervention have been well documented by scholars of Central America.[6] The United States provided military funding to right-wing regimes persecuting their citizens in El Salvador and Guatemala in the 1980s and destabilized Honduras by using it as a training ground for militias aimed to counter the Sandinistas in neighboring Nicaragua. In the 1990s, the United States incarcerated and then deported gang members to

Central America, introducing US gang culture into the very states it had destabilized, which fail to protect the basic human rights of their citizens.

US immigration policy has also exacerbated the vulnerability of Central American communities on both sides of the border. The historical bias against Central Americans in the US asylum process rooted in Cold War geopolitics has, to some extent, endured to this day, despite advocacy victories. Refugee recognition was denied not only to 98 percent of Guatemalans and Salvadorans in the 1980s, but also to many parents of today's unaccompanied minors, like mothers escaping domestic violence. Both unrecognized de facto refugees and other Central Americans—including those granted Temporary Protected Status on humanitarian grounds, following natural disasters—lack long-term legal status and family reunification rights. By separating Central American families for extended periods of time, US immigration policy places children left behind in sending countries at greater risk of exposure to violence. To bring their children to safety, family members have no option but to pay hefty fees to coyotes, who make dangerous unauthorized journeys to the United States possible.

The public debate needs to shift away from "crisis" management to instead focus on US accountability toward those individuals whom it had a role in displacing and, hence, has a responsibility to protect. In recent scholarship, political theorists have argued that states should grant asylum as a form of reparation for past harms.[7] In the aftermath of the Vietnam war, the US was willing to resettle large numbers of refugees, not only due to opportunistic Cold War geopolitics, but also because the government recognized its *responsibility* in producing the Vietnamese exodus through its military intervention. During the Cold War, granting asylum was a means for the outward condemnation of communist regimes, but this could also be inward looking, serving as an apology. With historical precedents like this in mind, political theorists argue that granting asylum can be a means for the party responsible to acknowledge wrongdoing.

By restoring the refugee-state relationship and granting access to a bundle of rights, including legal status and welfare benefits, asylum can play a compensatory role and redress past harms. Framing asylum as reparation can help gain public support for admitting more refugees because it creates a sense of responsibility, linking the national "us" to a particular refugee flow. Research in social psychology supports the idea that admitting culpability can be received in a positive way if it is framed as a possibility for learning and personal growth. Because the United States has the capacity to host more refugees, as a global superpower and the richest country in the world, and culpability in producing the Central American exodus, it follows that compassion should be treated as a resource in far more abundant supply in our asylum system moving forward.

The second myth that this book has sought to dispel is that of the devious unaccompanied minor and "bogus" refugee who take advantage of protective laws to "cheat" the system. These discourses are dangerous because they delegitimize protections that are the hard-won result of decades of advocacy work. Chapter 3 demonstrated that, before they migrate to the United States, most youths know almost nothing about asylum and US protections for unaccompanied minors. Even children and asylum seekers who know their rights are often unable to protect themselves from rights violations and illegal expulsions at the border, given their unequal power relationship with the state. When admitted, young asylum seekers struggle to understand complex asylum law that seldom coincides with their subjective understandings of why they fled.

Far from being unethical or somehow fraudulent, the lawyering strategies I described in this book are instead indispensable to enable de facto refugee youths to access rights and protections, including de jure refugee status, thus allowing the asylum institution to accomplish its stated goal: to protect those who fear returning to their home countries. These legal strategies help bridge the gap between asylum law and youths' lived experiences of migration. However, in light of an asylum system historically designed with male adults in mind, which does not take into account the best interests of the child, there is only so much that can be accomplished through ingenious lawyering. The protections that already exist for unaccompanied minors in the US asylum process mark a step in the right direction. Yet, as this book has shown, there is still much more work to be done.

HUMANE IMMIGRATION REFORM: LESSONS FROM THE CASE OF UNACCOMPANIED MINORS

In the spirit of the Convention on the Rights of the Child (CRC), protections for unaccompanied minors and other immigrant children should be *supplemental* to a baseline of rights for all immigrants in a more humane

US immigration system, as opposed to what they are today: *exceptions* to the restrictive, exclusionary, and legally violent norm. To achieve this goal, it is indispensable to both eliminate arbitrary forms of discrimination in the US asylum process for applicants of all ages and to strengthen legal protections for children on the move. Of course, any proposed overhaul of the asylum system will be largely meaningless for as long as the United States continues to use Title 42 or any other policy to evade its non-refoulment obligations and expel asylum seekers at the US-Mexico border. While unaccompanied minors, Ukrainians, and some other groups have been exempted, legal battles to end Title 42 are still playing out in the courts as this book goes to press.

To begin, ensuring that all asylum seekers—irrespective of age and mode of entry—have the right to first present their claims at the asylum office and, if denied, to access the full appeals process, would bring the United States into true compliance with international refugee law. As we have seen, the US asylum system discriminates between immigrants who are apprehended at the border and those who are not. Only the latter group is considered deserving of thorough due process. Conversely, except for unaccompanied minors, migrants apprehended at the border must apply for asylum in the adversarial immigration court process. This discrepancy in the treatment of asylum seekers is in line with the broader trend of focusing enforcement efforts at the US-Mexico border so that immigrants who cross the border on foot encounter more obstacles to legalize their status through all available pathways than those who overstay their visas.[8] This disparate treatment is also at odds with the Refugee Convention, which states that individuals who flee their homes should not be punished for crossing borders illegally rather than obtaining valid travel documents. Obtaining a visa to travel to the United States is indeed virtually impossible for poor residents of developing countries because of our immigration policies.

With its new Asylum Processing Rule, the Biden administration intends to make asylum officers responsible for deciding all asylum claims, regardless of the immigrant's mode of entry. This change would relieve pressure on the US immigration courts, where the backlog has reached a record of nearly two million pending cases, and overwhelmed immigration judges decide asylum cases that have life-or-death implications with resources akin to those of traffic court.[9] Asylum officers are extensively trained to apply refugee law, have resources to do independent research to grant individual cases, and they interview asylum seekers in a non-adversarial manner, which is far less retraumatizing for applicants than the trial setting of immigration court.

It is worth noting, however, that the asylum office has its own formidable backlog to tackle: over 470,000 pending cases as of March 2022. Moreover, some aspects of Biden's new rule have garnered criticism from advocates.[10] The application process will be expedited, giving asylum seekers less than forty-five days to prepare themselves for their interviews at the asylum office, a time frame that makes it exceedingly difficult to find legal representation and prepare complex claims. It is too early to examine the impact of the new Asylum Processing Rule, which has been implemented only on a very small scale at the time of this writing.[11] In the meantime, the tug of war between asylum opponents and advocates continues. On the one hand, pending conservative lawsuits could potentially scrap the new rule altogether.[12] On the other, advocates are still pressuring the administration to introduce more protections for asylum seekers in the new rule.

Next, the United States should provide universal legal representation to all immigrants in removal proceedings. A key lesson from this study is that children cannot be expected to prepare highly complex applications for humanitarian relief alone, nor can claimants of any age, for that matter. As chapter 3 demonstrated, when organizations have limited resources available to represent immigrants, case selection biases exacerbate inequalities in access to protection. This creates a dynamic where immigrants either access attorneys largely by chance or where they must compete for the scarce and coveted good of free legal aid. Since those without an attorney will most likely be denied relief, universal legal representation is crucial to ensure that individuals can access the humanitarian protections that already exist in US immigration law.

Further, binding national standards for how to conduct developmentally appropriate, child-sensitive asylum interviews and analyses of asylum cases should also be introduced in immigration court and during the appeals phase. While only asylum officers currently receive training on "child-friendly" interviewing practices and standards (see chapter 5), adjudicators in all agencies that decide asylum cases should receive this training and implement these standards. Research in developmental psychology suggests that individuals only reach cognitive maturity in their early twenties, which has implications for the ability to recall past experiences and tell the causal narratives necessary to win asylum. These findings suggest that developmentally appropriate interviewing accommodations are also needed for youths older than eighteen. Adjudicators in all agencies should consider developmental factors, not just when conducting interviews with young asylum seekers, but also to decide on the outcomes of their asylum cases.

In addition, in a world where children are increasingly crossing international borders to seek asylum alone, US asylum law must evolve to recognize the age-specific dynamics that cause persecution and youth migration today, as well as how age and gender—two key dimensions of social position—interact. I believe that social science research on migration decision-making in contexts of violence, which leverages theories developed in the field of international migration, as I did in chapter 2, can help inform legal developments. One of the lessons from that chapter is that the timing of escape plays out in paradoxical ways to mediate access to refugee status. Families assess and manage risk in the sending country through imperfect strategies, as acts of interpersonal violence can be inflicted suddenly, in ways difficult to predict. Preemptive flight is best for youths' well-being. It reflects the swift actions of loving and protective caretakers rather than irresponsible parents who abandoned their children or put them at risk by allowing them to migrate alone. In the current asylum system, preemptive flight poses challenges if youths have not accumulated *enough* experiences of suffering to allow attorneys to substantiate humanitarian capital. Yet if these youths are denied protection, they may very well risk harm in the future. When in doubt, asylum officers and immigration judges should decide cases to the benefit of the child.

The *types* of suffering that lead to refugee recognition in the US asylum process must also more closely mirror real-world dynamics. The Biden administration has undone Trump-era asylum case law that disqualified victims of domestic violence and those targeted due to their family ties, cases likely to win during the Obama years. Yet, as I have shown, even Obama-era asylum law excluded too many Central American de facto refugee youths. A further rethinking of how the law can be interpreted to protect children, youths, and other new categories of vulnerable people on the move today is both urgently needed and possible. The historical examples of the strides made to recognize sexuality- and gender-based forms of persecution (female genital mutilation, domestic violence) prove as much. If US asylum law evolves to recognize experiences of escape from violence as de facto refugee youths understand them, more vulnerable youths will access the protection they need. As we have seen, not all youths are equally well positioned to learn to reinterpret and tell their stories in the language of the law. Articulating the "right" type of suffering is especially challenging for youths with limited formal education, for those sheltered by protective caretakers from frightening family histories, and for younger applicants who do not have the same developmental ability as mature applicants to tell causal narratives, explaining not just *how* but *why* they fled.

What's more, the United States should finally catch up with the rest of the world by ratifying the CRC and adopting broader children's rights guarantees. In the current system, children who migrate with their parents are not granted the same protections as unaccompanied minors in detention and asylum proceedings, despite having the same developmental characteristics. Democratic and Republican administrations alike have sought to find ways to evade their Flores Settlement obligations in the cases of *accompanied* children in order to detain them with their parents. Yet, most of these families are seeking asylum, and detaining asylum seekers of any age without just cause is prohibited under international law. What's more, while measures like detention are ostensibly intended to deter future migration, research shows that these policies are ineffective when it comes to dissuading migrants fleeing violence in their home countries.[13] A simple solution is to do away with detention altogether.

Next, TVPRA protections at the border that allow unaccompanied minors to be admitted to the United States should not exclude Mexicans. This provision violates Article 2 of the CRC, which prohibits discriminatory treatment based on the child's nationality. The negative effects of excluding Mexican unaccompanied minors from this protection are clearly reflected in the low numbers of these youths who make it past Border Patrol screenings, despite having experienced similar forms of violence and victimization as Central Americans.[14] Policies such as this also increase the discretion of CBP, an agency focused on exclusion, which cannot be expected to implement provisions that protect children.

Indeed, CBP practices should, at the very least, be subjected to scrutiny by external observers to enforce compliance with existing child protection policies. Better yet, a different agency altogether, one that has a child protection mandate, could be entrusted with screening unaccompanied minors at the border. These types of reforms are necessary to guarantee that unaccompanied minors are being adequately identified, avoiding situations like those that Alicia and Manuel faced, both of whom might have been expelled if they had allowed CBP agents to intimidate them after questioning their age (chapter 3). Such reforms are also paramount to protect the rights of immigrant children at the US-Mexico border, which are repeatedly violated.[15] In the presence of these rights violations, seven children died in CBP custody in 2019.

For SIJS, legal advocates have pointed to two key reforms that would make an impactful difference. First, the expansive interpretations of child welfare laws used in California courts and other "immigrant-friendly" states could be used as best practices to reform decision-making in other parts of the country, where judges are wary of granting SIJS orders. Such changes would eliminate arbitrary geographical discrepancies in access to relief. Second, through minor changes to the Immigration and Naturalization Act, the yearly limitations on the number of green cards that can be granted through SIJS could be eliminated, ending the lengthy periods of legal limbo that place youths at risk. While neither of these changes have taken place at the time of this writing, a national coalition of advocates did achieve a major victory for SIJS applicants. [16] As of May 2022, SIJS applicants qualify for deferred action—work permits and a temporary stay on deportation—while their cases are pending. This change is expected to benefit both new applicants and the over forty-four thousand youths stuck in the SIJS backlog nationwide.[17] These youths would no longer face the added vulnerabilities that SIJS applicants experienced during the time of my research because they were ineligible for work permits (see chapter 6).

Next, the US government should commit to making reliable data on unaccompanied minors publicly available. The Trump administration severely undermined what was already limited data transparency on the treatment of unaccompanied minors in the United States. The number of youths in the SIJS backlog only became known to the public in 2021 thanks to data obtained by advocates through a FOIA request. These data were, in turn, essential to the advocacy efforts described above. In 2019, the asylum office stopped releasing statistics that it had previously shared on asylum cases (Figure 2), and administrative immigration court data on unaccompanied minors' cases has not been reliable since 2018.[18] The lack of consistent and reliable data on unaccompanied minors poses significant challenges for advocates and scholars seeking to identify, assist, and advocate on behalf of these youths and to monitor US compliance with laws protecting immigrant children.

Finally, Central American youths who escape from violence should be fully treated as refugees and receive the same ORR-funded integration support services that benefit refugees who arrive in the country through the US resettlement program. Less than 20 percent of those who win their asylum cases benefit from any ORR-funded integration support services.[19] Marking a step in the right direction, California announced in 2021 that it would be the first State to expand eligibility for resettlement services to all approved asylees. It is worth noting, however, that the United States invests roughly $2,000 per refugee to provide integration support through its resettlement agencies.[20] Conversely, the Trump administration spent $30,000 per child to separate children from their parents at the border.[21] The discrepancy between these two numbers is a stark expression of where the priorities of the current US immigration system lie.

Instead of investing taxpayer dollars in such inhumane enforcement practices, we could be supporting the integration and well-being of Central American youths to help them navigate school, work, and unfamiliar state systems. These resources would allow nonprofits to provide more services like those I describe in chapter 6 to better meet the needs of unaccompanied minors beyond the legal process. This funding could also support rights education work. For example, nonprofit staff educate youths about their right to stay in California high schools and finish their degrees until age twenty-one. This extra time is precious for youths who arrive as older teenagers with no English-language skills and often after interrupted schooling; they thus struggle to finish their high school degrees in just a few years. Through a more sustained effort to empower their clients and teach them about their rights, advocates and youths could work together to hold institutions like schools accountable and make them more inclusionary of this new and growing population of immigrant youths.

All systems of state selection of immigrants include some and exclude others, raising difficult questions about global inequality and social justice. A perfect system may very well be an unattainable goal. Yet working toward a better system is possible with reforms such as these. A host of policies could also be borrowed from other countries. For instance, the United States could introduce permits like those that exist in Europe that allow all unaccompanied minors under 18 to legally live, work, and study in the receiving country. More expansive approaches to refugee law have been heralded in Latin America and by the African Union, which could provide precedents for rethinking US asylum law so it can better protect those who flee violence today. Spending six years following immigration attorneys and advocates has convinced me that pursuing incremental, positive social change is an arduous but not unattainable goal. The United States can and should meet its legal and ethical responsibilities toward a population that it contributed to displacing and ensure that Central American refugee youths do not merely survive but can thrive in their new homes.

Methods Appendix

ETHNOGRAPHIC FIELDWORK, 2015–2019

I started this research serendipitously in January 2015. I initially wanted to study the implementation of an entirely different set of Obama-era immigration policies. I gained access to a legal aid organization in Los Angeles by offering to volunteer in addition to doing research. The organization was characteristically working under severe resource constraints, and they welcomed me as a fluent Spanish speaker who could help translate legal documents. Almost immediately after I started my fieldwork, a conservative lawsuit blocked the programs I had hoped to study. At the time, the legal aid organization was processing high volumes of asylum cases for Central American unaccompanied minors and families who had arrived at the border in increasing numbers during the previous summer, after which the Obama administration declared a "humanitarian crisis." Their cases had to be filed quickly due to strict deadlines imposed by the courts. The goal of my research shifted entirely when the director of the organization invited me to sit in as staff prepared these asylum applications. While I initially observed case preparation for adults and youths,[1] I later decided to concentrate on unaccompanied minors' cases.

Soon enough, I went from just observing case preparation and translating legal documents to being fully immersed in the organization's work as a volunteer legal assistant, helping attorneys prepare asylum cases for unaccompanied minors. I gradually expanded my project to conduct ethnographic fieldwork and volunteer with legal brokers in other legal aid organizations in Los Angeles and follow them to immigration court. I did research in multiple organizations to ensure that what I was observing was not the result of organizational idiosyncrasies but, rather, reflected the broader phenomenon of lawyering with unaccompanied minors. Interesting variations then emerged between organizations, which had an impact on lawyering strategies and on youths' access to legal representation, issues I discuss in chapter 3. In these various organizations, I shadowed a total of eighteen legal brokers: immigration attorneys, paralegals, case managers, and other support staff. I observed these staff members help seventy-eight Central American unaccompanied minors apply for asylum and/or SIJS and navigate challenges outside the legal realm. I was able to follow the cases of some of these youths through multiple stages of the legal process and over an extended period—months or sometimes years—or to learn the outcomes of their applications for relief from staff. Others, like those whose eligibility screening interviews I describe in chapter 3, I met only on one occasion.

In legal clinics, I explained to immigrants that I was a researcher and volunteer. I obtained verbal informed consent from immigrants for their participation in the study. When participants were under eighteen, I also obtained consent from their parents or other ORR sponsors. These adults always accompanied youths at least to their first meetings in legal clinics. This not only made it possible to obtain consent from adults for minors' participation in my study, but it also allowed me to ask caretakers questions and thus gain additional valuable insights into the lives of these families.

I was continuously surprised to find that, while some lawyers were guarded and refused to participate in my research, immigrant youths and their caretakers were almost always willing to allow me to sit in while they met with their attorneys and case managers. It certainly helped that a trusted person (an attorney, nonprofit staff) had vouched for me. I must have also seemed harmless due to my status as a graduate student—I was doing my PhD at UCLA—and my fluent and ambiguously accented Spanish, which led most to guess that I was Colombian or Argentinian. I did not actively try to "pass" as Latina, but this was what most immigrant clients assumed when they saw me, a petite brunette woman with brown eyes. When they asked, I told them about my Italian origins and that I too was an immigrant to the United States. This was a great rapport-building topic during my fieldwork and interviews. Youths and their family members also asked me questions about my role as a researcher and what I would do with their stories, such as how I was different from a journalist or a social worker, and whether I was writing a book. When immigrants declined to grant me research consent but the organization needed my help as a volunteer, I still worked on their cases, but I did not take any field notes.

As approved by the UCLA IRB, I did not record identifying information (real names, dates of birth, case numbers) in my fieldnotes, and I used pseudonyms

to refer to research participants to protect their identities.[2] I also use pseudonyms in this book to refer to immigrant study participants, and I removed or
(less often) altered small details to ensure the stories I share are not identifying.
Since the field of legal brokerage with unaccompanied minors is a relatively
small one, I omit the names of the organizations where I conducted my research
in the book. I also omit all identifying information for the legal brokers (e.g.,
national origin, age, professional trajectory). To mask legal brokers and organizations further, I identify all legal brokers as female. Most of them indeed were
women, as the profession of public interest immigration lawyering is highly
feminized.

RESEARCH ETHICS, MY POSITIONALITY AS AN ADVOCATE, AND BALANCING RESEARCH AND VOLUNTEER WORK

Questions about research ethics were ever present in my mind as I conducted this
study in an increasingly hostile political climate. During the Trump administration, unaccompanied minors and their families became much more vulnerable
and fearful. Legal brokers felt understandably defensive in a context where the
president himself had demonized asylum lawyering as a "big fat con job."[3] In a
famous methodological essay, Sociologist Howard Becker argues that it is impossible to do research "that is uncontaminated by personal and political sympa-
thies" and that the question that ethnographers should answer is not whether
they have taken sides but, rather, "whose side are we on?"[4]

This was certainly not research that I could do with the presumption of
neutrality. My positionality in the field was defined not only by my own immigrant background, politics, gender, and ethnicity but also, crucially, by my
work as a legal volunteer. This work clearly positioned me "on the side" of both
asylum-seeking youths navigating legal struggles for refugee recognition and
of the professionals helping them. My volunteer work shaped my own identity
as an advocate for these youths. It allowed me to build trust and relationships
with legal brokers through reciprocity and shared experience. My active involvement in the process I was studying helped me gain and retain access to different organizations and build my credibility with advocates as a trusted and
knowledgeable quasi-insider, which was especially important during the Trump
administration. Taking part in preparing asylum cases provided invaluable
information for this research by helping me understand firsthand how difficult
it is to obtain the information necessary to craft a successful asylum case from
traumatized youths.

Working in legal clinics was emotionally challenging. I understood the burnout and vicarious trauma that legal brokers talked about because I felt it myself.
Oftentimes, the stories of escape from violence that youths recounted were so

devastating that I could barely bring myself to write up field notes in the evening when I got home. I very much admired the legal brokers alongside whom I worked who cared deeply for their immigrant clients. They worked stressful and not very well-paid jobs, but they were motivated by their strong social justice convictions. Most had a personal connection to this phenomenon as Latinx immigrants and asylum seekers themselves or as the children of immigrants and asylum seekers. They had chosen their professions because they wanted to help other immigrants and give back to their communities. Some were seasoned attorneys, but many others were fresh out of law school and still learning the tricks of the trade while on the job. Legal brokers had their own critical analysis of the US immigration system and, sometimes, of their lawyering practices as well.

I was committed and spent countless hours on volunteer work. I thought, if there is such great need, why should I just study a phenomenon when there are people actually trying to help youths by working in the system? Yet, at the same time, I felt uncomfortable partaking in the extractive and inevitably retraumatizing interviewing that is part and parcel of preparing the asylum declaration. I also worried that if I got too deep into the volunteer work, it might compromise my research gaze. I found that a good way to reconcile the goals of helping out and collecting valuable information was to vary what I did in legal clinics as much as possible. When I realized that I was not learning much that was new in a particular role, I tried to change the type of volunteer work I did. I positioned my gaze to span the gamut from the active participant to the "fly on the wall."

As a volunteer legal assistant and active participant in the process I was studying, I filled out I-589 asylum application forms, interviewed asylum seekers to help attorneys prepare declarations, and put together proof and background materials, such as country reports and news clippings for the asylum application dossier. I also helped identify resources to address youths' needs outside the legal process. The types of fieldnotes that I took while engaged in my active volunteer role focused on youths' stories, conversations with colleagues about their cases, and on my reflexive impressions about the challenges of working with asylum-seeking youths. I also worked as a Spanish-English interpreter in legal clinics. This role allowed me to effectively take fieldnotes on attorney-client interactions and on how youths are prepared for their asylum interviews—this includes practicing with an interpreter—as well as to understand what gets lost in translation in the asylum application process and with what effects. Sometimes, attorneys took me along as a volunteer interpreter when their clients had their interviews at the asylum office, which was a means to get a glimpse into this black box that is normally off limits to researchers. Lack of access to the US asylum office for research purposes poses a significant challenge for scholars seeking to understand the legal and bureaucratic categorization struggles that have such a huge impact on the lives of asylum seekers. While I was at the asylum office, I was not able to take field notes since I was only a volunteer and due to the confidentiality of interviews between asylum officers and applicants. However, I took some autoethnographic notes after my visits, which focused, not on the details of individual cases, but on my experience working as an interpreter in that space and on the general challenges I observed.

In all the organizations where I did my fieldwork, I was also a "fly on the wall" at other times. In that position, I observed the naturally occurring interviews between attorneys (or paralegals, case managers) and their immigrant youth clients. While these interviews were taking place, I took notes frantically on a legal pad, writing down as much as I could of the verbatim conversation between the legal broker and the immigrant client. I also took notes about body language, reactions, expressions of emotion, and the "feel" of the room. I recorded information in Spanish, the language in which interactions usually took place. Most of the staff working in these organizations in Los Angeles were fluent or native Spanish speakers. In the evening when I got home, I transcribed my handwritten notes into a Word document and expanded on them while my memory was fresh. Short of using a tape recorder, which was not acceptable for this research given concerns about attorney-client privilege, this allowed me to collect rich data about social interactions between legal brokers and youths—the field note excerpts in the chapters that you have just read—and to record and analyze their discursive strategies.

It was possible for me to adopt all these approaches and position my gaze in different ways because I spent over four years doing ethnographic fieldwork, from January 2015 to April 2019. Leaving the field was difficult. An ethnographer is never really done with the work.[5] This is especially true for research on a contentious topic like asylum in the ever-evolving US political context. Policy changes were happening virtually nonstop, particularly under Trump. I felt that I needed to stay in the field longer to document and understand these changes. I also felt guilty for stepping out of the field because people were relying on me in my role as a volunteer. However, since I was adamant about finishing my PhD in a timely manner and getting an actual job, I stuck to the deadline that my dissertation advisor wisely gave me to wrap up my fieldwork.

Stepping out of the field, in my view, is important to take distance from the ethnographic material and to be able to write about it. Even during the more than four years of ethnographic fieldwork that I did, I took periodic breaks, during which I focused on writing up results to date. Writing was also somewhat therapeutic for me. It allowed me to recover emotionally from this difficult research with young survivors of trauma, which can lead not just practitioners but also researchers to deal with vicarious trauma and burnout. I wrote not just academic papers but also policy reports, research briefs, and op-eds. While I initially felt strongly that I should do more than "just study" this phenomenon, over the years, I made peace with the fact that my engaged role as a researcher could itself be a form of advocacy when combined with public-facing sociology.

After I finished my ethnographic fieldwork and while writing this book, I continued to monitor policy developments by reading legal briefs, policy reports, blogs by immigration lawyers and judges, and the websites of immigration advocacy organizations like CLINIC, AILA, NIJC, and the ACLU.[6] I also stayed in touch with many of my research participants. This allowed me to do a series of follow-up interviews between December 2020 and January 2021 (see below), getting back in touch with attorneys, case managers, and immigrant youths to document policy changes and their impact on youths and lawyering strategies through the end of the Trump administration.

THE INTERVIEWS (2016–2021)

To complement my ethnographic fieldwork, I conducted 122 in-depth semi-structured interviews. Through my legal aid organization entry points, and then through snowball sampling, I recruited and interviewed 28 immigration attorneys, thus getting a glimpse into almost all the legal aid organizations that work with unaccompanied minors in Los Angeles. Through snowball sampling, I also interviewed case managers and other legal clinic staff (n = 6), former ORR staff (n = 3), and asylum officers (n = 2). In January 2021, I did follow up interviews with 14 immigration attorneys and 2 case managers. Conducting these interviews between November 2016 and January 2021 allowed me to capture information about legal brokerage with unaccompanied minors and how policy developments shaped lawyering through the end of the Trump administration. Interviews with attorneys working in multiple organizations also allowed me to collect information about impact litigation that complemented what I was learning by shadowing attorneys who did direct client representation work.

Two years into my ethnographic fieldwork, I decided that it was important that I interview unaccompanied minors outside the space of the legal clinic. This was because my positionality as a legal volunteer had structured my interactions with youths and restrained the types of questions I could ask them. My research interviews with Central American unaccompanied minors allowed me to learn about how youths saw the legal process, as well as about their everyday lives navigating school, work, and family reunification. Youths' retrospective accounts also revealed important information about their experiences in institutional spaces where I did not have access, like ORR shelters and border holding facilities.[7] My selection criteria for immigrant youth interviewees were the following: (1) youths were apprehended at the US-Mexico border and entered the United States as unaccompanied minors; (2) they had been placed in removal proceedings; (3) they arrived in the United States during or after 2012; (3) they were from El Salvador, Guatemala, or Honduras.

I recruited my youth interview participants through referrals from a variety of legal aid and other types of organizations that work with unaccompanied minors in Los Angeles, as well as through attorneys working in private practice. I found that snowball sampling was not an effective means to recruit youth interviewees. I only obtained twelve referrals in this way, all of whom were either the parents, other caretakers, or siblings of my unaccompanied minor interviewees. I imagine that this was the case due to the sensitive nature of youths' past experiences. They were likely reticent to inform their friends and peers of their participation in a study about unaccompanied minors in removal proceedings and thus disclose their legal status and personal histories. Since snowball sampling was not an effective means to recruit youths, I was very reliant on referrals from advocates. One of my concerns was that advocates would refer only their favorite clients to me, the ones with inspirational stories or the "sweet" ones that fit the normative criteria of deserving and "assimilable" young immigrant behavior in the United States (see chapter 6). I used a few different strategies to work around these potential selection biases. In one organization, I had access to lists of clients who had just been granted or denied at the asylum office, and I used these lists to reach out to youths directly by phone to tell them about the possibility of being interviewed for my research. I was also able to distribute flyers in legal clinics and digitally, via bulk text messages, to large numbers of potential interviewees (some organizations use this means to communicate with their clients). Youths who saw the flyer then took the initiative of seeking me out to ask for more information about participating in the research.

While I was able to informally interview many parents and other ORR sponsors during my ethnographic fieldwork, recruiting them for formal interviews was very challenging. They had to find time in their busy schedules, which included work and multiple caretaking responsibilities, to meet with me. I had initially hoped to interview all the parents or other sponsors of my unaccompanied minor interviewees, but I was only able to interview ten of them (nine mothers and one aunt). In six of these cases, I interviewed youths and their caretakers together, at their request.

My main concern in conducting interviews with youths was to ensure an ethical research exchange. I wanted the interview to be a space for conversation outside of the emotionally charged encounters in legal clinics where the questioning that took place served the purpose of preparing high-stakes applications for asylum. To ensure they felt comfortable, I let youths choose where they wanted to meet me. They usually chose neighborhood parks or coffee shops, and occasionally, their homes.[8] I broke the ice by sharing stories of my own experience as an immigrant child in the United States. I thus let youths know that I understood what it meant to encounter a strange new land, with an intimidating new school. Of course, we were also very different. I was a researcher, someone older, and a privileged middle-class immigrant with a high-value European passport who had always had legal status. I did not live through, nor could I presume to understand firsthand what these youths had experienced as they suffered violence in their home countries and navigated dangerous journeys to the United States and arduous legal struggles for refugee recognition.

I structured my interviews with youths to deal with the least sensitive topics first. I started with a few rapport-building questions, such as: How would you/your friends describe your personality? Describe what you do during an average week of your life. I then moved on to asking about youths' everyday lives in Los Angeles, focusing on work or school, and then family, which was sometimes itself a sensitive topic (see chapter 6). Next, I asked youths about their interactions with the different bureaucracies that process unaccompanied minors in the United States, moving backwards through the process (the asylum office, immigration court, ORR, interactions at the border). Only at the end did I tackle questions about youths' countries of origin and their reasons for escape. (For more on this, see below.) On the day of the interview, I repeatedly stressed to youths that they could skip any and all questions they did not want to answer. Most youths answered all my questions, and some were especially loquacious, with a few interviews lasting over three hours. Some youths, however, chose to skip questions, most commonly about what had happened in their home countries to cause their escape. Giving youths the choice of whether or not to share accounts of escape and persecution with me was crucial to ensure that my research interviews were not retraumatizing. I phrased these questions as follows: "If you feel comfortable doing so, would you like to tell me something about why you left your home country/what happened to you before you left?" The tone of the interviews—during which youths felt that they could skip questions but also treated me with familiarity—made me confident that I was doing no harm while also collecting valuable information on young people's perspectives on the legal process.

In total, I interviewed forty-five youths from El Salvador, Guatemala, and Honduras who arrived in the United States as unaccompanied minors and were at different stages of their applications for asylum and SIJS (Table 8). Immigrant interviewees received a $30 Target gift card as a thank-you for their time. Interviews were audio recorded and transcribed in the original Spanish. I translated into English only the parts of interviews and field notes included in this book and research papers. I stayed in touch with many of the youths I interviewed over extended periods of time, either directly or through their attorneys and case managers, some of whom I was doing fieldwork with. Indeed, while for the purposes of simplification and description, I separate the ethnography from the interviews, there was a significant degree of overlap between these two study components.

I did follow-up interviews with twelve of these youths in December 2020 (Table 9). Roughly two years had passed since our first interview. Due to the COVID pandemic, I shifted my interviewing modality to video calls, conducted over WhatsApp or Zoom, which I recorded in audio only. Switching to online interviewing with youths (I also did this for advocate re-interviews) was effective because I was getting back in touch with young people who already knew

Table 8   Characteristics of immigrant youth, first round interviews

Country		Gender		Age at entry		Age at interview		Year of entry	
El Salvador	18	Male	25	12–14	8	12–14	2	2012–2013	3
Guatemala	16	Female	20	15–16	23	15–16	5	2014	8
Honduras	11			17	14	17	5	2015	14
						18+	33	2016	14
								2017	5
								2018	1

ORR sponsor		Occupation		Type of application for relief		Status of application	
Parent(s)	25	Studying	25	Asylum	25	Approved	17
Other family	18	Working	13	SIJS	8	Pending	21
Long-term foster care	2	Both	5	Asylum & SIJS	8	Denied	7
		Neither	2	T-visa/U Visa	2		
				None/aged out	2		

SOURCE: Formal interviews (n = 45).

and trusted me. Doing first-time interviews over video call would likely not have been possible with this population. In-person contact had been very important to establish rapport with youths: making small talk, going for a walk, sipping coffee together while not saying much initially, and answering their curious questions about me and my research.

During the second round of interviews, I asked youths about how their lives had changed in the two years since we last spoke: Had they finished high school? Were they working? Who did they live with now? Did the COVID pandemic create new challenges for them or their families? I also asked whether and how their immigration cases had progressed, and what their goals and aspirations for the future were. Tables 8 and 9 summarize the characteristics of immigrant youth study participants involved in the first and second round of interviews, respectively.

DATA VALIDITY, TRUTH, AND THE POLITICIZATION OF ASYLUM

I often get questions about whether youths misrepresented or exaggerated facts about their past experiences in the context of their asylum applications or during their interviews with me, given the rewards to be reaped by demonstrating

Table 9   Characteristics of youths re-interviewed in 2020

									Interview	
Nationality		Gender		Age		Occupation		Case status	I	II
El Salvador	6	Female	6	16	1	Studying	4	Granted	4	6
Guatemala	3	Male	6	20	5	Working	6	Pending	6*	4*
Honduras	3			21	3	Both	1	Denied	2	2
				22	3	Neither	1			

SOURCE: Formal interviews (n = 12).
* Includes one youth who was denied asylum but had a pending SIJS case.

victimhood in the asylum process. There is indeed some research that documents misrepresentation and even fraud in asylum proceedings. However, even that research finds that misrepresentation is usually not a devious strategy on the part of the asylum seeker.[9] Rather, it occurs due to misinformation about what asylum is and/or the more or less well-intentioned advice that asylum seekers receive from brokers like social workers and private attorneys, who mediate the process.

During my research in legal clinics, I did not find much evidence of either misrepresentation or fraud. When interviewing youths outside of legal clinics, I made it clear that I had no influence on the outcomes of their asylum cases and was not affiliated with the US government in any way, so youths did not have an incentive to portray their stories of escape in any particular way. Of course, I cannot look into the minds of my research participants or know exactly what happened to them. Neither can asylum officers, for that matter, even though youths seemed to think that adjudicators had an almost magical ability to tell whether they were lying. In fact, youths themselves have only inherently imperfect memories of the traumatizing past events that happened to them. Others have argued that truth is constructed rather than absolute in asylum proceedings because the reconstruction of past facts relies on memory, which is not necessarily reliable, particularly for young survivors of trauma.[10] Indeed, research in developmental psychology suggests that individuals who experience traumatic events tend to forget details, and those who experience childhood trauma tend to have poorer autobiographic memories. These findings suggest that *omissions* of accounts of past harm in asylum narratives are all too common.

Furthermore, I am especially confident about the material I collected because, in legal clinics, I was able to see the process of asylum case construction from start to finish. I observed how lawyers, youths, and family members prepared narratives together, as well as how youths' and lawyers' understandings of experiences of escape and past harm differed. Something I found quite striking was that, despite the fact that lawyers asked what could be construed as leading questions, youths did not uniformly say yes to these questions and parrot back the examples that lawyers told them. Rather, they selected the responses that they thought applied to them. Many youths also pushed back when lawyers inquired about past harm, such as child abuse, and they held their ground to say that this never happened to them (see chapter 5). During my fieldwork in legal clinics, I never heard stories that were "suspiciously" similar, although many were tragically motivated by the same structural dynamics that I describe in chapter 2. What's more, as I discussed in the empirical chapters, part of building the asylum dossier is compiling documentary evidence, country reports, and supporting testimonies from witnesses and family members, all of which are means to validate and verify youths' accounts. Of course, not everyone had the capacity to produce this proof, precisely due to their vulnerability, the quick circumstances of their flight, and the lack of protection by sending governments.

During my research interviews, I left for last the topic of flight and countries of origin. This was important in order to avoid retraumatizing youths. It was also another strategic means to try to hear youths' stories as they understood them, rather than how attorneys had taught them to recount these stories, in the language of the law. While some youths were more spontaneous, others wanted to tell me what I could often recognize as the causal and linear stories that they had learned to tell for their asylum interviews. However, it is wrong to assume that such accounts are untrue or fabricated. Rather, as I discuss at length in chapters 4 and 5, it takes work, particularly for young survivors of trauma, to understand *why* certain events and past harm took place, and how their personal stories fit within broader family histories and home country political dynamics. Most youths have the time, resources, and assistance to learn about these issues only *after* their escape, once they find safety in the United States. Former president Donald Trump has argued that asylum lawyers "sell" their clients stories. This book has shown what lawyers actually do: they teach their clients about how their personal experiences fit existing US legal frames; they teach young people with limited formal schooling about broader political issues in their home countries that they were not necessarily aware of beforehand; they teach youths how to use a legal, historical, cultural, and structural interpretive lens to talk about their lives. As we have seen, youths are especially vulnerable to deportation if they do not learn these valuable lessons.

In the context of their asylum applications or their interviews with asylum officers, did young asylum seekers "embellish" some more subjective aspects of their narratives, like how they felt at a certain time or during a certain event? Perhaps in some cases. The opposite also seemed to happen, however. For instance, reflecting traditional gender norms, boys oftentimes did not want to admit that they cried or felt scared, even after experiencing what, when described by them or others, sounded like horrible abuse and harm. Males, in particular, were often reticent to see and describe themselves as victims, despite the gains to be made by showing humanitarian capital in the US asylum process. Further, for the reasons I discuss in chapter 5, young asylum applicants are generally more reticent and less capable than adults to disclose information that could be relevant to their asylum claims. Because of this, in many cases, there was actually *less* material in youths' asylum applications than there could have been.

Discussing, and thus reliving, traumatic past events was daunting for many youths. When I interviewed Julio—a boy who lived in hiding for over a year in El Salvador after being threatened by MS-13—he told me that, when he arrived in the United States, all he wanted to think about was his future. It hurt him too much to think and speak about his past. So, Julio decided to skip questions about El Salvador during his interview with me. However, he gave me permission to read his asylum declaration—I was doing fieldwork in the legal clinic that prepared his asylum case—so I could know his story. He let me know that he had not even told the legal broker who prepared his case everything that had happened to him. At the asylum office, where Julio knew the stakes were high, he said that he had revealed more but, even then, not everything, because it was too scary and painful to relive the death threats and harm that he and his family had suffered.

In sum, while the problem of asylum fraud has been politicized and, in my view, blown out of proportion, nobody talks about cases like Julio's. I hope my research helps disrupt the problematic narrative of the "bogus" asylum seeker. To the best of my knowledge, my research participants were telling the truth. Because of all the dynamics I just described, I believe them. As scholars, when doing research with vulnerable young asylum seekers forced to navigate systems that view them with suspicion, we must position ourselves on their side and listen to them with empathy and trust. Such an approach is indispensable for conducting ethical and rigorous research with unaccompanied minors, asylum seekers, and other survivors of violence and trauma.

Notes

CHAPTER 1. EXCLUSION AND PROTECTION IN US IMMIGRATION LAW AND POLICY

1. To protect the identity of study participants, all the names in this book are pseudonyms.

2. *Coyote* is a Spanish term, used in Mexico and Central America to refer to the guides or smugglers who bring migrants to the United States.

3. I use the term *unaccompanied minors*, which is the norm in the academic literature. In US immigration law, this category of immigrants is formally referred to as "unaccompanied alien children" and defined as: "individuals with no lawful immigration status, under age eighteen, for whom no parents or legal guardians are available in the U.S. to provide care and physical custody" (6 U.S.C. 279(g)(2)).

4. See UNHCR (2014b). While children have always been a part of refugee flows, in the past, they either stayed in refugee camps in the Global South or arrived in countries like the United States in small numbers through government sponsored resettlement programs (Steinbock 1989).

5. In 2019, under Trump, the USCIS asylum office stopped releasing data on asylum cases, including unaccompanied minors' cases, which had been previously made publicly available during Quarterly Stakeholder Meetings. Under Biden, the asylum office resumed releasing limited data in 2021. As this book

goes to press, data on unaccompanied minors' asylum cases after 2019 is still unavailable.

6. The United States was not among the signatories of the 1951 Refugee Convention, but it ratified the 1967 Protocol. One hundred fifty countries worldwide have ratified either the Convention or the Protocol.

7. Fitzgerald (2019); Cuellar (2006); Arar (2017).

8. Heidbrink (2014); Terrio (2015).

9. Bhabha and Young (1999); Bhabha (2014); Pobjoy (2017); Arnold (2018).

10. Pound (1910).

11. Following De Genova (2002) and others, I use the term *illegal* in scare quotes because its use to describe immigrants is dehumanizing, and illegality is a condition that is actively produced by restrictive immigration policies rather than a natural attribute of individuals.

12. Galli (2018).

13. One exception is Michelle Statz's (2018) interview-based study of lawyers working with Fujianese unaccompanied minor trafficking victims. Statz argues that legal brokers assume that youths are not capable of determining their own best interests and thus do not see them as partners in cause lawyering.

14. In US immigration law, for the purposes of family reunification, children are considered derivatives on their parents' applications until age twenty-one. Young asylum seekers who migrate *with* their parents can likewise be considered derivatives on parents' asylum applications until age twenty-one.

15. The legal violence framework (Menjívar and Abrego 2012) has been applied extensively to study various groups of adults, including undocumented immigrants, temporary status holders, and asylum seekers (Abrego and Menjívar 2011; Abrego and Lakhani 2015; Dreby 2015; Enriquez 2015; Hsin and Aptekar 2022).

16. Massey, Durand, and Pren (2014); Dreby (2010); Menjívar, Abrego, and Schmalzbauer (2016).

17. De Genova (2002)

18. Menjívar (2006); Menjívar and Kanstroom (2003); Dreby (2016); Enriquez (2017); Gonzales (2016); Gonzales and Burciaga (2018); Brubaker (2015).

19. Wilson and Brown (2011).

20. See Dauvergne (2005) and Joppke (1997). Based on her research on US resettlement of Vietnamese refugees in the aftermath of the Vietnam war, Yen Espiritu (2014) takes this argument further to argue that refugee admissions also serve to sanitize past military intervention and erase the violence inflicted by US imperialism, by reframing the war as a benevolent humanitarian mission aimed at "saving" the citizens of repressive regimes.

21. Fassin (2011, 2013); Ticktin (2011); Perez (2021).

22. Ticktin (2011).

23. Nicholls (2013).

24. According to Zelizer (1985), this shift was consolidated in the United States between the 1870s and 1930s. See also Aries (1962) for a sweeping historical analysis of the emergence of childhood as a stage of the life course distinct from adulthood starting at the end of the Middle Ages.

25. In the United Kingdom, unaccompanied minors are granted permits until age seventeen and a half. For more on the reception of unaccompanied minors in Europe, see European Migration Network (2018) and Chase and Allsopp (2021).

26. Chavez and Menjívar (2010); Minow (1995); Statz and Heidbrink (2019).

27. Feld (1999).

28. TRAC (2014).

29. Lakhani (2013, 2014).

30. Coutin (2000).

31. Villalon (2010); Bhuyan (2008); Berger (2009).

32. Villalon (2010).

33. Coutin (1994, 2000).

34. IRCA allowed nearly three million undocumented immigrants to become lawful permanent residents if they met a minimum residency requirement.

35. Hagan and Baker (1993).

36. Bhabha (2014).

37. Hamlin (2021).

38. Miller, Keith, and Holmes (2014); Ryo and Peacock (2021).

39. Ramji-Nogales, Schoenholtz, and Schrag (2007).

40. See also Galli (2020a).

41. "Symbolic capital" can be defined as those resources that exist because they are "perceived by social agents endowed with categories of perception, which cause them to know, recognize, and give [them] value" (Bourdieu 1986: 47).

42. Fassin (2013).

43. This is unlike refugee resettlement—the process through which individuals are selected from refugee camps and brought to the United States—which is based on predetermined yearly quotas agreed upon by the White House and Congress.

44. Galli (2020a).

45. Fitzgerald and Arar (2018).

46. Richmond (1988); Menjívar (1993, 1994).

47. Richmond (1993); Fitzgerald and Arar (2018); Castles (2003).

48. Belloni (2020).

49. Crawley and Skleparis (2018); Hamlin (2021, 5).

50. Fitzgerald and Arar (2018).

51. Zolberg, Suhrke, and Aguayo (1989).

52. See Hamlin (2021). Cecilia Menjívar (2000) also positions Salvadorans who were denied refugee recognition in the 1980s and 1990s and who settled in Northern California as de facto refugees. This migrant group arrived with

disadvantages due to their experiences of escape and victimization. Unlike reset-tled refugees who receive integration support services from the state, Salvadorans were left to fend for themselves. The denial of refugee status and the associated state support have had lasting implications, leaving the migrant networks of Sal-vadorans with few resources and undermining intra-ethnic forms of solidarity.

53. Regional agreements in Africa and Latin America have expanded the ref-ugee definition to include victims of generalized violence.

54. Coined by Johann Galtung (1969), *structural violence* can be defined as the suffering that results from unequal social structures and institutions, such as economic inequality, racism, sexism, and ageism. Due to these forms of insti-tutionalized inequality, otherwise avoidable suffering is disproportionately in-flicted among disadvantaged members of society. On structural violence and the refugee definition, see also Rodriguez (2017); Betts (2013).

55. Gibney (2004); Bhabha (2014).

56. Freedman (2015); Hamlin (2014).

57. Orellana et al. (2001); Bloch, Sigona, and Zetter (2014).

58. Turner (1969).

59. UNESCO (2020).

60. US Department of Labor (2018).

61. ILO (2008a, 2008b, 2008c).

62. Heidbrink (2018).

63. Heidbrink (2020).

64. DeWaard, Nobles, and Donato (2018).

65. The concept of "waithood" was coined by Honwana (2014). See also Bellino (2017) and Belloni (2020).

66. Kandel and Massey (2002); Checa et. al. (2006).

67. Hernández León (1999); Horváth (2008); Lopez Castro (2007); Martinez (2019).

68. Kandel and Massey (2002).

69. Portes and Rumbaut (2001); Luthra, Soel, and Waldinger (2018).

70. Abrego (2011); Abrego and Gonzales (2010); Gonzales (2011, 2016).

71. Canizales (2015).

72. Thomas Jimenez (2017) has problematized the idea of a cultural "main-stream." In the classical scholarship on assimilation, the US mainstream was as-sociated with Anglo culture and Christian religion. Decades of immigration have transformed what mainstream means in the United States, and this composite, evolving culture is far more complex to capture for research purposes.

73. My goal with this book is not to examine assimilation *outcomes*, as doing so would require following youths over longer periods of time. Instead, I examine incorporation as a *process* whereby these young immigrants adapt to and claim membership rights in their new homes.

74. Trinkner and Tyler (2016: 417). I consider legal socialization to be a type of socialization process that pertains to the realm of laws and rules. More broadly, socialization is a concept that is attentive to the asymmetries of power through which structures of oppression are reproduced, and, hence, it is especially appropriate to study systematically marginalized communities such as immigrants and racial minorities (Guhin, Calarco, and Miller-Idriss 2021).

75. Tyler (1990); Fagan and Tyler (2005); Trinkner and Cohn 2014.

76. Ryo (2016); Ewick and Silbey (1998); Car, Napolitano, and Keating (2007); Chua and Engel (2019).

77. Suárez Orozco (1987); Roder and Mulau (2021).

78. Abrego (2011, 2019).

79. Nicholls (2013); Patler (2018).

80. Ryo (2017).

81. Abrego (2011); Gleeson (2010).

82. Menjívar (2000); Garcia (2006).

83. Coutin (2000).

84. Coutin (1994).

85. A type of impact litigation, class action lawsuits explicitly pursue advocacy goals by seeking rights and entitlements on behalf of groups of similarly situated people referred to as class members. Attorneys can also pursue lawsuits on behalf of a strategically selected individual with these same goals.

86. Coutin (2000).

87. Urrutia-Rojas and Rodriguez (1997).

88. Terrio (2015).

89. The 2002 Homeland Security Act transferred responsibility for the detention of unaccompanied minors from the Immigration and Naturalization Services (INS) to ORR. This change resolved the INS's prior conflict of interest as the agency that both detained unaccompanied minors and decided whether to grant them protection from deportation (Somers, Herrera, and Rodriguez 2010; Statz 2018).

90. For a full list of class action lawsuits in response to these restrictive changes, see American Immigration Lawyers Association (2019). At the time of writing, none of these changes have been implemented, and the Flores Settlement remains intact.

91. Schrag (2020).

92. Terrio (2015); Schrag (2020).

93. Canadian unaccompanied minors are also excluded but, unsurprisingly, given similar levels of economic development and security between the countries, there is no flow of child migrants from Canada to the United States.

94. UNHCR (2014a); (ORR 2020).

95. Carlson and Gallagher (2015).

96. The immigration court assesses the claims of those denied by the asylum office *de novo*. This means that immigration judges do not review the asylum officer's rationale for denying the case. Instead, they consider the petition anew on its merits. For more on this see note 10 in chapter 7.

97. The TVPRA also exempts unaccompanied minors from the one-year filing deadline (from the date of arrival) that adult asylum seekers are subjected to. Both the one-year filing deadline and the "two-tiered" asylum system that discriminates between border crossers and others (denying the former access to the asylum office) were introduced in 1996 with the Illegal Immigration and Immigrant Responsibility Act (Hamlin 2014).

98. In 2018, the Board of Immigration Appeals published new case law (Matter of M-A-C-O-), noting that the cases of unaccompanied minors who turn eighteen should be decided in immigration court instead of the asylum office, as had been the case prior to the Kim Memo of 2013. Next, USCIS issued the Lafferty Memo requiring asylum officers to determine whether previously designated unaccompanied minors continued to meet the UAC definition. The youth's age is considered at the time of filing the asylum application. Advocates sued and eventually obtained a preliminary injunction to the new policy (J.O.P v. DHS 409 F. Supp. 3d 367 (D. Md. 2019)). However, even with the injunction in place, new interpretations of the Kim Memo are imperiling unaccompanied minors' access to the asylum office. At the time of this writing, litigation in *J.O.P. v. DHS* is ongoing to restore protections to the Obama-era status quo. For more on this see, ILRC (2021).

99. Migration Policy Institute (2020); CLINIC (2019).

100. Human Rights First (2021).

101. ACLU (2020).

102. Human Rights First (2021); KIND (2020).

103. For statistics on apprehensions at the US border that disaggregate between those being admitted and those being expelled under Title 42, see www .cbp.gov/newsroom/stats/cbp-enforcement-statistics/title-8-and-title-42 -statistics and www.cbp.gov/newsroom/stats/custody-and-transfer-statistics.

104. Customs and Border Protection (2018).

105. The average amount of time that youths spend in ORR has varied widely, ranging from 35 days during the surge in arrivals under Obama in the summer of 2014 to 122 days in 2020 under Trump (Terrio 2015, ORR 2020).

106. The remaining 9 percent of unaccompanied minors are released to adults who are not their family members (ORR 2014). When no adults can be found to sponsor children, they may be placed in long term foster care arrangements (see chapter 3).

107. Immigration judges may administratively close the cases of immigrants who are waiting for decisions on their applications for deportation relief. Doing so does not confer legal status, but it does mean that immigrants are no longer actively facing removal proceedings and regularly reporting to immigration

court. Under Trump, it became far more difficult for judges to administratively close cases (see chapter 5). During the Obama years, immigration judges also had the power to grant immigrants who lost their asylum cases temporary work permits through prosecutorial discretion. The Trump administration eliminated this form of discretionary relief in 2017 but the Biden administration restored it shortly after taking office.

108. Human Rights Watch (2020).

109. The Los Angeles immigration court has jurisdiction over the cases of immigrants who are not detained and reside in the following counties: Los Angeles, Orange, Riverside, San Bernardino, Santa Clara, Kern, Ventura, Santa Barbara, and San Luis Obispo. If we consider only youths released to Los Angeles County, Harris County, Texas, surpassed Los Angeles County in recent years as the main destination for unaccompanied minor arrivals (Administration for Children and Families 2019). However, the sprawling LA metropolis does not neatly stop at the county line. Some of my research participants lived in these surrounding counties, and they attended immigration court in Los Angeles.

110. Grant rates for unaccompanied minors' cases at the asylum office were higher in Los Angeles (47%–66%) than the nation-wide average (28%–40%) between 2015 and 2019. See "Asylum Quarterly Stakeholder Meetings MPA and PRL Reports" (www.uscis.gov/outreach/).

111. Hlass 2014.

112. See TRAC (2019) "Unaccompanied Juveniles: Immigration Court Deportation Proceedings Data Tool" (https://trac.syr.edu/phptools/immigration/juvenile/). The representation rates reported above reflected whether unaccompanied minors had an attorney present at their last hearing ("current status"). Unaccompanied minor's representation rates for the first hearing in immigration court ("initial filing") were far lower: 35–55 percent nationwide and 51–68 percent in Los Angeles (2014–2017). This is unsurprising because it takes time for youths to find an attorney and immigration judges generally allow them time to do so (see chapter 3). Hence the former statistic is a more accurate measure of overall access to legal representation than the latter. Data on unaccompanied minors after 2017 are not reliable and hence are not reported in the TRAC data tool (for more on this, see chapter 7 and TRAC [2021]).

CHAPTER 2. CENTRAL AMERICAN YOUTHS ESCAPE FROM VIOLENCE

1. Homicide rates (measured as deaths per hundred thousand individuals) are commonly used to measure the prevalence of violence in society. In 2015, the homicide rate in the United States was 4.9 as compared to 103 in El Salvador. While homicide rates vary between El Salvador, Honduras, and Guatemala and

fluctuate over time (in El Salvador, they decreased after 2015), they remained much higher than in the United States overall during the years this research took pace. For example, in 2016, the homicide rates in Guatemala, Honduras, and El Salvador were 27.3, 59.0, and 27.3, respectively (Gagne 2017).

2. Massey, Durand, and Pren (2016); Chavez and Menjívar (2010).

3. Richmond (1988); Menjívar (1993); Menjívar (1994).

4. Taylor (1999).

5. Massey et al. (1990).

6. See Fitzgerald and Arar (2018).

7. Zolberg, Suhrke, and Aguayo (1989).

8. Coutin (2000).

9. Hiskey, Cordova, and Orces (2018).

10. Clemens (2017).

11. Doctors Without Borders (2020).

12. Physicians for Human Rights (2019).

13. Menjívar (2000).

14. Manz (2008).

15. Booth, Wade, and Walker (2005).

16. Rocha (2011).

17. Booth, Wade, and Walker (2005).

18. Menjívar (2011); Bruneau, Dammert, and Skinner (2011).

19. Booth, Wade, and Walker (2005).

20. Menjívar (2000, 2011); Bourdieu (1986).

21. Vogt (2013).

22. Betts (2013); Belloni (2019).

23. Menjívar (2011).

24. Manz (2008); ORMUSA (2019).

25. In Guatemala, over 2,500 women and girls were murdered between 2001 and 2006; in Honduras, one woman is murdered every fourteen hours, and feminicide rates increased by over 250 percent between 2005 and 2013; in El Salvador, the feminicide rate almost doubled between 1999 and 2006 (Gutierrez Rivera 2017).

26. Global Database on Violence against Women, see: https://evaw-global-database.unwomen.org/en; ORMUSA (2019).

27. Unidad de Proteccion a Defensoras de Derechos Humanos (2017).

28. Menjívar (2011).

29. Menjívar (1993, 1994, 2000); Abrego (2009, 2014); Booth, Wade, and Walker (2005).

30. Steffensmeier et al. (1989); Finkelhor (2008); UNDOC (2014).

31. ORR (2019).

32. Clemens (2017).

33. Zolberg, Suhrke, and Aguayo (1989).

34. Ladinos are the majority racial group in Guatemala, as well as in Honduras and El Salvador. They are "mestizos" or descents of the European colonizers

and the local indigenous populations. For more on race in Central America, see chapter 5.

35. Alicia's case was denied at the asylum office, which does not publish written decisions. This means that the exact rationale for case denials is, most often, unknown to both youths and their attorneys. For more on this, see chapter 5.

36. UNHCR (2010).

37. Fitzgerald and Arar (2018).

38. Menjívar (2000).

39. Menjívar (2000).

40. Coen (2017).

41. Hamlin (2014); Center for Gender and Refugee Studies (2014).

42. Wilson (1998).

43. Coutin (2000).

44. Fitzgerald (2019).

45. Gammeltoft-Hansen and Sorensen (2013); Hernández-León (2013).

46. Rosenblum and Ball (2016).

47. Garcia (2019).

48. Massey, Durand, and Pren (2014).

49. Separating minors from caretakers who are *not* their parents has always been US policy even before family separations made the headlines in the summer of 2018, and the Trump administration started taking children away from their parents. In 2022, the Biden administration announced plans to stop separating minors from their nonparent family members at the border.

50. In 2016, over 60 percent of unaccompanied minors were apprehended crossing the border in the Rio Grande valley area in Texas (GAO 2018).

CHAPTER 3. ENTER THE BUREAUCRATIC MAZE

1. Canizales (2015); Abrego (2011).

2. Merry (1990).

3. This chapter expands on and revisits material that has been previously published in article form in the journal *Social Problems*, published by Oxford University Press. See Galli (2020b).

4. Heidbrink (2014a); Terrio (2015).

5. De Genova (2002).

6. Menjívar and Abrego (2012).

7. Bourdieu and Wacquant (2004).

8. Abrego (2011).

9. Flores and Schachter (2018); Fassin (2013); Heidbrink (2014a).

10. Goffman (1963).

11. Dezenski (2017).

12. Advocates immediately sued the Trump administration over the rule that would have made everyone who entered the United States between ports of entry ineligible for asylum. After just ten days, a district court judge in San Francisco issued a temporary restraining order, and the government was unable to implement the regulation. In a separate case, a district court judge in Washington, D.C., also ruled that the rule violates federal law. The Trump administration appealed, but the ban never went into effect (Migration Policy Institute 2020).

13. Passing a credible fear screening allows immigrants to be classified as asylum seekers who have a well-founded fear of persecution in their home country, a legal mode of entry under US law. Unauthorized border crossers can instead be immediately expelled.

14. Seccombe et al. (1998); Waters (1999); Brown (2011).

15. Ebadolahi (2018).

16. I use the word *crisis* in scare quotes to problematize its use by the media and policy makers. Others have pointed out that countries in the Global North instrumentalize a language of crisis—using words like *waves, surges, swarms*—to restrict protections for asylum seekers, children, and other protected groups of immigrants (Lindley 2014; Mayblin 2017).

17. Schrag (2020).

18. Terrio (2015); Heidbrink (2014a).

19. Chase and Allsopp (2020).

20. Terrio (2015); Heidbrink (2014a); Ryo and Humphrey (2021).

21. Cummings (2018); Sherman (2018).

22. Jordan (2019).

23. Terrio (2015).

24. Bogado and Morel (2021).

25. Ryo and Humphrey (2021).

26. ORR (2019).

27. Abrego (2011).

28. Sands (2018).

29. Temporary Protected Status (TPS) is a renewable two-year work and residency permit that the US government gives to immigrants of certain nationalities on humanitarian grounds, for instance after natural disasters. Eighty-six thousand Hondurans and two hundred thousand Salvadorans were granted TPS following Hurricane Mitch (1999) and a series of earthquakes (2001), respectively.

30. American Immigration Council (2016).

31. Bohmer and Schuman (2008).

32. Negative experiences with legal institutions have similarly been found to cause other marginalized social groups, like racial minorities, to feel disenfranchised. The legal consciousness of disenfranchised social groups is "against the law" or characterized by the idea that legal systems cannot help them (Ewick and Silbey 1998). These findings are also in line with scholarship on procedural

justice that shows that individuals' perceptions about their treatment during past interactions with the state (e.g., with actors like the police) shape whether they understand the law as just and effective or even legitimate (Tyler 1990).

33. Ramji-Nogales, Schoenholtz, and Schrag (2007).

34. Bhabha (2014).

35. Seccombe, James, and Walter (1998); Waters (1999); Brown (2011).

CHAPTER 4. ACCESS TO LEGAL REPRESENTATION

1. The formal document initiating removal proceedings is called a Notice to Appear; this can be served to the immigrant by a US immigration enforcement officer or sent to them in the mail.

2. In Los Angeles, some immigration judges found a creative means around this by establishing a "status docket" for youths with pending cases. On a discretionary basis, youths could be placed on this docket, which did not require them to show up in court. Instead, their immigration attorneys could submit paperwork to update the court on the status of their asylum and/or SIJS petitions every six or twelve months.

3. Lakhani (2014).

4. TRAC (2014).

5. *C.J.L.G. v. Sessions.*

6. See TRAC's "Unaccompanied Juveniles: Immigration Court Deportation Proceedings Data Tool" (https://trac.syr.edu/phptools/immigration/juvenile/). Representation rates are for the years 2014 to 2017. The data do not disaggregate by type of legal representation (i.e., pro-bono versus full cost). Data after 2017 are not available (see TRAC [2021].)

7. Lakhani (2013, 2014); Coutin (1994, 2000); Hagan and Baker (1993).

8. Bhuyan (2008); Fassin (2011, 2012); Ticktin (2011).

9. Villalon (2010).

10. A deportation order can be issued "in absentia" when the respondent does not show up for court. This is, essentially, a formal warrant for the immigrants' arrest and deportation.

11. Noll (2005).

12. The Trump administration later tried to render family membership asylum claims ineligible with Matter of L-E-A, see chapter 5.

13. Because the U-Visa application process can take up to ten years, attorneys usually advised youths to apply for other forms of relief (asylum or SIJS).

14. Immigration judges may decide to grant a continuance, giving immigrants a later court date so they have more time to find an attorney, prepare an application for relief, or await the results of an application for relief.

15. Dery (1998).

16. See TRAC's "Immigration Court Backlog Tool" (https://trac.syr.edu /phptools/immigration/court_backlog).

17. Unaccompanied minors are also sorted into three different types of shelters ranging from high to low security (Terrio 2015; Ryo and Humphrey 2021). For more on this, see chapter 3.

18. Galli (2020a).

19. Farmer (2004).

20. Zolberg, Suhrke, and Aguayo (1989: 25).

21. Villalon (2010).

22. When youths were eligible for more than one type of relief, legal brokers' determination of the best strategy to pursue (i.e., which application to file or whether to file both) changed during the Obama and Trump administrations (see chapter 5).

23. Given-Wilson, Herlihy, and Hodes (2016).

CHAPTER 5. LAWYERING WITH UNACCOMPANIED MINORS

1. As quoted in the *Washington Post* (2017).

2. UNHCR (2010).

3. Coutin (2000); Lakhani (2013, 2014); Villalon (2010); Bhuyan (2008); Ticktin (2011); Fassin (2011); Fassin and d'Haullin (2011); Agustín (2007); Ong (2003).

4. For more on the differences between lawyering with youths and adults applying for asylum and other forms of humanitarian relief, see my previous work, Galli (2018, 2020a).

5. Zelizer (1985).

6. Bohmer and Shuman (2008).

7. Given-Wilson, Herlihy, and Hodes (2016).

8. Administrative processing priorities change frequently. During the Obama administration, recently arrived Central Americans were designated as the first processing priority in immigration court "*rocket-dockets*," a measure intended to deter future migration flows by quickly deporting those who lost their cases. The Trump administration changed processing priorities multiple times. In 2017, only unaccompanied minors detained in ORR for whom no sponsor could be found were still considered first processing priority in immigration court. The Trump administration also implemented a "last-in, first-out" policy at the asylum office (the most recent applications were assessed first). Yet this policy was implemented inconsistently; some cases were scheduled immediately, while others lagged for months before an interview.

9. These grant rates are for the period between fiscal years 2014 and 2017, based on administrative immigration court data (compiled by TRAC) and reports that the Asylum Office released during Quarterly Stakeholder Meetings.

These data have several limitations: mainly, the asylum office data on unaccompanied minors' asylum applications does not disaggregate by nationality. However, over 90 percent of all unaccompanied minors' asylum cases are filed by Salvadorans, Guatemalans, and Hondurans, making these numbers roughly comparable (USCIS 2015; DHS 2020).

10. Overall, the asylum office grants cases at higher rates than immigration court (Hamlin 2014).

11. USCIS (2019).

12. UNHCR (2009); UNCRC (2009); Frydman and Bookey (2018).

13. Legal scholars call this the nexus requirement: persecution must have taken place *on account of* one of the five protected grounds in the Refugee Convention.

14. KIND (2016).

15. The child-friendly criteria used at the asylum office are not binding in immigration court or at the appeals level in the circuit courts and at the Board of Immigration Appeals (BIA) (Frydman and Bookey 2018). While immigration judges receive minimal written guidelines about child-appropriate interview modalities and courtroom etiquette, they are not trained like asylum officers in this regard. Trainings for judges are considered voluntary and must be sought out proactively. Immigration court guidelines in place under Obama stressed that "docket demands" take precedent over voluntary trainings that judges might want to seek out and that the best interest of the child "cannot provide a basis to grant relief that is not sanctioned by the law" (EOIR 2007).

16. Given-Wilson, Herlihy, and Hodes (2016).

17. Vogler (2016).

18. Matter of Acosta was the decision that first defined the "social group" for the purposes of asylum eligibility, pointing to the visibility and recognizability criteria. This definition from US asylum law has been largely adopted by the international community but has since been subject to ongoing litigation in the United States.

19. TVPRA protections allow unaccompanied minors to first apply for asylum at the asylum office. Because of this, the lawyers I shadowed and interviewed had little experience preparing unaccompanied minors' cases for immigration court. Their clients' cases were either granted at the asylum office or, when denied, had often not yet been scheduled and heard in the immigration court due to high backlogs at the time of my research. For these reasons, most attorneys who had been practicing law and representing unaccompanied minors for one to three years sometimes had not yet had any experience with asylum in immigration court. While immigration court provides written decisions on asylum cases, the asylum office does not. It is possible to obtain such records from the asylum office by submitting a FOIA request, but nonprofit attorneys seldom did this.

20. Asylum seekers from the Middle East were also criminalized (in this case, as terrorist threats) and automatically sent to background checks during the Trump administration.

21. The Immigration and Naturalization Act contains a list of inadmissibility grounds that disqualify individuals from asylum eligibility, such as knowingly persecuting others or participating in terrorist activities (INA 212[a]).

22. See Coutin (2011) for a historical analysis of US asylum case law on gangs and its application in the cases of adults. See also Shiff (2022).

23. Bohmer and Schuman (2008).

24. As cited in Galli (2018).

25. Galli (2020a).

26. Moser-Mercer et. al. (1998).

27. In California, the SIJS order is requested in one of the following four types of state courts, depending on the circumstances: (1) Probate: when a nonparent is taking care of the child (guardianship is also requested in this case); (2) Delinquency: when the minor has committed a crime and is a ward of the delinquency court; (3) Dependency: when the child is in the foster care system, and the parent(s) have permanently or temporarily lost custody; (4) Family court: when one parent is seeking custody, and the other parent abused, abandoned, or neglected the child.

28. SIJS is subject to yearly per-country visa limitations. Applicants from the "high-demand" countries of El Salvador, Guatemala, and Honduras had the longest wait times to become permanent residents through SIJS (over 4 years), followed by Mexicans (2.6 years on average), during the time of this research. For all others, the wait time ranged between 6 months and 1.5 years (Davidson and Hlass 2021).

29. Hlass (2014).

30. *R.F.M. v Nielsen; J.L. v. Cissna, et al.*

31. This protection was introduced by the Kim memo in 2013, see chapter 1.

32. To grant cases based on "novel" PSGs, asylum officers must request approval from their supervisors at the asylum office headquarters. This process is far more onerous than granting cases based on existing PSGs.

33. Unlike a pending asylum application, a pending SIJS application (or approved SIJS order) is not a form of deportation relief. Immigration judges under Obama could administratively close the cases of SIJS applicants to avoid deporting youths on their dockets who were effectively waiting in line for permanent residency. Under Trump, administrative closure was no longer allowed, and, in principle, judges were expected to continue the deportation proceedings of youths with pending SIJS cases. For more on this, see note 2 to chapter 4.

34. The Biden administration has restored immigration judges' ability to manage their dockets, including by administratively closing and terminating cases, as well as by using prosecutorial discretion.

35. According to an asylum officer interviewed for this research, this change occurred through increased oversight of individual asylum officers by their new Trump-appointed supervisors, which directed their focus on fraud detection and credibility screenings. It also became less burdensome to deny the cases of

unaccompanied minors based on credibility: in their internal written decisions on these cases, asylum officers were no longer required to cite material from their "child-friendly" interview trainings and accommodations taking into account the developmental capacity of children.

CHAPTER 6. COMING OF AGE UNDER THE GAZE OF THE STATE

1. Hernández-León (1999); Massey et al. (1999); Monsutti (2007).

2. Berger Cardoso et. al. (2019); Menjívar and Perreira (2019).

3. Statz (2018).

4. Marrow (2009).

5. This number refers to the years in which my ethnographic fieldwork took place (2015–2019). Since then, more unaccompanied minors have become eligible for post-release services. However, due to limited funding, the support that social workers can provide beneficiaries is still insufficient to meet their needs (Migration Policy Institute 2021; Grace and Roth 2021).

6. Menjívar (2000).

7. Eligibility for Medi-Cal was expanded in 2016 to including undocumented immigrants under age nineteen. In 2020, eligibility was again expanded to undocumented immigrants under age twenty-six.

8. Some organizations in Los Angeles later took on family separation cases as well, helping separated children find their parents and/or apply for immigration relief.

9. Cisneros (2013); Golash-Boza and Sotelo (2013).

10. Chauvin and Garces Mascarenas (2012).

11. Berger Cardoso et al. (2017).

12. Gonzales (2016); Patler and Gonzales (2015).

13. Gonzales (2016); Nicholls (2013).

14. See also Diaz-Strong (2021).

15. Gonzales (2014).

16. Burke (2016).

17. Gonzales, Terriquez, and Ruszczyk (2014).

18. Gonzales (2016).

19. This reflects findings documented in the gender and migration scholarship. See for example, Abrego (2009); Curran and Saguy (2001); Dannecker (2005); De Jong (2000).

20. Gozdziak (2015).

21. In 2021, California announced that it would be the first state to provide integration support services to approved asylees as well as resettled refugees. The implementation of this policy is pending at the time of this writing. For more on this, see chapter 7.

22. Clements, Baird, and Campbell (2020).

23. While asylum seekers should obtain work permits 180 days after submitting their asylum applications, the moment the clock starts ticking may be delayed due to errors or the discretionary decisions of immigration bureaucrats (Penn State Law Immigrants' Rights Clinic and American Immigration Council's Legal Action Center 2010). In 2020, the Trump administration increased this waiting period and made it more difficult for asylum seekers to obtain work permits, but advocates found creative ways around this through impact litigation (https://help.asylumadvocacy.org/work-permit-updates/#3august2022-delays).

24. Berger Cardoso et al. (2019).

CHAPTER 7. BEYOND PRECARIOUS PROTECTIONS

1. Hernández-León (1999); Kandel and Massey (2002); Monsutti (2007); Martinez (2019).

2. Starting in May 2022, SIJS applicants with approved I-360s qualify for work permits. USCIS has also stated that SIJS applicant youths whose I-360s have been approved will no longer be automatically disqualified from adjusting their status to permanent resident when they get married before a visa number becomes available.

3. Fitzgerald (2019).

4. Galli (2020a).

5. 28 I&N Dec. 307 (A.G. 2021).

6. Abrego (2017); Menjívar (1994, 2000); Rocha (2011); Garcia (2006).

7. Souter (2014); Coen (2017).

8. Menjívar, Abrego and Schmalzbauer (2016).

9. TRAC (n.d.b).

10. While most advocates agree that allowing all asylum seekers to apply at the asylum office is a positive change, the new rules have also been criticized in other ways for undermining due process. Under the new rule, claims denied at the asylum office and referred to the immigration court would be "streamlined," meaning that immigration judges could potentially deny a case based on the record produced by the asylum officer. This is different from the current system where judges assess cases *de novo* on their merits, considering new evidence submitted by the applicant. For more on this, see note 97 to chapter 1.

11. Between March and August 2022, about 1,400 individuals were processed using the new rules in a small pilot program run out of a Texas detention center (National Immigration Project 2022). For up to date information on the implementation of the new Asylum Processing Rule, see: https://www.dhs.gov/immigration-statistics/special-reports/asylum-processing-rule-report.

12. Texas v. Mayorkas; Arizona v. Garland.

13. Hiskey, Cordova, and Orces (2014).

14. UNHCR (2014a).

15. Ebadolahi (2018).

16. For more on the End SIJS Backlog National Coalition, see: https://www.sijsbacklog.com.

17. See Davidson and Hlass (2021) for more information on the SIJS backlog and for a list of INA amendments and other policy changes that would end or alleviate the harms of the SIJS backlog.

18. The asylum office previously held Quarterly Stakeholder Meetings and released data on adults' and unaccompanied minors' cases (number of cases filed and pending, grant rates), which were publicly available online (for the last report, dated March 2019, see https://www.uscis.gov/outreach/notes-from-previous-engagements/asylum-division-quarterly-stakeholder-meeting). For more on this, see note 5 to chapter 1. Further, due to changes in how the immigration courts tracked unaccompanied minors (EOIR 2017), the data released by EOIR on unaccompanied minor's cases in immigration court are no longer considered reliable following 2018 (see TRAC 2021).

19. Migration Policy Institute (2021).

20. Fee (2019).

21. Schrag (2020).

METHODS APPENDIX

1. See Galli (2018, 2020a).

2. For immigrant interview participants, I kept their first names and phone numbers on an encrypted and password-protected drive.

3. *Washington Post* (2019).

4. Becker (1967).

5. See Stuart (2016: Methodological Appendix)

6. For example: https://immigrationcourtside.com; www.asylumist.com; https://cliniclegal.org; www.aclu.org/issues/immigrants-rights; https://immigrantjustice.org.

7. Susan Terrio (2015) and Lauren Heidbrink (2014a) conducted their ethnographies of ORR shelters in 2012 prior to the first increase in arrivals of Central American unaccompanied minors at the US-Mexico border. After that, ORR facilities became off limits for researchers.

8. Like I did for the ethnographic study component, I obtained consent from youths directly for their participation in interviews if they were over eighteen. If they were younger, I first obtained consent from their parents or other adult caretaker sponsors, over the phone or in person. The study design described in this appendix was approved by the UCLA IRB.

9. Ordoñez (2015); Constable (2014); Hsin and Aptekar (2021).

10. Fassin (2013).

References

Abrego, Leisy. 2009. "Economic Well-Being in Salvadoran Transnational Families: How Gender Affects Remittance Practices." *Journal of Marriage and Family* 71 (4): 1070–85.

———. 2011. "Legal Consciousness of Undocumented Latinos: Fear and Stigma as Barriers to Claims-Making for First- and 1.5- Generation Immigrants." *Law & Society Review* 45 (2): 337–70.

———. 2014. *Sacrificing Families: Navigating Laws, Labor, and Love Across Borders*. Stanford, CA: Stanford University Press.

———. 2017. "On Silences: Salvadoran Refugees Then and Now." *Latino Studies* 15(1): 73–85.

———. 2019. "Relational Legal Consciousness of US Citizenship: Privilege, Responsibility, Guilt, and Love in Latino Mixed-Status Families." *Law & Society Review* 53(3): 641–670.

Abrego, Leisy, and Roberto Gonzales. 2010. "Blocked Paths, Uncertain Futures: The Postsecondary Education and Labor Market Prospects of Undocumented Latino Youth." *Journal of Education for Students Placed at Risk* 15 (1–2): 144–57.

Abrego, Leisy, and Cecilia Menjívar. 2011. "Immigrant Latina Mothers as Targets of Legal Violence." *Journal of Marriage and the Family* 37 (1): 9–26.

Abrego, Leisy, and Sarah Lakhani. 2015. "Incomplete Inclusion: Legal Violence and Immigrants in Liminal Legal Statuses." *Law & Policy* 37(4): 265–93.

ACLU (American Civil Liberties Union). 2020. "District Court Blocks Trump Administration's Illegal Border Expulsions. www.aclu.org/press-releases /district-court-blocks-trump-administrations-illegal-border-expulsions.

Administration for Children and Families (ACF). 2019. "Minors Released to Sponsors by County." www.hhs.gov/programs/social-services/unaccompanied -children-released-to-sponsors-by-county-september-2019.html.

Agustín, Laura. 2007. *Sex at the Margins: Migration, Labour Markets and the Rescue Industry*. New York: Zed Books.

American Immigration Council. 2016. "Children in Immigration Court: Over 95 Percent Represented by an Attorney Appear in Court." www.american immigrationcouncil.org/research/children-immigration-court-over-95 -percent-represented-attorney-appear-court.

American Immigration Lawyers Association. 2019. "Documents Relating to *Flores v. Reno* Settlement Agreement on Minors in Immigration Custody." www.aila.org/infonet/flores-v-reno-settlement-agreement.

Arar, Rawan. 2017. "The New Grand Compromise: How Syrian Refugees Changed the Stakes in the Global Refugee Assistance Regime." *Middle East Law and Governance* 9 (3): 298–312.

Aries Philippe. 1962. *Centuries of Childhood: A Social History of Family Life*. New York: Random House.

Arnold, Samantha. 2018. *Children's Rights and Refugee Law: Conceptualising Children within the Refugee Convention*. London: Routledge.

Becker, Howard S. 1967. "Whose Side Are We On?" *Social Problems* 14 (3): 239–47.

Bellino, Michelle. 2017. *Youth in Postwar Guatemala: Education and Civic Identity in Transition*. New Brunswick, NJ: Rutgers University Press.

Belloni, Milena. 2019. *The Big Gamble: The Migration of Eritreans to Europe*. Oakland: University of California Press.

———. 2020. "Family Project or Individual Choice? Exploring Agency in Young Eritreans' Migration." *Journal of Ethnic and Migration Studies*. 46 (2): 336–53.

Berger, Susan. 2009. "(Un)Worthy: Latina Battered Immigrants under VAWA and the Construction of Neoliberal Subjects." *Citizenship Studies* 13 (3): 201–17.

Berger Cardoso, Jodi, et. al. 2019. "Integration of Unaccompanied Migrant Youth in the United States: A Call for Research." *Journal of Ethnic and Migration Studies* 45 (2): 1–20.

Betts, Alexander. 2013. *Survival Migration*. Ithaca, NY: Cornell University Press.

Bhabha, Jacqueline. 2014. *Child Migration and Human Rights in a Global Age*. Princeton, NJ: Princeton University Press.

Bhabha, Jacqueline, and Wendy Young. 1999. "Not Adults in Miniature: Unaccompanied Child Asylum Seekers and the New U.S. Guidelines." *International Journal of Refugee Law* 11: 84–125.

Bhuyan, Rupaleem. 2008. "The Production of the 'Battered Immigrant' in Public Policy and Domestic Violence Advocacy." *Journal of Interpersonal Violence* 23 (2): 153–70.

Bloch, Alice, Nando Sigona, and Roger Zetter. 2014. *Sans Papiers: The Social and Economic Lives of Young Undocumented Migrants*. London: Pluto Press.

Bogado, Aura and Laura Morel. 2021. "'I'm going to tase this kid': Government Shelters Are Turning Refugee Children Over to Police." *Reveal News* (June 8).

Bohmer, Carol, and Amy Shuman. 2008. *Rejecting Refugees: Political Asylum in the 21st Century*. New York: Routledge.

Booth, John A., Christine J. Wade, and Thomas W. Walker. 2005. *Understanding Central America: Global Forces, Rebellion, and Change*. Boulder, CO: Avalon Publishing.

Bourdieu, Pierre. 1986. "The Forms of Capital." In *Handbook of Theory and Research for the Sociology of Education*, edited by Maureen T. Hallinan, 241–58. New York: Springer.

———. 1998. *Practical Reason: On the Theory of Action*. Stanford, CA: Stanford University Press.

———. 2004. "Gender and Symbolic Violence." In *Violence in War and Peace: An Anthology*, edited by Nancy Scheper-Hughes and Philippe Bourgois, 339–42. Malden: Blackwell Publishing.

Bourdieu, Pierre, and Loïc Wacquant. 2004. "Symbolic Violence." In *Violence in War and Peace*, edited by Nancy Scheper-Hughes and Philippe Bourgois, 272–74. Malden, MA: Blackwell.

Brown, Hana. 2011. "Refugees, Rights, and Race: How Legal Status Shapes Liberian Immigrants' Relationship with the State." *Social Problems* 58 (1): 144–63.

Brubaker, Rogers. 2015. *Grounds for Difference*. Cambridge, MA: Harvard University Press.

Bruneau, Thomas, Lucía Dammert, and Elizabeth Skinner. 2011. *Maras: Gang Violence and Security in Central America*. Austin: University of Texas Press.

Burke, Garance. 2016. "AP Exclusive: Migrant Children Kept from Enrolling in School." Associated Press (May 1 2016).

Byrne, Olga, and Elise Miller. 2012. *The Flow of Unaccompanied Children Through the Immigration System: A Resource for Practitioners, Policy Makers, and Researchers*. New York: Vera Institute of Justice.

Canizales, Stephanie. 2015. "American Individualism and the Social Incorporation of Unaccompanied Guatemalan Young Adults in LA." *Ethnic & Racial Studies* 38 (10): 1831–47.

Carlson, Elizabeth, and Anna Marie Gallagher. 2015. "Humanitarian Protection for Children Fleeing Gang–Based Violence in the Americas." *Journal on Migration and Human Security* 3 (2): 129–58.

Carr, Patrick, Laura Napolitano, and Jessica Keating. 2007. "We Never Call the Cops and Here Is Why: A Qualitative Examination of Legal Cynicism in Three Philadelphia Neighborhoods." *Criminology* 45 (2): 445–80.

Castles, Stephen. 2003. "Towards a Sociology of Forced Migration and Social Transformation." *Sociology* 37 (1): 13–34.

CBP (Customs and Border Protection). 2018. "Family Unit Subject and UAC Apprehensions." www.cbp.gov/newsroom/stats/sw-border-migration.

Center for Gender and Refugee Studies. 2014. "Domestic Violence." https://cgrs .uchastings.edu/our-work/domestic-violence.

Chase, Elaine, and Jennifer Allsopp. 2020. *Youth Migration and the Politics of Wellbeing: Stories of Life in Transition*. Bristol, UK: Bristol University Press.

Chauvin, Sébastien, and Blanca Garcés-Mascareñas. 2012. "Beyond Informal Citizenship: The New Moral Economy of Migrant Illegality." *International Political Sociology* 6 (3): 241–59.

Chavez, Lilian, and Cecilia Menjívar. 2010. "Children without Borders: A Mapping of the Literature on Unaccompanied Migrant Children to the United States." *Migraciones internacionales* 5 (18): 71–111.

Checa, Francisco, Ángeles Arjona, Juan Carlos Checa Olmos, and Ariadna Alonso. 2016. *Menores tras la frontera: Otra inmigración que aguarda*. Barcelona, Spain: Icaria Editorial.

Chua, Lynette J., and David M. Engel. 2019. "Legal Consciousness Reconsidered." *Annual Review of Law and Social Science* 15: 335–53.

Cisneros, Natalie. 2013. "Alien Sexuality: Race, Maternity, and Citizenship." *Hypatia* 28 (2): 290–306.

Clemens, Michael A. 2017. "Violence, Development, and Migration Waves: Evidence from Central American Child Migrant Apprehensions." Center for Global Development Working Paper 459. https://www.cgdev.org/publication /violence-development-and-migration-waves-evidence-central-american -child-migrant.

Clements, Kathryn A. V., Diane Baird, and Rebecca Campbell. 2020. "'It's Hard to Explain.': Service Providers' Perspectives on Unaccompanied Minors' Needs Based on Minors' Forms of Immigration Relief." *Journal of International Migration and Integration* 21 (2): 633–48.

CLINIC (Catholic Legal Immigration Network, Inc). 2019. "Recent Updates on the Administration's Assault on Asylum." https://cliniclegal.org/resources /asylum-and-refugee-law/recent-updates-administrations-assault-asylum.

Coen, Alise. 2017. "Capable and Culpable? The United States, RtoP, and Refugee Responsibility-Sharing." *Ethics & International Affairs* 31(1): 71.

Constable, Nicole. 2014. *Born Out of Place: Migrant Mothers and the Politics of International Labor*. Oakland: University of California Press.

Coutin, Susan B. 1994. "Enacting Law as Social Practice: The U.S. Sanctuary Movement as a Mode of Resistance." In *Contested States: Law, Hegemony, and*

Resistance, edited by Susan F. Hirsch and Mindie Lazarus-Black, 282–303. New York: Routledge.

———. 2000. *Legalizing Moves: Salvadoran Immigrants' Struggle for U.S. Residency*. Ann Arbor: University of Michigan Press.

Crawley, Heaven, and Dimitris Skleparis. 2018. "Refugees, Migrants, Neither, Both: Categorical Fetishism and the Politics of Bounding in Europe's 'Migration Crisis.'" *Journal of Ethnic and Migration Studies* 44 (1): 48–64.

Cuellar, Mariano-Florentino. 2006. "Refugee Security and the Organizational Logic of Legal Mandates." *Georgetown Journal of International Law* 37 (4): 583–724.

Cummings, Williams. 2018. "Migrant Children Describe Abuse, Being Forcibly Medicated at Youth Shelters: Lawsuit." *USA Today* (June 21).

Curran, Sara R., and Abigail C. Saguy. 2001. "Migration and Cultural Change: A Role for Gender and Social Networks?" *Journal of International Women's Studies* 2 (3): 54–77.

Dannecker, P. 2005. "Transnational Migration and the Transformation of Gender Relations: The Case of Bangladeshi Labour Migrants." *Current Sociology* 53 (4): 655–74.

Dauvergne, Catherine. 2005. *Humanitarianism, Identity, and Nation: Migration Laws of Australia and Canada*. Vancouver: University of British Columbia Press.

Davidson, Rachel L., and Laila Hlass. 2021. "Any Day They Could Deport Me: Over 44,000 Immigrant Children Stuck in the SIJS Backlog." https://www.sijsbacklog.com/any-day-they-could-deport-me.

De Genova, Nicholas P. 2002. "Migrant 'Illegality' and Deportability in Everyday Life." *Annual Review of Anthropology* 31 (1): 419–47.

DeJong, Gordon F. 2000. "Expectations, Gender, and Norms in Migration Decision-Making." *Population Studies* 54 (3): 307–19.

Dery, David. 1998. "'Papereality' and Learning in Bureaucratic Organizations." *Administration & Society* 29 (6): 677–89.

DHS (Department of Homeland Security). 2020. "Refugees and Asylees: Annual Flow Report." https://www.dhs.gov/sites/default/files/2022-03/22_0308_plcy_refugees_and_asylees_fy2020_1.pdf.

Diaz-Strong, Daysi Ximena. 2021. "'She Did Not Find One That Was for Me': The College Pathways of the Mexican and Central American Undocumented 1.25 Generation." *Harvard Educational Review* 91 (1): 83–108.

DeWaard, Jack, Jenna Nobles, and Katharine M. Donato. 2018. "Migration and Parental Absence: A Comparative Assessment of Transnational Families in Latin America." *Population, Space and Place* 24 (7): 2166.

Dezenski, Lauren. 2017. "Sessions: Many Unaccompanied Minors Are 'Wolves in Sheep's Clothing.'" *Politico* (September 21, 2017).

Doctors Without Borders. 2020. "No Way Out: The Humanitarian Crisis for Migrants and Asylum Seekers Trapped between the United States, Mexico and the Northern Triangle of Central America."www.doctorswithout borders.org.

Dreby, Joanna. 2010. *Divided by Borders: Mexican Migrants and Their Children.* Berkeley: University of California Press.

———. 2015. "US Immigration Policy and Family Separation: The Consequences for Children's Well-Being." *Social Science & Medicine* 132: 245–51.

Ebadolahi, Mitra. 2018. "Neglect and Abuse of Unaccompanied Immigrant Children by U.S. Customs and Border Protection." ACLU/IHRC (American Civil Liberties Union and International Human Rights Clinic, University of Chicago), May 23. www.aclusandiego.org/civil-rights-civil-liberties/.

Enriquez, Laura. 2015. "Multigenerational Punishment: Shared Experiences of Undocumented Immigration Status within Mixed-Status Families." *Journal of Marriage and Family* 77 (4): 939–53.

———. 2017. "A 'Master Status' or the 'Final Straw'? Assessing the Role of Immigration Status in Latino Undocumented Youths' Pathways out of School." *Journal of Ethnic and Migration Studies* 43 (9): 1526–43.

EOIR (Executive Office for Immigration Review). 2007. "Guidelines for Immigration Cases Involving Unaccompanied Alien Children." Memorandum 07-01.

———. 2017. "Guidelines for Immigration Cases Involving Juveniles, Including Unaccompanied Alien Children." Memorandum 17-03.

Espiritu, Yen Le. 2014. *Body Counts: The Vietnam War and Militarized Refugees.* Oakland: University of California Press.

European Migration Network. 2018. "Approaches to Unaccompanied Minors following status determination in the EU plus Norway." https://ec.europa.eu/.

Ewick, Patricia, and Susan S. Silbey. 1998. *The Common Place of Law: Stories from Everyday Life.* Chicago: University of Chicago Press.

Fagan, Jeffrey, and Tom R. Tyler. 2005. "Legal Socialization of Children and Adolescents." *Social Justice Research* 18 (3): 217–41.

Farmer, Paul. 2004. "On Suffering and Structural Violence: A View from Below." In *Violence in War and Peace: An Anthology*, edited by Nancy Scheper-Hughes and Philippe Bourgois, 281–89. Malden, MA: Blackwell.

Fassin, Didier. 2011. "Policing Borders, Producing Boundaries. The Governmentality of Immigration in Dark Times." *Annual Review of Anthropology* 40 (1): 213–26.

———. 2013. "The Precarious Truth of Asylum." *Public Culture* 25 (1): 39–63.

Fassin, Didier, and Estelle d'Halluin. 2017. "Critical Evidence: The Politics of Trauma in French Asylum Policies." *Ethos* 35 (3): 300–329.

Fee, Molly. 2019. Paper Integration: The Structural Constraints and Consequences of the US Refugee Resettlement Program. *Migration Studies* 7 (4): 477–95.

Feld, Barry C. 1999. *Bad Kids: Race and the Transformation of the Juvenile Court*. New York: Oxford University Press.

Finkelhor, David. 2008. *Childhood Victimization: Violence, Crime, and Abuse in the Lives of Young People*. New York: Oxford University Press.

Fitzgerald, David Scott. 2019. *Refuge Beyond Reach: How Rich Democracies Repel Asylum Seekers*. New York: Oxford University Press.

FitzGerald, David Scott, and Rawan Arar. 2018. "The Sociology of Refugee Migration." *Annual Review of Sociology* 44 (1): 387–406.

Flores, René D., and Ariela Schachter. 2018. "Who Are the 'Illegals'? The Social Construction of Illegality in the United States." *American Sociological Review* 83 (5): 839–68.

Freedman, Jane. 2015. *Gendering the International Asylum and Refugee Debate*. New York: Palgrave McMillan.

Frydman, Lisa, and Blaine Bookey. 2018. "Applying the Refugee Definition to Child-Specific Forms of Persecution." In *Research Handbook on Child Migration*, edited by Jacqueline Bhabha, Jyothi Kanics, and Daniel Senovilla Hernández. Cheltenham, UK: Edward Elgar Publishing.

Gagne, David. 2017. "InSight Crime's 2016 Homicide Round-Up." *InSight Crime* (blog). www.insightcrime.org/news/analysis/insight-crime-2016-homicide-round-up/.

Galli, Chiara. 2018. "A Rite of Reverse Passage: The Construction of Youth Migration in the US Asylum Process." *Ethnic and Racial Studies* 41(9): 1651–71.

———. 2020a. "Humanitarian Capital: How Lawyers Help Immigrants Use Suffering to Claim Membership in the Nation-State." *Journal of Ethnic and Migration Studies* 67 (4): 763–81.

———. 2020b. "The Ambivalent US Context of Reception and the Dichotomous Legal Consciousness of Unaccompanied Minors." *Social Problems* 46 (11): 2181–98.

Galtung, Johan. 1969. "Violence, Peace, and Peace Research." *Journal of Peace Research* 6(3): 167–91.

Gammeltoft-Hansen, Thomas, and Ninna Nyberg Sorensen, eds. 2013. *The Migration Industry and the Commercialization of International Migration*. New York: Routledge.

GAO (Government Accountability Office). 2018. "Border Patrol: Issues Related to Agent Deployment Strategy and Immigration Checkpoints." www.gao.gov/assets/gao-18-50.pdf.

———. 2020. "Unaccompanied Children: Actions Needed to Improve Grant Application Reviews and Oversight of Care Facilities." www.gao.gov/products/gao-20-609.

García, Angel Escamilla (2019). "Learning to Look Mexican." In *Deadly Voyages: Migrant Journeys across the Globe*, edited by Veronica F. Bruey and Steven W. Bender, 3–18. Lanham, MD: Lexington.

Garcia, Maria Cristina. 2006. *Seeking Refuge: Central American Migration to Mexico, the United States, and Canada.* Berkeley: University of California Press.

Gibney, Matthew J. 2004. *The Ethics and Politics of Asylum: Liberal Democracy and the Response to Refugees.* Cambridge, UK: Cambridge University Press.

Given-Wilson, Zoe, Jane Herlihy, and Matthew Hodes. 2016. "Telling the Story: A Psychological Review on Assessing Adolescents' Asylum Claims." *Canadian Psychology/Psychologie Canadienne* 57 (4): 265.

Gleeson, Shannon. 2010. "Labor Rights for All? The Role of Undocumented Immigrant Status for Worker Claims Making." *Law & Social Inquiry* 35 (3): 561–602.

Goffman, Erving. 1963. *Stigma: Notes on the Management of Spoiled Identity.* New York: Simon & Schuster.

Golash-Boza, Tanya, and Pierrette Hondagneu-Sotelo. 2013. "Latino Immigrant Men and the Deportation Crisis: A Gendered Racial Removal Program." *Latino Studies* 11 (3): 271–92.

Gomberg-Muñoz, Ruth. 2015. "The Punishment/El Castigo: Undocumented Latinos and US Immigration Processing." *Journal of Ethnic and Migration Studies* 41(14): 2235–52.

Gonzales, Roberto. 2011. "Learning to Be Illegal: Undocumented Youth and Shifting Legal Contexts in the Transition to Adulthood." *American Sociological Review* 76 (4): 602–19.

———. 2016. *Lives in Limbo: Undocumented and Coming of Age in America.* Oakland: University of California Press.

Gonzales, Roberto G., and Edelina M. Burciaga. 2018. "Segmented Pathways of Illegality: Reconciling the Coexistence of Master and Auxiliary Statuses in the Experiences of 1.5-Generation Undocumented Young Adults." *Ethnicities* 18 (2): 178–91.

Gonzales, Roberto G., Veronica Terriquez, and Stephen P. Ruszczyk. 2014. "Becoming DACAmented: Assessing the Short-Term Benefits of Deferred Action for Childhood Arrivals (DACA)." *American Behavioral Scientist* 58 (14): 1852–72.

Gozdziak Elzbieta. 2015. "What Kind of Welcome? Integration of Central American Unaccompanied Minors into Local Communities" Institute for the Study of International Migration at Georgetown, Report Prepared for the Kaplan Fund.

Grace, Breanne L., and Benjamin J. Roth. 2021. "Bureaucratic Neglect: The Paradoxical Mistreatment of Unaccompanied Migrant Children in the US Immigration System." *Journal of Ethnic and Migration Studies* 47(5): 3455–72.

Guhin, Jeffrey, Jessica M. Calarco, and Cynthia Miller-Idriss. 2021. "Whatever Happened to Socialization?" *Annual Review of Sociology* 47: 109–29.

Gutierrez Rivera, Lirio. 2017. "Female Asylum Seekers from Honduras." In *Race, Criminal Justice, and Migration Control: Enforcing the Boundaries of Belonging,* edited by Mary Bosworth, Alma Parmar and Yolanda Vazquez, 43–60. Oxford: Oxford University Press.

Hagan, Jacqueline Maria, and Susan Gonzalez Baker. 1993. "Implementing the U.S. Legalization Program: The Influence of Immigrant Communities and Local Agencies on Immigration Policy Reform." *International Migration Review* 27 (3): 513–36.

Hamlin, Rebecca. 2014. *Let Me Be a Refugee: Administrative Justice and the Politics of Asylum in the United States, Canada, and Australia.* Oxford: Oxford University Press.

———. 2021. *Crossing: How We React to and Label People on the Move.* Stanford, CA: Stanford University Press.

Heidbrink, Lauren. 2014a. *Migrant Youth, Transnational Families, and the State: Care and Contested Interests.* Philadelphia: University of Pennsylvania Press.

———. 2014b. "Unintended Consequences: Reverberations of Special Immigrant Juvenile Status." *Journal of Applied Research on Children* 5 (2): 9.

———. 2018. "Circulation of care among unaccompanied migrant youth from Guatemala." *Children and Youth Services Review* 92 (September): 30–38.

———. 2020. *Migranthood: Youth in a New Era of Deportation.* Stanford, CA: Stanford University Press.

Hernandez-Leon, Ruben. 1999. "A la aventura! Jóvenes, pandillas y migración en la conexión Monterrey–Houston." In *Fronteras Fragmentadas*, edited by Gail Mummert, 11–143. Zamora, México: El Colegio de Michoacán.

———. 2013. "Conceptualizing the Migration Industry." In *The Migration Industry and the Commercialization of International Migration,* edited by Thomas Gammeltoft-Hansen and Ninna Nyberg Sorensen, 24–44. New York: Routledge.

Hiskey, Jonathan, Abby Cordova, and Diana Orces. 2018. "Leaving the Devil You Know: Crime Victimization, U.S. Deterrence Policy, and the Emigration Decision in Central America." *Latin American Research Review* 53 (3): 429–47.

Hlass, Laila L. 2014. "States and Status: A Study of Geographical Disparities for Immigrant Youth." *Columbia Human Rights Law Review* 46: 266.

Honwana, Alcinda. 2014. "'Waithood': Youth Transitions and Social Change." *Development and Equity* 2: 28–40.

Horváth, István. 2008. "The Culture of Migration of Rural Romanian Youth." *Journal of Ethnic and Migration Studies* 34 (5): 771–86.

Hsin, Amy, and Sofya Aptekar. 2022. "The Violence of Asylum: The Case of Undocumented Chinese Migration to the United States." *Social Forces* 100 (3): 1195–217.

Human Rights First. 2021. "Delivered to Danger: Trump Administration Sending Asylum Seekers and Migrants to Danger." https://deliveredtodanger.org.

Human Rights Watch. 2020. "Deported to Danger." www.hrw.org/report/2020 /02/05/deported–dangerunited–states–deportation–policies–expose –salvadorans–death–and.

ILRC (Immigrant Legal Resource Center). 2021. "Current Status of UC Asylum Jurisdiction and JOP v. DHS." www.ilrc.org/matter-m-c-o-and-jurisdiction -over-uc-asylum-claims.

ILO (International Labour Organization). 2008a. "El Salvador: child labor data country brief." https://www.ilo.org/.

———. 2008b. "Guatemala: child labor data country brief." https://www.ilo.org/.

———. 2008c. "Honduras: child labor data country brief." https://www.ilo.org/.

Jimenez, Tomas. 2017. *The Other Side of Assimilation: How Immigrants are Changing American Life*. Oakland: University of California Press.

Joppke, Christian. 1997. "Asylum and State Sovereignty: A Comparison of the United States, Germany and Britain." *Comparative Political Studies* 30 (3): 259–98.

Jordan, Miriam. 2019. "Migrant Children Are Spending Months Crammed in Temporary Facility in Florida." *New York Times* (June 26).

Kandel, W., and D. S. Massey. 2002. "The Culture of Mexican Migration: A Theoretical and Empirical Analysis." *Social Forces* 80 (3): 981–1004.

KIND. (Kids in Need of Defense). 2016. "Improving the Protection and Fair Treatment of Unaccompanied Children." https://supportkind.org/.

———. 2020. "Remain in Mexico: Unlawful and Unsafe for Children." https:// supportkind.org/wp-content/uploads/2020/01/Remain-in-Mexico-Fact -Sheet-FINALv2-1.29.20.pdf.

Lakhani, Sarah. 2013. "Producing Immigrant Victims' 'Right' to Legal Status and the Management of Legal Uncertainty." *Law & Social Inquiry* 38 (2): 442–73.

———. 2014. "From Problems of Living to Problems of Law: The Legal Translation and Documentation of Immigrant Abuse and Helpfulness." *Law & Social Inquiry* 39 (3): 643–65.

Lindley, Anna. 2014. *Crisis and Migration: Critical Perspectives*. New York: Routledge.

Lopez Castro, Gustavo. 2007. "Niños, socialización y migración a Estados Unidos." In *El país transnacional: Migración mexicana y cambio social a través de la frontera*, edited by Marina Ariza and Alejandro Portes, 545–70. México, D.F: Universidad Nacional Autónoma de México, Instituto de Investigaciones Sociales.

Luthra, Renee, Thomas Soehl, and Roger Waldinger. 2018. *Origins and Destinations: The Making of the Second Generation*. New York: Russell Sage Foundation.

Manz, Beatriz. 2008. "Central America: Patterns of Human Rights Violations." www.refworld.org/pdfid/48ad1eb72.pdf.

Marrow, Helen. 2009. "Immigrant Bureaucratic Incorporation: The Dual Roles of Professional Missions and Government Policies." *American Sociological Review* 74 (5): 756–76.

Martinez, Isabel. 2019. *Becoming Transnational Youth Workers: Pathways of Survival and Social Mobility*. New Brunswick: Rutgers University Press.

Massey, Douglas S., Rafael Alarcon, Jorge Durand, and Humberto González. 1990. *Return to Aztlan: The Social Process of International Migration from Western Mexico*. Berkeley: University of California Press.

Massey, Douglas S., Jorge Durand, and Karen A. Pren. 2014. "Explaining Undocumented Migration to the U.S." *International Migration Review* 48 (4): 1028–61.

Mayblin, Lucy. 2017. *Asylum after Empire: Colonial Legacies in the Politics of Asylum-Seeking*. London: Rowman and Littlefield.

Menjívar, Cecilia. 1993. "History, Economy, and Politics: Macro and Micro-level Factors in Recent Salvadorian Migration to the US." *Journal of Refugee Studies* 6 (4): 350–71.

———. 1994. "Salvadorian Migration to the United States in the 1980s: What Can We Learn about It and from It?" *International Migration* 32 (3): 371–401.

———. 2000. *Fragmented Ties: Salvadoran Immigrant Networks in the America*. Berkeley: University of California Press.

———. 2006. "Liminal Legality: Salvadoran and Guatemalan Immigrants' Lives in the United States." *American Journal of Sociology* 111 (4): 999–1037.

———. 2011. *Enduring Violence: Ladina Women's Lives in Guatemala*. Berkeley: University of California Press.

Menjívar, Cecilia, and Leisy J. Abrego. 2012. "Legal Violence: Immigration Law and the Lives of Central American Immigrants." *American Journal of Sociology* 117(5): 1380–421.

Menjívar, Cecilia, Leisy J. Abrego, and Leah C. Schmalzbauer. 2016. *Immigrant Families*. Cambridge: Polity Press.

Menjívar, Cecilia, and Daniel Kanstroom, eds. 2013. *Constructing Immigrant 'Illegality': Critiques, Experiences, and Responses*. New York: Cambridge University Press.

Menjívar, Cecilia, and Krista M. Perreira. 2019. "Undocumented and unaccompanied: children of migration in the European Union and the United States." *Journal of Ethnic and Migration Studies* 45(2): 197-217.

Merry, Sally Engle. 1990. *Getting Justice and Getting Even: Legal Consciousness among Working-Class Americans*. Chicago: University of Chicago Press.

Miller, Banks, Linda Camp Keith, and Jennifer S. Holmes. 2014. *Immigration Judges and US Asylum Policy*. Philadelphia: University of Pennsylvania Press.

Migration Policy Institute (MPI). 2020. "Dismantling and Reconstructing the U.S. Immigration System: a catalog of changes under the Trump Presidency." www.migrationpolicy.org/research/us-immigration-system-changes-trump -presidency.

———. 2021. "Biden Administration Asylum Processing Revamp at the U.S. Border Could Be a Game Changer." www.migrationpolicy.org/news/biden -asylum-processing-proposed-rule.

Minow, Martha. 1995. "What Ever Happened to Children's Rights." *Minnesota Law Review.* 80: 267.

Monsutti, Alessandro. 2007. "Migration as a Rite of Passage: Young Afghans Building Masculinity and Adulthood in Iran." *Iranian Studies* 40 (2): 167–85.

Moser-Mercer, Barbara, Alexander Künzli, and Marina Korac. 1998. "Prolonged Turns in Interpreting: Effects on Quality, Physiological and Psychological Stress." *Interpreting* 3 (1): 47–64.

National Immigration Project. 2022."Biden's Asylum Processing Rule—Three Months In, What Practitioners Need to Know." https://nipnlg.org/PDFs /2022_7Sept-FAQs-asylum-processing-rule.pdf.

Nicholls, Walter. 2013. *The DREAMers: How the Undocumented Youth Movement Transformed the Immigrant Rights Debate.* Stanford, CA: Stanford University Press.

Noll, Gregory. 2005. Proof, Evidentiary Assessment and Credibility in Asylum Procedures. *Refugee Survey Quarterly* 24 (4): 169–69.

Ong, Aihwa. 2003. *Buddha Is Hiding: Refugees, Citizenship, the New America.* Berkeley: University of California Press.

Ordóñez, Juan Thomas. 2015. "Some Sort of Help for the Poor: Blurred Perspectives on Asylum." *International Migration* 53 (3): 100–110.

Orellana, Marjorie Faulstich, Barrie Thorne, Anna Chee, and Wan Shun Eva Lam. 2001. "Transnational Childhoods: The Participation of Children in Processes of Family Migration." *Social Problems* 48 (4): 572–91.

ORMUSA (Observatorio de Violence contra Mujeres). 2019. *Indicadores de violencia.* San Salvador, El Salvador. https://observatoriodeviolencia .ormusa.org.

ORR (Office of Refugee Resettlement). 2014. "Office of Refugee Resettlement Annual Report to Congress 2014." www.acf.hhs.gov/orr/resource/office-of -refugee-resettlement-annual-report-to-congress-2014.

———. 2020. "Facts and Data Related to ORR's Unaccompanied Alien Children's Services Program." www.acf.hhs.gov/orr/about/ucs/facts-and-data.

Patler, Caitlin. 2018. "Undocumented Youth Organizations, Anti-Deportation Campaigns, and the Boundaries of Belonging." *Social Problems* 65 (1): 95–115.

Patler, Caitlin, and Roberto G. Gonzales. 2015. "Framing Citizenship: Media Coverage of Anti-deportation Cases Led by Undocumented Immigrant Youth Organisations." *Journal of Ethnic and Migration Studies* 41 (9): 1453–74.

Penn State Law Immigrants' Rights Clinic and American Immigration Council's Legal Action Center. 2010. "Up Against the Asylum Clock: Fixing the Broken Employment Authorization Asylum Clock." *Center for Immigrants' Rights Clinic Publications* 7.

Perez, Marta. 2021. "Emergency Frames: Gender Violence and Immigration Status in Spain." *Feminist Economics* 18 (2): 265–90.

Physicians for Human Rights (2019). "'There is no one here to protect you': Trauma among Children Fleeing Violence in Central America." https://reliefweb.int/report/united-states-america/there-no-one-here-protect-you-trauma-among-children-fleeing-violence.

Pobjoy, Jason. 2017. *The Child in International Refugee Law*. Cambridge: Cambridge University Press.

Portes, Alejandro, and Rubén G. Rumbaut. 2001. *Legacies: The Story of the Immigrant Second Generation*. Berkeley: University of California Press.

Pound, Roscoe. 1910. "Law in Books and Law in Action." *American Law Review* 44: 12–36.

Ramji–Nogales, Jaya, Andrew I. Schoenholtz, and Philip G. Schrag. 2007. "Refugee Roulette: Disparities in Asylum Adjudication." *Stanford Law Review* 60: 295.

Richmond, Anthony H. 1988. "Sociological Theories of International Migration: The Case of Refugees." *Contemporary Sociology* 36 (2): 7–25.

———. 1993. "Reactive Migration: Sociological Perspectives on Refugee Movements." *Journal of Refugee Studies* 6 (1): 7–24.

Rocha, Jose Luis. 2011. "The Street Gangs of Nicaragua." In *Maras: Gang Violence and Security in Central America*, edited by Thomas Bruneau, Lucia Dammert, and Elizabeth Skinner, 105–22. Austin: University of Texas Press.

Röder, Antje, and Peter Mühlau. 2012. "Low Expectations or Different Evaluations: What Explains Immigrants' High Levels of Trust in Host-Country Institutions?" *Journal of Ethnic and Migration Studies* 38(5): 77792.

Rodriguez, Naomi Glenn–Levin. 2017. *Fragile Families: Foster Care, Immigration, and Citizenship*. Philadelphia: University of Pennsylvania Press.

Rosenblum, Marc R., and Isabel Ball. 2016. "Trends in Unaccompanied Child and Family Migration from Central America." Migration Policy Institute. www.migrationpolicy.org.

Ryo, Emily. 2016. "Fostering Legal Cynicism through Immigration Detention." *Southern California Law Review* 90: 999.

———. 2017. "Legal Attitudes of Migrant Detainees." *Law & Society Review* 51 (1): 99–131

Ryo, Emily, and Reed Humphrey. 2021. "Children in Custody: A Study of Detained Migrant Children in the United States." UCLA Law Review 68: 136–211.

Ryo, Emily, and Ian Peacock. 2021. "Represented but Unequal: The Contingent Effect of Legal Representation in Removal Proceedings." *Law & Society Review* 55(4): 634–56.

Sands, Geneva. 2018. "ICE Arrested 170 Potential Sponsors of Unaccompanied Migrant Children." CNN (December 10). https://www.cnn.com/2018/12/10/politics/ice-potential-sponsors-arrests/index.html.

Schrag, Philip G. 2020. *Baby Jails: The Fight to End the Incarceration of Refugee Children in America*. Oakland: University of California Press.

Seccombe, Karen, Delores James, and Kimberly Walter. 1998 "The Social Construction of the Welfare Mother." *Journal of Marriage and the Family* 60 (4): 849–65.

Sherman, Carter. 2018. Exclusive: How the Trump Administration Tries to Stop Undocumented Teens from Getting Abortions. *Vice News* (February 28, 2018).

Shiff, Talia. 2022. "Regulating Organizational Ambiguity: Unsettled Screening Categories and the Making of US Asylum Policy." *Journal of Ethnic and Migration Studies* 48 (7): 1802–20.

Somers, Aryah, Pedro Herrera, and Lucia Rodriguez. 2010. "Constructions of Childhood and Unaccompanied Children in the Immigration System in the United States." *UC Davis Journal of Juvenile Law & Policy* 14: 311–82.

Souter, James. 2014. "Towards a Theory of Asylum as Reparation for Past Injustice." *Political Studies* 62 (2): 326–42.

Statz, Michele. 2018. *Lawyering an Uncertain Cause: Immigration Advocacy and Chinese Youth in the U.S.* Nashville, TN: Vanderbilt University Press.

Statz, Michele, and Lauren Heidbrink. 2019. "A better "best interests": Immigration policy in a comparative context." *Law & Policy* 41(4): 365–386.

Steffensmeier, Darrell J., Emilie A. Allan, Miles D. Harer, and Cathy Streifel. 1989. "Age and the Distribution of Crime." *American Journal of Sociology* 94 (4): 803–31.

Steinbock, Daniel J. 1989. "The Admission of Unaccompanied Children into the United States." *Yale Law & Policy Review* 7 (1): 137–200.

Stuart, Forrest. 2016. *Down, Out, and Under Arrest: Policing and Everyday Life in Skid Row*. Chicago: University of Chicago Press.

Suárez-Orozco, Marcelo. 1987. "Becoming Somebody": Central American Immigrants in US Inner-City Schools." *Anthropology & Education Quarterly* 18 (4): 287–99.

Taylor, Edward J. 1999. "The New Economics of Labour Migration and the Role of Remittances in the Migration Process." *International Migration* 37 (1): 63–88.

Terrio, Susan. 2015. *Whose Child Am I? Unaccompanied, Undocumented Children in US Immigration Custody*. Oakland: University of California Press.

Ticktin, Miriam I. 2011. *Casualties of Care: Immigration and the Politics of Humanitarianism in France*. Berkeley: University of California Press.

TRAC (Transactional Records Access Clearinghouse). 2014. "Representation for Unaccompanied Children in Immigration Court." https://trac.syr.edu/immigration/reports/371/.

———. 2017. "Unaccompanied Juveniles: Immigration Court Deportation Proceedings Data Tool." https://trac.syr.edu/phptools/immigration/juvenile/.

———. 2021. "Immigration Court's Data on Minors Facing Deportation Is Too Faulty to Be Trusted." https://trac.syr.edu/immigration/reports/669/.

———. n.d.a. "Asylum Decision Tool." https://trac.syr.edu/phptools/immigration/asylum/.

———. n.d.b. "Immigration Court Backlog Tool Pending Cases and Length of Wait by Nationality, State, Court, and Hearing Location." https://trac.syr.edu/phptools/immigration/court_backlog/.

Trinkner, Rick, and Ellen S. Cohn. 2014. "Putting the 'Social' Back in Legal Socialization: Procedural Justice, Legitimacy, and Cynicism in Legal and Nonlegal Authorities." *Law and Human Behavior* 38 (6): 602–17.

Trinkner, Rick, and Tom R. Tyler. 2016 "Legal socialization: Coercion versus consent in an era of mistrust." *Annual Review of Law and Social Science* 12: 417–39.

Turner, Victor. 1969. *The Ritual Process: Structure and Anti-structure.* New York: Routledge.

Tyler, Tom. 1990. *Why People Obey the Law.* New Haven, CT: Yale University Press.

UNCRC (United Nations Committee of the Rights of the Child) (2005). "General Comment Number 6: Treatment of unaccompanied and separated children outside of the country of origin." https://www2.ohchr.org/english/bodies/crc/docs/GC6.pdf.

UNDOC. 2014. "Global Study on Homicide 2013." Vienna: United Nations Office on Drugs and Crime. www.unodc.org/documents/gshpdfs2014_GLOBAL_HOMICIDE_BOOK_web.pdf.

UNESCO. 2020. Education Database. http://data.uis.unesco.org/.

UNHCR. 2009. "Guidelines on International Protection: Child Asylum Claims under Articles 1(A)2 and 1(F) of the 1951 Convention and/or 1967 Protocol relating to the Status of Refugees." https://www.unhcr.org/50ae46309.pdf.

———. 2010. "Considerations in Regard to Eligibility for International Protection in the Context of Gangs and Other Groups Involved in Crime." www.refworld.org.

———. 2014a. "Children on the Run: Unaccompanied Children Leaving Central America and Mexico and the Need for Protection." www.unhcr.org/en-us/children-on-the-run.html.

———. 2014b. *UNHCR Statistical Yearbook.* www.unhcr.org/en-us/statistical-yearbooks.html.

Unidad de Protección a Defensoras de Derechos Humanos. 2017. Informe annual 2017 por el derecho a defender derechos. https://udefegua.org/informes/informe-anual-2017-dddh-en-guatemala.

Urrutia-Rojas, Ximena, and Nestor Rodriguez. 1997. "Unaccompanied Migrant Children from Central America: Sociodemographic Characteristics and

Experiences with Potentially Traumatic Events." In *Health and Social Services among international Labor Migrants: A Comparative Perspective*, edited by Antonio Ugalde and Gilberto Cardenas, 151–66. Austin: University of Texas Press.

USCIS (United States Citizen and Immigration Services). 2015. "The 2014 Humanitarian Crisis at Our Border." www.uscis.gov/tools/resources -congress/testimonies-and-speeches/2014-humanitarian-crisis-our-border -review-governments-response-unaccompanied-minors-one-year-later -senate-committee-homeland-security-july-2015-associate-director-joseph-e -langlois.

———. "Children's Claims: Training Module." USCIS: Refugee, Asylum, and International Operations Directorate (RAIO)—Officer Training. www.uscis .gov/sites/default/files/document/foia/Childrens_Claims_LP_RAIO.pdf.

US Department of Labor. 2018. Child Labor and Forced Labor Reports. https:// www.dol.gov/agencies/ilab/resources/reports/child-labor/el-salvador.

Vera Institute. 2018. "The Case for Universal Representation." https://www.vera .org/advancing-universal-representation-toolkit/the-case-for-universal -representation-1.

Villalon, Roberta. 2010. *Violence Against Latina Immigrants: Citizenship, Inequality, and Community*. New York: New York University Press.

Vogler, Stefan. 2016. "Legally Queer: The Construction of Sexuality in LGBQ Asylum Claims." *Law & Society Review* 50 (4): 856–89.

Vogt, Wendy A., 2013. "Crossing Mexico: Structural Violence and the Commodification of Undocumented Central American Migrants." *American Ethnologist* 40 (4): 764–80.

Washington Post. 2019. "Trump: 'Asylum Is a Big Con Job.'" (April 15). www.washingtonpost.com/video/politics/trump-asylum-is-a-big-con-job /2019/04/15/542fea86-6077-4078-aa3e-7400aa3f0c30_video.html.

Waters, Mary. 1999. *Black Identities*. Cambridge, MA:: Harvard University Press.

Wilson, Richard Ashby, and Richard D. Brown, eds. 2011. *Humanitarianism and Suffering: The Mobilization of Empathy*. Cambridge: Cambridge University Press.

Wilson, Tamar Diana. 1998. "Weak Ties, Strong Ties: Network Principles in Mexican Migration." *Human Organization* 57 (4): 394–403.

Zelizer, Viviana A. 1985. *Pricing the Priceless Child: The Changing Social Value of Children*. Princeton, NJ: Princeton University Press.

Zolberg, Aristide, Suhrke Astri, and Sergio Aguayo. 1989. *Escape from Violence: Conflict and the Refugee Crisis in the Developing World*. Oxford: Oxford University Press.

Index

Abrego, Leisy, 70–71

accompanied children, 23; obligations in the cases of, 223

acculturation, process of, 22, 23, 212

agency, in migration decision-making as not binary (forced or voluntary), 16, 38

Alejandro (research participant), 49–50

Alicia (research participant), 47–48, 76–78, 85–86, 91–92

American Baptist Church (ABC) versus Thornburg, 25

Andres (research participant), 81

Antonio (research participant), 190–91, 205

"architecture of repulsion," the, 63

asylum, 213, 223; asylum protections, scope of, 166; commonsense understanding of, 2, 131–32, 208; differences of from SIJS, 159–60; and the role of asylum officers, 140, 252–53n35. *See also* asylum claims/cases; asylum law; asylum seekers; asylum system/process

asylum claims/cases, 118–19, 130; applications for, 216–17; qualifications/criteria for, 6–7, 108–9, 135, 141–45

asylum law, 112–13, 131, 132–33, 152, 222, 223; contradictions of, 153; infantilizing asylum case law, 18, 132, 170

Asylum Office, 255n18; release of grant rates by, 250–51n9

Asylum Processing Rule, 220–21, 254n11

asylum seekers, 3–4, 6, 8, 12–13, 17, 23, 26, 28, 49, 53, 66, 230–31, 248n16, 254n23, 254n10, 152–53, 156, 215, 217, 219, 220, 248n13, 254n10, 254n23; adult asylum seekers, 75, 139*fig*, 153, 244n97; Central American, 109, 152–53, 225–26; Guatemalan, 25; Salvadoran, 12, 25; young asylum seekers, 134, 145, 214, 222, 237, 238, 240n14

asylum system/process, 131–32, 169–71, 220; and asylum case law, 112–13; asylum system failures, 18–19, 39–40; increasing volatility of under the Trump administration, 111–12; protection for unaccompanied minors under, 27–28, 29*tab*, 138, 139*fig.*, 140, 141–45

BAR license cards, 114–15

Barrio 18, 37

Becker, Howard, 229

Biden administration, 30, 177, 217, 239–40n5, 252n34; and the Asylum Processing Rule, 220–21

Board of Immigration Appeals (BIA), 220, 251n15

Founded in 1893,
UNIVERSITY OF CALIFORNIA PRESS
publishes bold, progressive books and journals
on topics in the arts, humanities, social sciences,
and natural sciences—with a focus on social
justice issues—that inspire thought and action
among readers worldwide.

The UC PRESS FOUNDATION
raises funds to uphold the press's vital role
as an independent, nonprofit publisher, and
receives philanthropic support from a wide
range of individuals and institutions—and from
committed readers like you. To learn more, visit
ucpress.edu/supportus.